AN EPIC
SWINDLE

Brian Reade is a *Daily Mirror* columnist, Kop season ticket holder and author of the book *43 Years With The Same Bird*. He lives in Liverpool.

AN EPIC SWINDLE

44 MONTHS WITH A PAIR OF COWBOYS

BRIAN READE

Quercus

First published in Great Britain in 2011 by Quercus

This paperback edition published in 2012 by

Quercus
55 Baker Street
Seventh Floor, South Block
London
W1U 8EW

The article quoted from on pp.57–58 is by Mihir Bose and was
originally published in the *Daily Telegraph* on 27 December 2006.

The article quoted from on pp.76–77 is by David Conn and was
originally published in the *Guardian* on 14 March 2007.

Every effort has been made to contact copyright holders
of material reproduced in this book. If any have been inadvertently
overlooked, the publishers will be pleased to make restitution
at the earliest opportunity.

A CIP catalogue record for this book is available
from the British Library

ISBN 978 0 85738 600 7

10 9 8 7 6 5 4 3 2 1

Text designed and typeset by Ellipsis Digital Limited, Glasgow

Printed and bound in Great Britain by Clays Ltd, St Ives plc

To The Noise that refused to be dealt with

'This was a valuable asset that was swindled away from me in an epic swindle'

– Tom Hicks, October 2010, on failing to make a profit out of the sale of Liverpool FC

'They have presented a grotesque parody of the truth'

– Lord Grabiner, QC, October 2010, on Hicks's and George Gillett's attempts to make that profit

'I want to put a tag of shame on the greedy bastards who are responsible for this.'

– John Steinbeck, 1939, on the American capitalists who caused the Great Depression and inspired *The Grapes of Wrath*

ACKNOWLEDGEMENTS

John Aldridge, Tony Barrett, Chris Bascombe, David Bick, Roy Boulter, Owen Brown, Jamie Carragher, Mick Carroll, Tony Evans, Steven Gerrard, Peter Hooton, Steve Horner, Alan Kayll, David Luxton, John Mackin, James McKenna, Richard Milner, Steve Monaghan, Danny Nicolson, Rick Parry, Phil Reade, Paul Rice, Paul Tyrrell and everyone who cannot be named. Thank you all.

CHAPTER ONE

'Give us a little time. We're gonna have some fun together'

— George Gillett

There had been other surreal moments at Anfield.

Bill Shankly's and Kenny Dalglish's resignations spring to mind as does the grim League Cup draw with Chesterfield on a cold autumn night in 1992. There I stood on a half-empty Kop, Graeme Souness's finest making me want to pour lukewarm tea on my nuts and wire them up to the floodlights, when a stranger in a red Harry Enfield Scouser's wig, with an East Midlands accent, tried to start an Istvan Kozma chant ('Iiiiiiiiiiiist-van') and accused *me* of being a plastic tosser for not joining in.

But nothing in the history of this 'wonderful, storied club' (copyright Thomas Ollis Hicks) seemed as foreign as the events of 6 February 2007.

One snapshot which sums up this most bizarre of afternoons came when the new American owners caressed the This Is Anfield sign, despite being the antithesis of everything it stood for, barely able to comprehend their luck or contain their glee.

Behind the bank of flashing cameras which captured this Shankly grave-spinning image, their frat-brat sons, new red woollen scarves sitting uneasily on stiff suits, stared gormlessly at photos of Liverpool's past glories, like men forced to peruse *Bella* magazines in a dentist's waiting room.

Minutes later, the six of them squeezed their all-American frames down the tight players' tunnel, back-slapping as they went, past the dugouts into the harsh late-winter sun, and formed a line near the centre circle with the Kop as a backdrop.

There was George with son Foster, Tom, Tom Jr., and his brothers Mack and Alex, all giving out false, nervous laughs at Gillett's poor man's Ernie Wise act. They had fixed, white-teethed grins, gleaming vitamin-powered skin and wore red ties under identical pin-striped grey suits which all had a single button done up. You'd have thought it a Seventh Day Adventist Bible-Sellers Convention if it wasn't for the signed LFC ball Tom Jr., the tallest of them in centre shot, held uncomfortably.

As the flashbulbs died down and the line broke up I half expected an American version of Michael Knighton's notorious Old Trafford ball-juggling act. Hicks shouting: '22-21-18-32' as the boys hitched up the flaps on their suit jackets and showed him their butts, while Gillett sprinted on to the pass and did a touchdown by the Kemlyn Road corner flag, threw the ball back over his head and leapt, bicycle-kicking into the Kop.

That's how weird it seemed.

Yet if a suspicion started to grow that something wasn't quite right about these unknown American strangers taking over Liverpool Football Club, it was drowned out by a primeval scream for change.

Since Roman Abramovich arrived and pumped millions of petro-dollars into a near-bankrupt Chelsea, it was as clear as the seventeen-year gap on the league-winners' section of our honours' board that someone with deep pockets needed to take the keys out of owner David Moores' hands and make Liverpudlians believe again.

Many were so relieved that dithering David had been ousted, that the Americans' promise of the earth just seemed a bonus. And buddy was that earth promised. Revisiting what they vowed at that infamous February 2007 press conference should be compulsory reading for apprentice comedy-writers, because here was the ultimate masterclass in irony.

Gillett said he loved meeting people. **'If they want to do me harm, they don't need to wait until match day. My name is in the phone book. Call me.'** How long would it be before all numbers and email addresses were changed due to harm being pledged?

'When I go to Anfield I'm going to be on the streets in front of the stadium talking to the fans.' Soon he'd be hustled into Anfield from speeding blacked-out vans for fear the fans wanted more than just a word with him.

'We're not people to come here and milk the fans.' We'll never know how much dairy produce they claimed on their multimillion-pound expense sheets but I'm guessing there was some in there.

'We are passionate about winning and will do everything we can to ensure Liverpool wins plenty of trophies here in England and in Europe.' They won precisely none during their time in charge.

'This club is not far from being the best in the world.' True.

Back then they were en route to their second Champions League Final in three years. When they left they were in the relegation zone.

'It is not just about spending money.' True. You never spent any. Of your own anyway.

'I must have an identical evil twin if the rumours I met Everton's board to discuss a groundshare are true.' You do. Sitting next to you. Name of Hicks.

What Gillett unleashed that day wasn't so much a charm offensive as a fully fledged land-and-sea charm invasion. Codename: Operation Bullshit. He did most of the schmoozing but when he was flagged up, George W. Bush's side-kick, Tom Hicks, unleashed Operation Shock and Awe.

'This is not a takeover like the Glazer deal at Manchester United. There is no debt involved.' Oh yes there was. Every goddam cent.

'We believe that as custodians of this wonderful, storied club we have a duty of care to the tradition and legacies of Liverpool.' A duty so shamelessly neglected Evertonians raised a flag after they'd left saying 'Agents Hicks and Gillett: Mission Accomplished.'

'Liverpool is like buying the Boston Red Sox in baseball, they are the biggest and the best.' When the New England Sports Ventures eventually paid off Hicks's debt to the banks and took over the club he claimed, 'There's better owners than the Boston Red Sox out there.'

'We want to build the greatest stadium facility in world football.' They didn't even build the greatest stadium facility in Subbuteo football.

When asked when this magnificent edifice would rise in

nearby Stanley Park Gillett answered: 'The shovel needs to be in the ground in the next sixty days.' The shovel still sits, with a 'reserved' sticker on, under till three at B&Q's Speke branch.

And here's my favourite from Georgie boy: 'I want to earn the respect of the fans. My message to them is to give us a few years and we'll see where it takes us. Give us a little time and we are going to have some fun together.' I'm sorry but this is way, way past irony now.

The phone started to throb. It was the *Daily Mirror* Features desk. I'm guessing that the way the day is panning out they want me to do an I'm Feeling Yankee Doodle Dandy now we're Beverly Hills Kopped piece.

Don't answer. Think this through.

What's really nagging away is the memory of Anfield's last joint press conference, when Roy Evans and Gerard Houllier were thrown before the microphones and ordered to sell us a bright new future. That literally ended in tears (from Evans' eyes) at another conference four months later.

Was this also a shotgun marriage of financial, if not foot-balling, convenience? Watching Foster Gillett refusing to speak a word to the Hicks boys should have told us that the families may both have been from the same country but geographically and culturally they were thousands of miles apart.

Besides, what did we really know about them?

Gillett had been sniffing around the Premier League for a while. He may have owned ski-resorts and ice-hockey teams but clearly knew puck-all about football. Plus he couldn't have a mountain of his own cash or he wouldn't have had to beg Hicks to wade in with his cheque book.

Why had the Texan only come in at the last minute? What did we know of him other than he ran a couple of US sports teams, once owned Dr Pepper and gave big bucks to George W. Bush? Yes, that George W. Bush. And the main man in our boardroom bankrolls him? Nice. Where does that leave Shankly's quote about the socialism he believed in meaning everyone having a share of the rewards? Or was I coming over all studenty? Was I forgetting that if you want the best capitalists to run your club the chances are they're not going to sell copies of *Socialist Worker* in their spare time?

And anyway, didn't the last manager to win the League, Kenny Dalglish, dress on the right-hand side? Wasn't the last successful chairman, John Smith, bluer than the broken veins on Churchill's conk? Hadn't Rafa Benitez been desperate for a world-class right-winger since he joined?

The language was grating, though. Who'd have imagined we would one day hear the club's owners pretending to talk with passion about the 'Liverpool Reds', 'goal-minders' and 'defence-men'?

Having said that, Liverpool had nearly been bought by bent Thai dictator Thaksin Shinawatra, meaning we could have been sitting there hearing him tell Amnesty International why he doesn't deserve to be fending off homosexual advances in a prison cell doing time for human rights abuses.

They could have been the Glazers who had piled millions of pounds of debt on Manchester United. But they weren't, were they? Hadn't they themselves just told us that? Hadn't the chief executive Rick Parry confirmed it?

They've met Jamie Carragher, Steven Gerrard and Rafa Benitez who've all given the thumbs-up. You have to go with the judgement of those who've met them. As Moores and Parry say, you only get to sell the family silver once and you have to get it right. I know they've made some calamitous decisions in the past – look at Parry's perm, look at Moores' moustache – but surely, surely, they've got this right?

Of course the Yanks were only here for the potential fortunes to be had beaming football into every slum from Caracas to Chongqing. Are we that naive to think they've watched black-and-white YouTube footage of the Kop on *Panorama* singing 'Anyone Who Had a Heart' and thought 'Ah love those wacky, sentimental Scousers so much I want to hand them all my lahf savings to make them happy again?'

Besides, where's the evidence that says all Yanks are bad? For every Glazer at United there's Randy Lerner at Aston Villa whom the Brummies love.

We're going to have to back them now the deal is done. Think glass half-full. They wouldn't pay all this cash for a club to *not* make it successful would they? And where would we be if we hadn't sold to them? The Dubai crowd have walked off, meaning we'd be stuck with Moores and his empty pockets watching Chelsea and United ride over the hills and far away.

The phone goes again. It's getting on for five o'clock. They're impatient. I answer.

'So what do you think about your new best buddies then?'

'I really don't know. They look like aliens in suits and the little one keeps calling Liverpool a franchise. Like we're part of a chain of friggin' fried chicken shops.'

'That's how they speak.'

'It's not how *we* speak, is it?'

'So you want them doing Dick van Dyke Scouse?'

'They've brought their families too. It's creepy. All they're doing is flashing their gnashers and giving off lurrr-ve. If Shirley Jones was here we could re-form the Partridge Family.'

'Well they seem to be talking a good game.'

'They're definitely saying the right things.'

'Well, give them a big welcome then.'

'We can't be sure though, can we? For all we know this could—'

'Typical Scouser. You spend years saying all you need is someone with serious money and you'll be winning everything again, and when your sugar daddies come along all you can do is moan and take the piss out of them. Go with the flow, eh? Anyway the editor's splashing on it under the headline 'We could not walk alone any more' and he wants your words with it. So knock out 300 for the front page.' – *click*.

So that's what I gave them. Three hundred and twenty-six to be precise. Three hundred and twenty-six glass-half-full words that would haunt this Liverpool fan of forty-four years for the next forty-four months.

Bless me, Shankly, for I have sinned. It is four decades since my last confession, and I accuse myself of … criminal naivety:

> It was surreal watching a pair of Fred Flintstone and Barney Rubble characters, sitting in Anfield, chuckling at the prospect of Liverpool FC being their new plaything.
>
> Especially when they thanked the Royal Bank of Scotland for helping them secure ownership of this exciting 'franchise'. How easy it would be to dismiss them as opportunists and lament that the Liverpool Way had been flogged for a fistful of dollars.

But that would be to miss the point. Since Bill Shankly's arrival in 1959, Liverpool had always been about continuity but as with the famous Boot Room the boardroom had reached the end of the line.

Put simply, in a sport where success equates to cash in the bank, Liverpool didn't have any. Which is one of the reasons you have to go back seventeen years to last find them champions of England. Something radical needed to be done to make sure the club had more than a fabulous past.

They had to find new investors with the clout and vision to compete with Europe's best, and with no billionaire Scousers able to step in, it had to be outsiders.

Unparalleled amounts will soon pour into the global game. Gillett and Hicks know the elite will cream it off unless they catapult Liverpool back into that bracket.

The fans feel vulnerable. But maybe they should remember another pair of Yanks, Rodgers and Hammerstein, whose song You'll Never Walk Alone has inspired the club down the ages.

Or simply remember that at the very least the club's debt will go, the new stadium will be built, and men with serious money, knowledge of sport and business intent will be in charge. Men who say they understand the club's traditions and intend to respect them.

Whether they have the desire and commitment for the long-haul remains to be seen.

But until they see evidence to the contrary, most Liverpudlians will give them the benefit of the doubt. And dream.'

Saying a million Hail Marys and a billion Our Fathers could not absolve my sins.

The only consolation I can take is I wasn't the only one to be done up like a kipper as the banner headline on the next day's *Liverpool Echo*: 'Rafa: We're in Good Hands' confirmed.

Plus, I could have been the fan who daubed the following words on to a red bedsheet and proudly held it up on the Kop:

> *Match ticket … £32*
> *New Anfield … £220m*
> *Rafa Benitez … priceless*
> *For everything else …*
> *there's George and Tom*

Indeed, virtually everyone in English football and the English media swallowed it. The logic being the Liverpool board couldn't be that stupid, even though we had ample proof that they could.

It was as though we'd all been in the trenches for so long that when the war was over everyone looked up the line assuming that the men a rank above had checked out the terms of the armistice and handed us a peaceful, prosperous future with our paternal American allies.

Who proceeded to drive their tanks onto our lawn and blast us to hell.

CHAPTER TWO

'The more I looked, the more I became convinced
it was an opportunity to buy a crown jewel of sports
at a modest price'

– Tom Hicks

'A bee-bah-bow-ba-ba-ba-ba-bow … how yawl doin' out there
in pop-picker-land. You're listenin' to Steve King, The Weekend
Wonder Boy on K-O-L-E, the station that makes sure you don't
feel alone in the Lone Star State. Now I wooden know if *you*
have a wooden heart but I most definitely do *not* have a wooden
heart. Cos this daddio's gotta heart full of lurrrrve for all you
crazee cats out there. Which is why your very own King of
Texas is gonna get your beat-feet a-poppin' as he spins you the
latest hot disc from, you guessed it … Dixie's finest … the
Pelvis himself …'

I might be wrong, but that's how I imagine fifteen-year-old
Tom Hicks in 1961 sitting behind the decks of his father's KOLE
radio station, zits popping out of plump baby-faced cheeks
under a greased-back jelly-roll haircut, in his DJ persona as
Steve King The Weekend Wonder Boy.

He'd been doing menial jobs at the station since he was

thirteen, but his dad's decision to give him his own show led to his first big pay-day. And twenty dollars a week in 1961 was nothing to be sniffed at. As Steve King, Hicks was already indulging his lifelong passions of talking big and turning a quick buck while letting others do the donkey work. In this case the likes of Elvis, Del Shannon and Buddy Holly.

Thomas Ollis Hicks was born in Houston on 7 February 1946 and spent his early childhood in Dallas where his father, John, was an advertising salesman for TV and radio stations.

In the late 1950s John Hicks bought out the KOLE radio station in the small, oil-refinery city of Port Arthur, ninety miles outside Houston. The city's only claims to fame were that it was a hot-bed of racial segregation and Janis Joplin's birthplace.

Hicks went to Thomas Edison Junior High and then Thomas Jefferson High School where he was a modestly successful American footballer. Admirers say it was these teenage years spent dee-jaying and playing gridiron that inspired his later investments in sport and media. Others refuse to see past that twenty bucks a week, as it was clear making money was where his heart lay.

After high school, he studied finance at the University of Texas, earning a Bachelor of Business Administration degree in 1968 and two years later he added a Master of Business Administration degree from University of Southern California. While at university he became a brother of the secret-letter Sigma Phi Epsilon fraternity in which he remains to this day, living by its three guiding principles of – no sniggering at the back, please – 'Virtue, Diligence and Brotherly Love'.

His first job on leaving university was with Continental

Illinois in Chicago, where he helped set up a venture capital division. Hicks took to venture capital like a vampire to blood and soon he was in Wall Street, working in the investment departments at first Morgan Guaranty Trust Company and then J.P. Morgan.

In 1974, he moved back to Texas to serve as President of First Dallas Capital Corporation and three years later, at thirty-one, Hicks created Summit Partners to do his first leveraged buyout – the technique of buying low with borrowed money, then selling high at a huge profit, which he perfected so spectacularly it made him a billionaire. The same technique he would employ thirty years later to buy Liverpool. Shame about the profit.

In the greed-is-good 1980s, Hicks was like a (non-criminal) Gordon Gecko, filling his cowboy boots through the gains of leveraged buyouts, with partner Bobby Haas. In one deal alone, they bought Dr Pepper and 7Up for $646 million and sold it on for $2.5 billion.

Hicks and Haas were pulling off coup after coup in media, oil, gas, food and soft drinks, mainly through buying up firms with similarities and putting them together, utilising economies of scale. But the investment world started to change as fund managers came to the fore and in 1989 the pair split because Hicks wanted to raise huge pools of cash to invest in big ventures while Haas preferred to work on individual deals.

One former Hicks and Haas employee who stayed close to both men told Bruce Schoenfeld of US magazine publisher Street & Smith's *SportsBusiness Journal* that Haas had made enough money to last him the rest of his life and wanted out. Not so Hicks.

'It wasn't important for Bobby Haas to be on the Forbes List (the US rich-list) but Hicks cared about such things. He was the quintessential businessman who loved keeping score. He loved doing big deals, showing off his success.'

According to Schoenfeld, Hicks had always been a gambler, but a clued-up one who calculated the odds carefully. The occasional losses were simply seen as the cost of doing business.

Luke Bateman, a Dallas-based investment banker, explained his thinking: 'If you're interested in big money, in big business, raising billion-dollar funds is the way to do it. You can't win in Vegas playing small stakes.'

With Haas gone, Hicks sought partners who shared his desire to reach for the stars. In 1989, he co-founded the investment firm that was to grow into Hicks, Muse, Tate & Furst, with former Prudential Securities banker John Muse.

The firm raised $250 million, with early investments including life insurance company Life Partners Group. In 1991, Morgan Stanley's Charles Tate and First Boston's Jack Furst became partners. During the time that Hicks was chairman (1989 to 2004), the firm raised $12 billion of private equity funds, broke more than $50 billion of leveraged acquisitions, and grew into one of the largest private investment firms in the USA.

Their first few funds were hugely successful, enabling a buoyant Hicks to buy Dallas's prestigious Crespi estate with its historic centrepiece mansion, and turn it into the most elegant, most expensive and most-envied house in Dallas.

Schoenfeld, who interviewed Hicks there in May 2010, when his sports empire was unravelling, describes it thus:

The 28,996-square-foot home connects with George W. Bush's off the back lawn. The Matisse on the library wall looks utterly appropriate, and why not?

The Hicks house is bigger, and more tastefully appointed, than most art museums. At an estimated value of $41 million, down from a high of more than $60 million, it remains the most expensive house in Dallas, which is an achievement in a place that isn't shy about showing off its wealth. Turn into the sweeping driveway, glide past the manicured lawns, and it comes upon you like a Bordeaux chateau, all turrets and greenery.

Hicks owns some $100 million of real estate and controls multiple businesses. His net worth was estimated by Forbes last year at $1 billion, which should keep the Matisse hanging on the wall for a while.

Throughout the 1990s everything Hicks touched turned to gold as he rode the wave of new media with stunning success. He invested $2 million with Mark Cuban's Broadcast.com and turned that into $55 million in less than a year. But when he tried to take a stake in the emerging internet boom his luck changed.

'We were making bets in another exploding industry we knew nothing about,' Hicks told Schoenfeld.

The profits were becoming so huge so quickly, and thus the bets so tempting, he was buying up companies without arranging the capital to run them. 'It was a huge mistake,' said Peter Brodsky who worked for Hicks & Muse and is now a principal at HM Capital. 'By the time we were raising the money, the dot-com bubble had burst.

'Tom Hicks has an iron stomach for risk. As a result, his successes are big, and his failures are big.'

Suddenly, everything the Texan touched was turning brown. His telecom investments ended up losing more than $1 billion, a South American sports channel and other Latin investments went broke and the internet investments never regained anything close to their value.

'In hindsight, where I personally had my biggest success was with middle-market companies,' Hicks told Schoenfeld. 'When we became a bigger institution and started doing larger deals, those were not as successful. I made my money in leveraged buyouts, and gave a lot of it back in money management.'

In 2004, he left Hicks, Muse, Tate & Furst, saying he wanted to spend more time with his family – art dealer wife Cinda and his six children, four from a previous marriage, and, more importantly, his sports firms.

As the dollars rolled on a non-stop conveyer belt towards his tax-minimised accounts during the nineties, Hicks bought into three different sports – baseball, ice hockey and, let's commit blasphemy here, soccer.

Observers say his intentions were twofold. He'd made a billion out of unsexy, unseen deals, but they didn't give him a big profile outside business circles. They didn't boost the view he had of himself as a patrician figure, a pillar of the community to be loved and respected for putting something back. In short, he thought it was time to buy into the ego-massaging industry.

Of course, there was also the small issue of sport becoming big business. Ball games were no longer about how many dollars you took from your local blue-collar workers on the gate or at the burger-stand. It was about how much you could take from companies, from selling on the brand via sponsorship, corporate packaging and TV and internet rights. With Hicks's vast experience and huge portfolio in broadcasting, it seemed natural to him that building and exploiting sports franchises was the future. But when you cut through the hype, spin and rewriting, he only ever enjoyed one major success during fifteen years' investment in sport: winning ice hockey's Stanley Cup with the Dallas Stars.

Meanwhile, there was such a litany of failure and broken promises Hicks would eventually be a leading contender for the title of America's Worst Sports Owner.

According to Schoenfeld, Hicks enjoyed owning sports teams and being saluted as a philanthropic public figure. When things went well he liked the adulation and revelled in beating America's other multimillionaires.

'When I look in the mirror, I see a very competitive guy,' Hicks said. 'I like to win. And what I say about sports is, you get instant feedback. You either win or lose that night.'

But, says Schoenfeld, what matters most to Hicks is the ultimate feedback of a big black number on his financial statement, and all of his investments in sports franchises are primed to pay him handsome returns.

It was why he treated all of the criticism he received – and he received it wherever he went – like water off a shark's fin: 'I've been doing high-risk, high-return investment since 1977. It's all I've ever done,' said Hicks.

'So I'm used to having some deals be great and some not work out. I don't get devastated because, at the end of the day, whatever happens, it's a deal. These are sports teams, so

I have to read about it in the newspaper. That's the only difference.'

He bought the National Hockey League's Dallas Stars in 1996 for $82 million, inheriting a club on the up, with a strong core of home-grown talent, in a hot southern city which was just starting to fully embrace a sport usually loved by cold northerners.

In 1999 they won, for the first time, ice hockey's biggest club accolade, the Stanley Cup, and for a short while in the early 2000s, Dallas Stars was the league's highest-grossing team. Together with Ross Perot Jr., who owned the NBA's Dallas Mavericks, Hicks built the American Airlines Center at a cost of $325 million which was widely hailed the most attractive of its generation of arenas. But the Stars never recaptured the turn-of-the-millennium glory days and went into decline. By the end of season 2009–10, with a skint Hicks trying to bail out and starving them of funds which left their wage bill way below their rivals, they finished last in the Pacific Division.

It was the first time the franchise had failed to make the play-offs for two consecutive seasons since moving to Dallas in 1993. Hicks wanted out and the feeling could definitely be described as mutual.

There was a different kind of star rising in Texas in the 1990s called George W. Bush, a piece of whom Hicks quickly realised he had to have. Down in the Lone Star state, their relationship is still viewed, by many, with suspicion.

In 1994, Hicks switched sides in the state governorship race, moving his hefty financial backing from the Democrat Ann

Richards to Republican Bush, pumping so much into the future president's coffers he became part of an elite group of donors called Bush Pioneers.

When elected, Hicks persuaded Governor Bush to form a private investment company called The University of Texas Investment Management Company (UTIMCO), which awarded lucrative contracts from public funds to private firms, including ones connected to Hicks.

UTIMCO's board consisted of Bush Pioneers and Yale University connections, and operated without any disclosure or public scrutiny until the Texas Legislature intervened. By then UTIMCO had lost a fortune in failed investments in Enron and WorldCom stock. Investigations revealed a pattern of cronyism with substantial investments going to a group of companies with close ties to Bush and Hicks.

In 1999 Hicks was forced to resign after the Houston *Chronicle* exposed these dealings. Award-winning investigative journalist (and massive Liverpool fan) Ed Vulliamy, who was the *Observer*'s man in America, says:

> After Bush made him a regent of the University of Texas Board in return for a hefty donation to his campaign coffers, Hicks revolutionised the way the university invested its funds.
>
> He 'privatised' some $9 million of assets into UTIMCO, which also guaranteed good salaries for Hicks and his fellow regents on the board.
>
> UTIMCO soon went into politics. The company placed $10 million with the Carlyle Group merchant bank in Washington, whose chairman was Frank Carlucci, Ronald

Reagan's former Defense Secretary. George W. Bush had
a seat on Carlyle's board.

There was no criminality, but analysts see Hicks, who became
Bush's fourth biggest campaign donor, as one of the President's
Texan 'Good ol' Boys' cronies.

And he certainly looked after his political friend. In 1998
when Hicks bought the Texas Rangers baseball team for $250
million, from a group headed by Bush, Dubya received a bonus
of $12.6 million on top of the $2.3 million he earned from his
$606,000 investment in the franchise, thus boosting his wind-
fall to $14.9 million.

As Vulliamy notes: 'Tom Hicks was the man who really made
George W. Bush rich.'

But when asked about their friendship at his first Anfield
press conference, Hicks, conscious that he was now in a city
that could never be described as natural Bush territory, replied:
'Certain media would say I'm one of his closest friends. I'm
not in his inner circle. I know his dad.

'But he is a big baseball fan and once every two years I bring
my star players to the White House to meet him. Would I do
the same with Liverpool? Sure, if they're in the neighbourhood.'
Fortunately they never were.

After Hicks took over the Texas Rangers things went relatively well. They won their local division titles in 1998 and 1999
but failed to make any impact on baseball's coveted World Series.

Hicks knew that if he was to win kudos and make a financial killing he had to do a deal that would make American sport
believe there was a new mogul in town. A mogul with balls
bigger than Texas. So in the winter of 2000 he lured Alex

Rodriguez, the best player in baseball, to the Texas Rangers with a ten-year, $252 million contract, which was the most generous in the history of the game. Hicks's plan was to make A-Rod, as he was known, the cornerstone of a franchise which would sweep all before it.

'I like to win. I like to build things, whether it's a $2 billion corporate acquisition or a chance to win the World Series,' Hicks said at the time. 'This is a chance for our team to win a World Series and leapfrog into an area where we've never been before.'

What a shame this deal went down as the worst ever in modern baseball. What an even greater shame it led one American newspaper to christen Hicks 'Tom Dumb'.

It was a spectacularly reckless transaction made by a man who clearly understood very little about sport. A-Rod was a big star, but no other club had been willing to pay within $100 million of that sum for him, meaning Hicks had outbid himself on a grand scale. But it didn't stop there. By busting the bank for A-Rod there was no cash left for much-needed investment in the rest of the squad. With no funds available for quality pitchers, which are vital to decent teams, the Rangers had the seventh-highest payroll yet one of the worst teams.

By the end of the 2003 season it was clear the only way the Rangers were going to be successful was by selling Rodriguez and using the proceeds to rebuild the entire squad. At this point the comedy turns to farce. After tortuous negotiations to sell A-Rod to the Boston Red Sox failed, Hicks made him captain and announced he'd see out his full ten-year contract (which would have taken him up to the age of thirty-five).

'A benefit of Alex now being the official leader of our team is that our fans are now confident he is going to be here,' said Hicks. 'If we don't win, the fans are going to be mad. But we're going to win.'

A couple of weeks later he moved Rodriguez to the New York Yankees in a deal that left egg splattered all over his face. He had to pay them to take A-Rod off his hands. With $179 million still owed to Rodriguez, Hicks paid him $67 million to leave, allowing the Yankees to sign him for a mere $16 million a year.

Hicks had believed he could buy the World Series simply by bribing a megastar to shine in a team of average players, but all he bought was acute embarrassment and confirmation of his own sporting ignorance. Fair play to A-Rod though. All in all, he took Hicks for $140 million, giving him in return three seasons where the Rangers finished bottom of the league every time.

You can blame the world's most famous Viagra salesman for getting Hicks involved in football – that's the football of WAGs not moms.

In March 1998 the Pele Law, named after the legendary player, was passed to attract outside investment into Brazil's debt-ridden national sport. The top twenty teams were more than £250 million in the red, most paying it down by selling the transfer rights to their best players to foreign, mainly European teams. In 1999 a staggering 658 Brazilian professionals were sold abroad. The inherent problem was that Brazilian teams were legally bound to be run in a feudal manner, as social and athletic clubs rather than businesses. Pele Law changed that, allowing them to become corporations and negotiate their own commercial deals.

Hicks, Muse, Tate & Furst were quick to spot an opening.

'It's hard to imagine a better sector in which to invest in Brazil,' said Charles Tate at the time. 'If you add up all the fans of professional baseball, basketball, football and hockey in the United States, that number is lower than the number of Brazilians who are soccer fans.'

HMT&F invested more than £40 million in Corinthians in the first year of what was supposedly a ten-year partnership deal. So confident were they of striking it rich in Brazil that, six months after their investment in Corinthians, they took over the business operations of Cruzeiro, a first-division team from the east-central city of Belo Horizonte.

The plan was to buy up the cream of Brazilian football, broadcast their games all over Latin America on the Hicks-owned TV station PSN, sit back and watch the dollars roll in.

Just as he did at Liverpool, Hicks & co. talked Texan Big when Corinthians was bought. There were promises of bringing in the best players and the building of a 45,000-seater stadium in the suburbs of São Paulo, and at first they gave the fans hope. They tied down the best players with new contracts, found the cash to bring in decent additions like Dida and Luizao and signed a $12 million, two-year sponsorship deal with Pepsi.

On the pitch things were going well mainly because Corinthians were a side on the up. They had won the Brazilian championship in 1998, which they retained, as well as winning the FIFA Club World Championship in 2000.

But not long after that prestigious victory things began to go downhill. Corinthians weren't bringing in the returns quickly enough to satisfy HMT&F, so they sold transfer rights to two of the star players, which brought in $12 million. Money which wasn't reinvested in the team. Fans were enraged, especially when stories emerged of plans to change their famous black-and-white kit, and the anti-Hicks & co. protests began.

One Brazilian source said at the time: 'The Americans came into Corinthians with money but did not understand the way football works. They brought in a strong team of advisers to administer the club but the way they did things was very American, in the crudest sense. The model they wanted does not function here. Things had to be done their way.'

In a scenario familiar to Kopites, Hicks finally bailed out in 2003 after three years of ultimate failure amid boardroom in-fighting, fan resentment, accusations that its local partner in Brazil had 'misappropriated funds' and legal wrangling which dragged on for another four years.

Corinthians, Brazil's second-most popular club with a reputed following of twenty million fans, were left on a downward spiral. MSI took over the club's management but, despite a league title in 2005, the financial problems initiated by HMT&F proved too much of a burden and they were relegated to the second tier of Brazilian football for the first time in their history in 2007. The fans never saw that new stadium.

When Hicks was desperately trying to sell Liverpool for an over-inflated price in 2008, he issued a prospectus to financial companies describing himself as 'a master of purchasing and growing professional sports teams'.

Fans of Corinthians, the Texas Rangers, the Dallas Stars and Liverpool might disagree with that. After they've employed a surgeon to pick them off the floor and stitch up their split sides.

*

When the bailiffs finally came for George Nield Gillett Jr., taking his collection of thirty classic cars and his 235,000-acre Oregon ranch, the personal humiliation was beyond devastating: 'I had ten days to get out of my house,' said the father-of-four. 'I had to buy back my clothes. I had to buy back my dogs.'

In 1992, as Liverpool sank to their worst league finish for twenty-seven years, Gillett was plunging even lower. For a quarter of a century the rich kid from Wisconsin had been building a billion-dollar empire, spread across the sports, media and meat industries.

But it was an empire built on high-risk borrowing which was always one big, godawful deal away from ruin. That deal was buying Storer Communications' six TV stations, which went so badly wrong it left his businesses with debts of $1 billion and a personal bankruptcy to the tune of $66 million.

Back then he admitted he had 'caused the problem' that led to the downfall of Gillett Holdings because of an 'error in judgement and timing' about the Storer deal. To be specific he had overpaid, on money borrowed via high-risk 'junk bonds', for the stations just as the TV industry was going into recession. When those junk bond rates soared past 17 per cent he couldn't pay. Or as he puts it: 'When the notes came due, we were dead.'

Gillett's riches-to-rags-to-riches story uncannily mirrors the rise and fall of the world money markets since the 1960s. Like Tom Hicks, Gillett saw no point in thinking small. He loved the chase and got high on the risk, playing the markets, schmoozing the clients, sealing the deal. If that risk was being determined by monetary forces outside his control, so be it. He could brave it out. The prize was all.

Time magazine wrote in 1997 about the keen downhill sloper's penchant for building his business ventures on a mountain of junk securities: 'Gillett personally relishes skiing "steep and deep" which is not a bad metaphor for his investment style.'

When Gillett confessed to the interviewer of his weakness for moving too fast and buying too much – 'I've lived my dreams, but then I blow them up' – *Time* sarcastically noted: 'How comforting that must be to his bond-holders.'

He was born in 1938, in Racine, Wisconsin, a small, affluent city on the shore of Lake Michigan, sixty miles north of Chicago. His mother came from a rich Milwaukee family, his father owned a car dealership and was a prominent surgeon. It's fair to say the economic ravages of America's 1930s Great Depression never paid a visit to the Gillett front door.

He went to the exclusive independent prep school Lake Forest Academy before attending the private Amherst College in Massachusetts. His first jobs were as a salesman before becoming a management consultant with McKinsey & Company, where he learnt the stratagems and slick gimmicks of the business world. As a leading Whitehall mandarin said of McKinsey & Co. when Tony Blair hired them to restructure his Cabinet Office: 'They're basically people who come in and use PowerPoint to state the bleeding obvious.'

In 1966, aged twenty-eight, he decided to invest in sport, and made a speculative call to Pete Rozelle, the Nation Football League (NFL) commissioner, to ask about potential opportunities.

Rozelle, believing he was an heir to the Gillette toiletries empire, and thus the best his sport could get, gave him a lead on an emerging expansion franchise called the Miami Dolphins. Gillett bought 22 per cent and became the team's business manager. Two years later, he and two partners bought the Harlem Globetrotters, the fabled basketball team, whose popularity had begun to wane. This was the kind of opportunity that stirred Gillett's juices. A historic sports institution, on its uppers, which was failing to move with the times but which had massive potential. Ring any bells?

Even in the late-sixties Gillett realised the way to make money out of a sports brand was to maximise the power of television, which led him to come up with an inspirational idea: turning the team into a cartoon series. Hanna-Barbera's *Harlem Globetrotters* began on CBS in 1970 and was an instant hit, boosting the appeal of the team and bringing advertisers to the table. Gillett used the Globetrotter franchise to build his first firm, Globetrotter Communications, which included the basketball team, the animated TV show, a marketing division, and a golf equipment manufacturer.

In 1969, Gillett bought two radio stations in Cleveland. When Globetrotter Communications went public in 1971, he used the cash to buy three other radio stations, two in Chicago and one in Detroit. Gillett sold out his stake in the Globetrotters for $3 million and began searching for companies that could be turned around rapidly.

He bought more small radio stations in Sioux Falls, South Dakota; Erie, Pennsylvania; and Bakersfield, California. He took over Packerland Packing Company, a failing beef plant in Green Bay, Wisconsin. The beef industry of the late 1970s was plagued by overproduction and a market hampered by increasingly health-conscious Americans, so Gillett shifted the focus of the company towards production of lean, low-cholesterol meats. Packerland became the first company to win the US Food and

Drug Administration's 'light' beef classification. Packerland's sales soared, which impressed Gillett's bankers, who provided him with a steady source of cash for acquisitions elsewhere. The Gillett Group, as it was then known, was born.

Early in 1981 Gillett bought his first major television station, WSMV-TV in Nashville, Tennessee. The station was the top-ratings channel locally, and competition to buy it was intense, but through a combination of charm, hard-sell and a commitment to move his family to Nashville, Gillett sealed the deal.

By now he was developing his own unique strategies for buyouts. He convinced the owners of WSMV, an insurance company, that it would save on taxes and net a higher profit if they simply gave him the station in exchange for $42 million in notes that would not pay out until 1986. The price was twenty-one times the station's annual earnings, but within five years it was worth $180 million. Gillett was praised not just for his savvy but for his laid-back management style.

Gillett's ownership of WSMV was marred when an investigative news series critical of government meat inspections mentioned three supermarket chains that did $100 million annual business with Packerland. But the scandal did little to halt Gillett's success.

Between 1980 and 1986, WSMV's operating cash flow increased from $2 million to $11.2 million, and Packerland had become a steady source of revenue for other acquisitions, providing over $100 million cash.

Gillett's new-found wealth enabled him to buy a prestigious piece of real estate – Colorado's huge Vail and Beaver Creek ski resorts. He started to spend his summers and winters there

– often posing as a ski-lift employee to get feedback from customers – flying by private jet to the family home in Nashville.

In 1986, Gillett sought the assistance of junk bond king Michael Milken to raise over $650 million, and snapped up a dozen TV stations in the wake of liquidations and mergers throughout the broadcasting industry.

Like Hicks, Gillett was doing remarkably well (mostly with other people's money) out of the greed-is-good eighties. He had built his multi-faceted empire during a time of deregulation and junk bond financing, and was beginning to feel indestructible. Which is never a good thing.

He had long coveted Storer Communications' six TV stations, having known the company's chairman, Peter Storer, since the late 1970s. Despite warnings from Milken that, at fifteen times cash flow, the price for Storer Communications was too high, Gillett bought the stations in partnership with Kohlberg Kravis Roberts (KKR). The structure of the arrangement, like Gillett's Nashville deal, was unique in broadcasting. Gillett Holdings and KKR each contributed $100 million in equity, and the remaining $1.1 billion of the purchase price was financed by $600 million in bank loans, and $550 million in junk bonds – most of them paying no interest for seven years, but maturing at an astounding 17.5 per cent.

The six stations were held by a new company, SCI Television, of which Gillett Holdings owned 51 per cent and KKR the remaining 49 per cent. But as the Storer deal was being done in November 1987 the television industry peaked. Viewers and advertisers were moving into video and cable, earnings began to fall and Gillett Holdings' junk bonds plunged to 80 per cent of their original value.

By late 1989, Gillett Holdings was in trouble: Gillett sold WSMV-TV for $125 million and used most of the proceeds to pay down bank loans. Meanwhile, Storer Communications defaulted on $153 million in interest on public debt. But rather than force Storer Communications into bankruptcy, Gillett managed to convince bond-holders to restructure the subsidiary's more than $500 million bonded debt.

Storer's financial woes bounced onto Gillett Holdings, which had serious problems of its own. By 1990 the company's bonds had become so insecure that some traded as low as seventeen cents on the dollar. Then, in August, Gillett Holdings defaulted on over $450 million of debt. By February 1991, bond-holders frustrated with Gillett's half-hearted attempts at restructuring filed an involuntary bankruptcy petition. When the company failed to meet the resulting court-imposed deadline it was forced into Chapter 11 bankruptcy. However, in the company restructuring that followed, savvy Gillett negotiated a $1.5 million annual salary to manage the Vail skiing operation, plus some stock options, $5 million in Gillett Holdings securities, and $125,000 per year in life insurance premiums.

With the little capital he had, he started again. After floating the Vail stock options he walked away with $32 million, which was enough to rebuild his empire.

In 1994 he bought back the meat-packing firm he'd lost and snapped up more meat-packing companies, moving beyond beef into the poultry market. He added a barge business in the Pacific and some golf courses in Montana. In 1996 he formed Booth Creek Ski Holdings, acquiring or expanding ski resorts in Wyoming, New Hampshire, California and Washington. By 2000, eight years after bankruptcy, Gillett had clawed back half of the billion-dollar fortune he'd lost through bankruptcy. And as a new century dawned he set his sights on doing what he believed he did best, and where he believed there was big money to be made – owning sports teams.

He tried to buy the Denver Nuggetts basketball team and the Colorado Avalanche ice hockey franchise, along with the stadium they play in, but was rebuffed. In 2001 he paid $185 million for an 80 per cent share in the Montreal Canadiens ice hockey team, and its 21,000-seater Bell Centre arena.

Its motto should raise a smile among Liverpool fans: 'To you from failing hands we throw the torch. Be yours to hold it high.' As should the track record since Gillett's takeover of the National Hockey League's most successful club: they've won nothing of note.

'We went into a relatively hostile environment in Montreal, culturally at least,' said Gillett. 'We didn't come from that community. A lot of the people knew that the club was for sale and none of the locals bought it so you obviously go in with a level of suspicion. Your first reaction is there must be something wrong with it.

'Rather than saying to the fans "I come with the answer", I clearly don't. I think you'd be terribly presumptuous to come into a community like Montreal with twenty-four Stanley Cups and say "I can do it better". I don't think we came with an answer. I think we came with questions.'

They also arrived in the wake of another US sports owner, Jeffrey Loria, who had bought the Montreal Expos from local interests when no one else wanted them, said all of the right things about being committed to the city and to making baseball work in Montreal, before moving the franchise to Washington.

Loria was cast as a cartoon villain, the cynical foreign opportunist. And now here was another American, apparently a friendlier one, but one whose motives were instantly called into question simply because of what had gone before.

'For the first year in Montreal, more than half the articles were about whether we were like Loria or not,' says George's son Foster Gillett, who moved to Montreal to help run the Canadiens (as he did with Liverpool although some would question the use of the words 'help' and 'run').

'It took us a while to stand on our own two feet and not be continually compared to these Americans who came before us.'

Winning the locals over was a task Gillett warmed to, and he could often be seen in the Bell Centre taking up empty seats and chatting to the fans, listening to their concerns, dishing out soda pops and flattery. The Wisconsin Kid has always used charm and flattery to get his way, as the wooing of Rick Parry, David Moores and his wife, and the opening Anfield press conference were to testify. He calls people 'sweetie', the women who work in the offices 'gorgeous' and almost every English sports journalist who dealt with him tells of a similar greeting whenever they needed hard answers from him: 'You know you're my favourite writer. I really love your stuff ...'

Gillett is small, gregarious, thinks he has a neat sense of humour and tries to disarm all-comers with an intense personal connection. When once asked why he never wears a watch he replied: 'It's a personal philosophy of relationships. Whomever I'm with is the most important person in my life at that time.' Which could have come straight out of the McKinsey manual of How To Perfect Blue-sky Thinking, Corporate Bollock-Speak. He'd go out of his way to have you believe he was the guy next door who was also your best friend 'You can always contact me,' he'd say, 'my number's in the phone book, but you'd better have a good question when you call.' But underneath was a hard, shrewd operator. If a little mad.

Ask most English people what they made of him and you get a puzzled look, a laugh, a head-shake and an admission they could never quite work him out. He was always acting weird, spouting oblique ideas, giving rhetorical and ambiguous answers. A constantly chattering clockwork mouse, who never really told you anything.

Gillett somehow managed to perfect an evasive style which was both self-effacing and self-congratulatory at the same time. This was his reply when asked why he went into the sports business:

'Each person in life has their own comfort zone. Some people jaywalk. And we see people dive across interstates. Other people only cross at the intersection and only do it with the lights. Maybe I've crossed against red more often than I should have.'

What freaked many was every time they met him he wore walking boots under his suit. The comfort footwear was down to him having both knees replaced after skiing injuries, but the muddy hikers were nonetheless off-putting.

Having been encouraged by the success of the Canadiens and bullish on the prospects of blue-chip professional sports franchises, Gillett decided it was time to think big. So he looked across the Atlantic to the country and the sport that was raking in the greenbacks like no other.

What made English football so attractive to American investors like the Glazer family, Randy Lerner and Gillett was the ease of entry. Investors could execute rapid takeovers through leveraged buyouts, dealing with a few key shareholders, and then take advantage of revenue streams that legislation in North America forbids. Selling club-branded credit cards and having lucrative links with gambling firms are examples. They also saw untapped financial opportunities in stadium management, with seven-day earning potential, and an absence of established naming rights.

America's population was becoming more Hispanic and thus more football-obsessed. In 2007 there were 42 million Hispanic Americans. By 2020 a quarter of Americans will be of Hispanic origin or ethnicity. Therein lies potential for English clubs to make money in America. Then, of course, there are the phenomenal TV deals falling into the laps of Premier League clubs.

Gillett had been circling the Premier League for a few years, looking for prey. Foster, a passionate sports fan, was a driving force. Gillett's three other sons, Geordie, Alex and Andrew, became involved in other aspects of the family business.

'We started looking for clubs that had a very strong fan base that perhaps weren't as well developed as they might have been,' says Gillett. He refuses to admit he failed to buy Aston Villa, losing out to another American, and owner of NFL's Cleveland Browns, Randy Lerner.

But he did. As Villa's then chairman Doug Ellis explains, he was desperate to buy him out. All that stopped it happening was Ellis realising Gillett wanted to borrow money to buy Villa, thus putting the debt on the club.

'The *Birmingham Evening Mail* ran the headline "Doug Will Sell" and this attracted a lot of predators,' says Ellis. 'The independent valuation was £115 million. As I thought I was on my death bed, this was reduced by £30 million.

'Gillett badly wanted the club, and was willing to meet the new asking price. On his second visit, I told him that at a community club such as Aston Villa the owner should live in situ. He said he could not, but that his son would.

'All but one of the suitors, I was informed by Rothschild's, were borrowing money to strike the deal. I do not believe in borrowing. It is against my principles. And I do not believe it is the way a football club should be run. The exception was Randy Lerner. When he came over to see me, he was soon followed by his bank manager.

'I was impressed by Lerner's demeanour and by his record. On his third visit, he said he would pay £20 million less than the asking price – but in cash. He asked me to trust him when declining to pay £20 million into a fund to spend on players.

'I could have benefited by £20 million but I did not wish to saddle the club I had run since 1968 with debt. I believed Randy was the right man and so far I have been proved right.

'As for Liverpool, it is not the way I would have run it. Gillett is a nice enough fellow but he and Hicks were hardly ever there. I never met them in the Anfield boardroom.'

After losing out on Villa, the investment banker Gillett had been working with alerted him to Liverpool and he liked what he saw, particularly as the club was still basking in the afterglow of the 2005 Champions League victory in Istanbul. Here was a fanatical supporter base that would surely fill every seat in a new stadium, a glorious history that had made them one of football's global brands, a consistent Champions League participant and thus a prime benefactor of the TV billions pouring into the game.

There was only one problem. He didn't have the £450

million needed to buy out the Liverpool shareholders and build a new stadium. He had several meetings with Rick Parry and David Moores (during which his case wasn't helped by rumours emerging that he had floated the idea of a groundshare with Everton), but due to his lack of serious wealth was always seen as a non-starter. It came as no surprise in late 2006 when Liverpool announced they were selling to the infinitely-wealthier Dubai Investment Capital, which led to a typical piece of Gillettian wit: 'I lost to an entire country.'

But he refused to give up. After Parry called, in November, to tell him he was going with DIC, he switched his efforts to finding a wealthy partner to move in for the kill if the Arab bid fell through. What better partner than Tom Hicks, with whom he had worked in 2002 to pull off a series of mergers and form meat-packers Swift & Co., the second largest pork and beef processor in the world?

On the surface, the effervescent, jokey northern boy and the serious, dead-eyed Texan seemed unlikely soulmates. But they had plenty in common, and not just a love of cutting a deal, pocketing a huge profit and getting out.

They shared interests in art: Hicks's wife, Cinda, was a former New York dealer, while Gillett's wife, Rose, bought him a set of eighteenth-century landscape paintings one Christmas. They already owned sports clubs and, despite being in their sixties, enjoyed participating: Gillett was an ace skier while Hicks played golf and shot pheasant. Put them together and you've got James Bond. Look at them separately and you've got Tom and Jerry.

They bumped into each other at the annual convention for ice-hockey owners and Gillett filled Hicks in on Liverpool, telling him there were signs of uncertainty over the Dubai bid. How they'd spent an eternity on due diligence. How David Moores was having sleepless nights worrying about the deal, especially after the *Daily Telegraph* leaked a report which claimed DIC were planning to sell Liverpool after seven years.

Gillett convinced Hicks this was a once-in-a-lifetime opportunity, the crowning glory of their careers. What they'd 'always dreamed of.' By putting together Liverpool with the Dallas Stars, Texas Rangers and Montreal Canadiens they could answer the needs of any potential client, whether in Europe, the States or Far East.

'We'll be able to show the world something new and different,' said Gillett.

Hicks went away and Googled Liverpool and was taken aback by their history. He studied the Premier League's recent £2.7 billion TV deal, realised its worldwide potential and couldn't believe the figures that were leaping off the screen: 'The more I looked,' said Hicks, 'the more I became convinced it was an opportunity to buy a crown jewel of sports at a modest price.'

Within forty-eight hours their shotgun wedding was mutually blessed. They went back to Liverpool, armed with Hicks's billionaire ranking on the Forbes List, and piled on the promises to buy the shares at £500 more than the Arabs were offering, build the stadium, provide money for players, safeguard the club's traditions and generally make Anfield heaven on earth.

By the time they were having dinner with Moores and his wife Marge, and laying on the charm with a Texan-sized trowel, it was already game over.

Now, unless your name is Wayne Rooney, and the print is too small for you, it's probably taken you less than thirty minutes to read this chapter. Half an hour, at most, to discover that Tom Hicks was a serial asset-stripper and a failed sports entrepreneur whose game plan wherever he went was to make huge profits leveraging the price of a failing institution, using someone else's money to do it. George Gillett was a bankrupt who did have a pot to urinate in, but it was so small it could be filled by a Lilliputian after a vicar's tea party.

If it took you thirty minutes to discover that about the people Liverpool FC were selling the family silver to, where were the eyes, the ears and the brains of the directors and shareholders who had been entrusted with that precious cargo?

Why did they, after years of searching for and rejecting potential suitors, decide at the eleventh hour to ditch Sheikh Mohammed's Dubai Investment Capital, whose accountants had spent more than a year doing due diligence, in favour of a couple of Americans, one completely unknown to them, who didn't even ask to see the books?

As the *Guardian*'s Paul Hayward wrote at the time: 'A club synonymous with the earthy virtues of Shankly, Paisley and Dalglish rebuffed a suitor wealthier than Roman Abramovich to foxtrot with George Gillett and a partner who showed up later than a mystery man in a Hollywood thriller.

'Picture the scene in a secret location.

'"Who's your friend?" the Anfield money men ask Gillett as an exuberant cap-wearing Texan called Tom Hicks joins the negotiations.

'"Don't worry. This guy's for real. He's George Dubya's buddy."

'And before you know it, Sheik Mohammed suddenly knows what it's like to make a generous offer for a house in Fulham only to be told by an eighteen-year-old estate agent that a City boy with a bonus has just blown him out of the water.'

CHAPTER THREE

'I'm handing it over to safe hands. This is not someone coming over just to make a quick buck. They are in it for the long term'

– David Moores

The coaches from Krakow, Warsaw, Lodz and Wroclaw had been pulling up all morning in the car parks around Old Trafford. It was October 2005, and eight thousand Poles had passed over land and sea in the hope of seeing their country knock England off the top of their World Cup qualifying group. After mooching around the ground in the rain, and staring at Ryan Giggs bedside lamps in the United megastore for shelter, hundreds drifted back to the coaches, woke the drivers from their back-seat kip and asked a favour.

How would they fancy, in return for a fistful of Zlotys, taking them down the road to a real footballing shrine? How about an afternoon at Anfield?

To work out how hot Liverpool were around this time think of a nude Heidi Klum sitting in a sauna after a gallon of water has been lashed on the coals. That stunning, emotional Champions League triumph five months earlier in Istanbul had inspired a tidal wave of support. Indeed an official Europe-wide survey of fans that summer named Liverpool the continent's most popular second team.

Three countries in particular had been bitten by the bug. Spain, because of Rafa Benitez, Xabi Alonso and Luis Garcia; Italy, because most of the nation were grateful for Liverpool breaking the hearts of Silvio Berlusconi's AC Milan; and Poland, because of Jerzy Dudek, the boy from the small Silesian city of Rybnik, whose goalkeeping heroics during extra time and the penalty shoot-out had made him a national sporting legend.

Make that a saint, after he dedicated his Istanbul performance to the former goalkeeper, Polish Pope John Paul II, who had died a month before the final.

That's why the boys from Warsaw and Lodz didn't want to stare at Wayne Rooney bedspreads, the Matt Busby statue or the Munich clock. They wanted to see Anfield, home of the famous Kop, and its trophy room, home to the European Cup, which had become theirs to keep after winning it for the fifth time.

How could the drivers refuse, especially if there was a chance of getting their photo taken in the Kop goal doing the Dudek?

And so to Anfield.

'Sorry, lads. The only way you can get inside the ground is on a stadium tour and they're fully booked.'

'But we've come all the way from Poland.'

'As I say. Nothing I can do.'

'Can't we just go into the museum?'

'You've got to have a ticket for the stadium tour to get in, and we're fully booked.'

'But there are lots of us and we just want to have a look inside the ground.'

'As I say ...'

'But what if' – pulls out a tenner – 'we all pay you, just to let us in and take photographs standing in front of the Kop. It won't take long, then we will go.'

'As I say, the stadium tours are fully booked today. The club shop's open, though.'

'Can we get a drink and a meal?'

'Er' – stares at watch – 'the cafe down the road might be open.'

Welcome to the European Capital of Football, folks. Not so much the Nou Camp as the No Chance.

The Polish hordes drifted off disappointed and bemused into the club store to grab the last few remaining Dudek mugs, before strolling around the outside of the ground. The only surface on which to sit and view one of the most iconic football stadiums in the world was a small stretch of wall facing the Kop.

The only place to take photographs was standing on the other side of Walton Breck Road, hoping a 26 bus didn't fly past, spraying your Kodak with gutter-rain and blocking out your smiling pal under the Paisley Gates.

Back to Manchester they travelled, without getting a glimpse of the European Cup or the Kop, wondering where all that garbage came from about Anfield being a warm and special place, the proud heartbeat of the world's most popular club. Outside and inside Old Trafford was where they spent their money and took home presents and memories. Never mind, lads. If you bought a Wayne Rooney bedspread and managed to keep it stainless, you've probably got a collectors' item.

This is just one of countless examples of how Liverpool's commercial department has been a laughing stock for years when compared to the smooth-running, big-hitting, all-singing, all-dancing operation down the M62. Throughout the 1990s, Old Trafford was Harrods, while Anfield was a corner shop. As this century progressed, United's brand, fired by repeated Premier League wins and Champions League successes, grew even stronger. While Liverpool's flat-lined.

As screenwriter and Kop season-ticket holder Roy Boulter put it: 'We weren't even a corner shop by comparison. We were the greasy-haired hot-dog seller who used to stand outside the Arkles pub, a wheel missing from his stand, flicking ash into his watery onions. Doing trade only when he felt like and only with the desperate.'

All you need to know about Liverpool's non-ability to cash in on its global brand is contained in the following sentence. On 26 May 2005, when all of Europe woke up with the previous night's Istanbul images imprinted on their minds, Liverpool's club shop remained shut all day. Clearly the hot-dog man had a hangover.

For years Liverpool's commercial and marketing operation had been derided by fans, rival teams and suppliers. But the feeling was, after Istanbul, Liverpool were looking at a huge open-goal even they could not miss. It turned out they had more misses in them than Emile Heskey.

The problems were they had few staff, most of whom were overworked and demotivated. There was no proper management structure and they outsourced most of their operations, meaning other businesses were left to exploit the Liverpool brand and cream off a nice profit. George Davies did the merchandising, Paul Heathcote the catering, Granada the TV, etc.

Fans abroad (remember that global fan base Liverpool smugly refer to) would complain about a baffling inability to buy products online, due to the store nearly always being out of stock. It wasn't that baffling when you saw how the system worked. Online ordering was done via virtual buckets. For example, there would be a bucket containing large-sized home shirts. Whenever the bucket emptied someone had to spot it and manually transfer new shirts over from stock.

No one had bothered to work out, or maybe chose to ignore, that when staff went home at five thirty p.m. and the other side of the world was waking up, if the bucket was empty, regardless of whether large-sized home shirts were stacked to the warehouse ceiling, customers were told there were none left. And, even more criminal from a business perspective, the system wasn't asking for details so they could get back and sell it to them when it arrived in stock.

The logic behind this award-winning customer care campaign was that Liverpool didn't really want you to shop online. Due to outsourcing, it was more lucrative to sell through the official club shop because Liverpool kept 100 per cent of the profit. Anything sold online went through Granada, who took 33 per cent.

No one had stopped to think that if you live on the other side of the world the chances are you won't get to the club shop, or be near a computer between nine a.m. and five thirty p.m. GMT, and therefore 66 per cent of profit on a shirt was better than no profit at all.

The amateurish approach to sponsorship was even worse.

Back in 1979, under the stewardship of Peter Robinson and John Smith, Liverpool became the first English club to have sponsors' names on their shirts, after a deal was sealed with Hitachi.

At the time of Istanbul they were getting £3 million a year from Carlsberg, which eventually went up to £7 million in 2007. Manchester United were getting £15 million, and were about to trade up to £20 million. I have heard both former sponsors and managers of radio stations who cut deals with Liverpool brag how they knew all along that they were paying vastly under the odds for their access.

It was small wonder some sponsors left. An executive at one former sponsor found after the deal was over that his firm had been entitled to have an end-of-season game on the Anfield pitch. When he asked the club why he hadn't been told about the perk, the answer was: 'Well, you never asked us.'

There were few management meetings, but then there were few staff. Or if we're being generous, there were roughly as many staff as Wigan Athletic employed, but with no structure. Just everything going through an over-burdened chief executive, Rick Parry, whose chairman, David Moores, let him get on with it.

As a senior Anfield source put it: 'With David it was all about having an easy life. Not because he was a bad person, and certainly not because he didn't care about Liverpool. But because all he wanted to do was turn up, park his car, have a smoke in the boardroom, go to the match, be around the players and the club, and go back home. If you confronted him with a problem he'd wave you away with the words 'see Rick'. As for Rick, he just took on far too much. Any commercial prowess he'd had when he joined Liverpool had probably been beaten out of him during his time there.'

And it wasn't just on the commercial side where the club bumbled along in an amateurish way. It extended to the dealings with the manager, staff and players. Take the dismissal of manager Gerard Houllier in the summer of 2004. As early as the Marseille game in March, journalists were talking about Houllier being finished and Valencia's Rafa Benitez, who had been approached behind-the-scenes by Liverpool, as the next manager.

A few days after the final game of the season, a board meeting was held during which David Moores reluctantly proposed parting company with Houllier. Within forty-five seconds he was unanimously backed by the board. The next item on the agenda was Houllier's review of the season and his plans for the next one. Not only did they usher the Frenchman in and allow him to spend the next two hours detailing where things had gone wrong and how he would put them right, he was grilled by board members on his assessments and proposals. Despite knowing they'd just decided to bid him au revoir.

When Moores was asked when he was going to do the honourable thing he said he couldn't do it that week because he'd invited Houllier and his wife to his Lake District home the following weekend for a get-together. So Houllier turned up and had a good time believing everything was right with the world. All because his chairman didn't have the bottle to tell him the board had voted to dismiss him. On it went into a second week, and when the deed was eventually done it was Parry who did it. Was Moores a too-decent man, a too-weak man, or both? Opinion was divided.

Behind this terminal indecision lay a sad myth you're going to read a lot about in this book: The Liverpool Way. Or rather the phrase 'It's not The Liverpool Way'. That great smokescreen that has given every excuse-seeker shelter during the many barren title-less years. The Get Out Of Jail Free card for every director, manager, executive, player or ex-player who is too afraid to admit deficiencies in themselves and the system, and embrace change. It tells you more about why Liverpool didn't move on while all the big teams around them did.

Moores was reluctant to say to Houllier, 'Thanks for six years' service, we feel we need a new direction, so we're letting you go,' because Liverpool hadn't sacked a manager for almost fifty years. So they couldn't start now. It wasn't The Liverpool Way. The same irrelevant, self-serving tripe that kept Moores' first manager Graeme Souness in a job two years after he should have been sacked for a multitude of sins.

Moores didn't want it on his charge sheet that he'd sacked a manager. He was hoping that Houllier would feel the negative vibes and offer his resignation. He believed this offered him more dignity.

During that period of indecision between deciding Houllier was history and actually telling him, the leak-fuelled rumour mill went into overdrive. Houllier was phoning up reporters and quizzing staff at Melwood about whether they'd heard he'd been sacked. Dignity The Liverpool Way. Benitez, on the other hand, had second thoughts about going to a club which couldn't even dismiss a manager a week after the board had unanimously decided to do so. This is a manager who has three clubs, including Inter Milan, begging him to join on the back of his second La Liga title and a UEFA Cup triumph. Eventually

Houllier agreed an over-generous payout, and with not a little personal vanity involved, went along with the parting-by-mutual-consent line.

Was it The Liverpool Way that almost saw its finest home-grown son, Steven Gerrard, walk out on them weeks after captaining the club to its greatest hour of glory?

After heavy interest from Jose Mourinho at Chelsea, the then 25-year-old had been thinking about his future going into the Champions League Final and the club braced itself for a huge bid. Immediately after Liverpool's triumph Gerrard came out with the immortal line, 'How can I leave after this?' The obvious thing to do was to capitalise on the moment, get a contract drawn up and thrust it at him as he waited in Liverpool the next day for the open-top tour of the city.

But clearly that was not The Liverpool Way. Too slick. Too modern. A week passed, and with no mention of a new contract and Chelsea cranking up the pressure Gerrard began to believe that maybe Liverpool didn't want him. Maybe they wanted the money instead.

So he did a piece with the *Liverpool Echo* saying he wanted to stay and get it all sorted as soon as possible. Meanwhile Rick Parry was on holiday in Barbados, telling inquiring journalists not to worry about Stevie because, as he said himself after Istanbul, how can he leave now? Translation: He's given us his word. He understands The Liverpool Way.

Gerrard, a hyper-critical, insecure self-analyst at the best of times, then believed they clearly didn't want him. He only had two years left on his contract, a point where negotiations usually begin, and he'd gone public saying he wanted to stay but still they hadn't rung. One of the most sought-after players in the world then went into pre-season training after a summer of mental turmoil, during which no one at the club had offered reassurance, expecting to be dragged into an office and handed a contract.

Nothing. He was convinced they wanted him out and decided to jump before he was pushed by announcing his desire for a transfer. All hell broke loose, in which thousands of fingers were pointed at Gerrard as he was told that what he'd done was not The Liverpool Way. Go figure.

As the son of Cecil Moores and nephew of Sir John Moores, Littlewoods heir David Moores inherited a lot of money, a love of football and a dutiful compulsion to put something back into the community. The Moores family had been ingrained into the fabric of Liverpool life since before the Second World War. Retail giants, pools millionaires, football club owners and cultural benefactors, the dynasty established by the autocratic Sir John stayed true to its roots and received the ultimate loyalty repayment by having the city's second university named after its patriarch.

John and Cecil believed passionately that what was good for Liverpool and Everton was also of huge benefit to the community on which all their business success was based. And they poured their money into both clubs.

Sir John, the son of a Mancunian bricklayer, started in business in the 1920s outside Old Trafford, selling pools coupons. After a shaky start, his pools scheme caught on. He and his brother Cecil added a mail order business in 1932 and chain stores five years later, and thus was born the Littlewoods Organisation – the largest privately owned company in Britain at the time. In 1961 the family took control of Everton. Sir John became chairman and made it his first task to sack the then manager, John Carey, and replace him with Harry Catterick, during a ten-minute taxi ride to the Football League's AGM.

In business circles he was perceived as a hard, some would say brutal, operator, but across Merseyside the family were revered for their financial support of both clubs and their backing for arts and charities. While other members of the Moores family followed their elders into commerce, David, the only clan member who spoke with a Scouse accent, was drawn to football. Here was a rich man who had worked for a while in minor roles for Littlewoods, but who spent most of his life indulging two passions forged in Sixties Liverpool – music and the Reds. Indeed, according to Companies House, in the early 1990s he tried his hand at moving into the music industry, though he hardly emerged as the next Brian Epstein.

Goalaction was a recording studios venture, which he formed in September 1990. The company was dissolved and struck off in June 1993. And Dry Communications was formed in March 1991 to promote the singer Thomas Lang. In its first seventeen months of business, the company lost £50,000, then ceased trading before being dissolved and struck off the company register in July 1994. Maybe that's why Moores stuck to Liverpool FC. It was a 1991 share issue aimed at raising money to redevelop the Kop after the Taylor Report that allowed him to buy a 51 per cent controlling interest and realise a lifelong dream of becoming the club's largest shareholder and chairman.

As he took up the post, one of his predecessors, John Smith, paid a warm, if somewhat ironic, tribute: 'The Moores family have been great benefactors to Merseyside football. David's appointment will keep the predators at bay.' And the predators were certainly circling, smelling the carcass of one of the world's biggest football clubs which had failed to move into the new money-fuelled Premier League era.

In 1999, the year Manchester United did their famous treble of League, FA Cup and Champions League sending their 'brand recognition' moonwards, Moores realised he had to bring in outside capital to keep the club hanging on to their rivals' coat-tails. A lack of trophies, worsening performances on the pitch, boardroom rows and shareholder revolts forced him to bring in investment bankers Schroders to examine the club's future. This was a tough decision for a man who not only felt he would be letting the Moores family down by selling off part of the city's cultural heritage but someone who disliked bankers intensely.

A year before bringing in Schroders, Moores had said: 'I don't see why we should have people in the City who have no love for Liverpool telling us what to do with our club. You only have to look at other football clubs who have got City people on board telling them what they can and can't do. If you're interested in a player, you've got to go to them and it will take days, weeks even, before someone can be signed.'

His reservations were made increasingly irrelevant by the changing face of football. In 1999, Granada snapped up 9.9 per cent of the club's shares for £22 million, taking over media and corporate catering responsibilities but it was clear that would never be enough if Liverpool wanted to get back on an equal financial footing with the best in Europe.

A new ground was needed, not just to boost capacity but also to take advantage of the boom in corporate entertaining which was transforming match-day revenue. At a minimum cost back then of £150 million, David Moores was never going to be able to fund a new ground. The club needed men at the top with clout and cash. Men like billionaire Roman Abramovich, who in 2003 bought Chelsea and changed the role of football club owner for ever.

Moores, petrified of being slaughtered by Liverpool fans for not keeping up with the Chelseas, decided he could go no further. In 2004 he told Rick Parry he was selling up, and nothing would change his mind.

Cue the battle for hearts, minds and Amnesty International approval, between Garston builder Steve Morgan and the Thailand Prime Minister Thaksin Shinawatra. And the beginning of embarrassment and disillusion among fans as they saw, for the first time, boardroom warfare made public.

Shinawatra had a charge sheet to make Al Capone envious. Back then he faced allegations of electoral fraud, corruption, authoritarianism, treason, press censorship, tax evasion, selling national assets to international investors and human rights abuses. Far worse than all that in Liverpudlian eyes, he was a Manchester United fan who'd once held up a Red Devils shirt bearing his name next to Satan himself, Alex Ferguson.

Rick Parry flew out to Bangkok to meet him, and realised pretty quickly due to the massive media coverage of their talks that he was being exploited by Shinawatra's electioneering PR machine.

When fans' opposition grew to his human rights record and it surfaced that his investment would come from the Thai people paying into a public lottery, he was quickly dropped. Parry now refers to the cringeful saga as 'a lot of froth'.

The Steve Morgan tussle was nothing of the sort though.

Here was a lifelong Liverpudlian, former building-site worker, club shareholder and self-made multimillionaire who had built a personal fortune through Redrow Homes and the De Vere Hotel group, who wanted to put down the cash, and utilise his own expertise to get the new stadium built, while strengthening the first-team squad. Here was the chief rebel at the stormy AGMs who had taken the battle to Moores.

But from the word go he met stiff opposition from the chairman, who believed he was being ousted from his Anfield fiefdom on the cheap. It was personal between Morgan and Moores. The builder had been hugely critical in public of Liverpool's inability to exploit its commercial opportunities. He ridiculed Moores' lack of business experience and demanded to know why so much of the £73 million offer he had tabled had to go into shareholder's pockets, when every Liverpudlian knew they needed every spare million they could get to rebuild.

Not surprisingly, he received massive support from fans who identified with both him and his criticisms. The *Liverpool Echo* ran a poll which claimed 87 per cent of Liverpool supporters wanted the Redrow man to run the club, and before the final game of the 2004 season against Newcastle, pro-Morgan banners were unveiled and the odd chant was audible. Small wonder Moores was loath to sell to a fellow Scouser who had so quickly won a place in fans' affections by claiming to be everything Moores was not. Especially when it would almost certainly signal his exit from the club with a drastically reduced windfall.

After six month's negotiations, with the cost of the planned stadium rising, Morgan wanted to give the shareholders £20 million instead of a proposed £35 million, with the rest going to the club. It would have meant Moores picking up a mere £10 million.

The deal was dead and Morgan walked away in the autumn of 2004. When he eventually took a seat in the Anfield direc- tors' box, as Wolves chairman, on Boxing Day 2009, he pointed the finger of blame for Liverpool's money troubles at Moores: 'The fact is David Moores wanted what was best for David Moores, not the club. He was entitled to do that but it's his decision that has led to the situation Liverpool are in now.' Moores, though, with some justification, could ask why Morgan so readily sold his shares to Hicks and Gillett.

Over the next couple of years other suitors would knock on Moores' door, notably Northern Irish property developer John Miskelly and US tycoon Robert Kraft, but no one seriously got their feet under the table. That is, until Parry got tickets to the 2005 Champions League Final for Dubai International Cap- ital's chief executive and long-time Liverpool fan, Sameer Al Ansari.

Within a fortnight of Istanbul the Arabs were asking to see Liverpool's books, which led Moores and Parry to believe that in Sheikh Mohammed bin Rashid Al Maktoum, the absolute monarch of Dubai, they'd found their own Abramovich.

By the autumn, however, the Arabs appeared to have got cold feet. Maybe it was the price. Moores valued the club at £200 million, with another £200 million needed for the new stadium and £50 million for new players. With costs and debt- servicing any prospective buyer was looking at £500 million. Maybe it was a glimpse at the books which showed those sums didn't add up. Or maybe Dubai's appetite to move into Eng- lish football wasn't shared by the man at the top.

Over the next year DIC would come back in, drift out, then come back in again, before telling Parry in August 2006 that they were ready to do business. But by now George Gillett had come on the scene and was turning the charm-setting up to max.

In November he invited Moores and Parry to see his Montreal set-up. Moores didn't want to go because he hates flying more than a few hours as it means he can't have a smoke. So Gillett sent his private jet to pick him up, scoring quite a few Brownie points in the process.

He scored plenty more in Montreal by wheeling out his executives, players, stadium developers and commercial team who all, naturally, spoke highly of him. When Moores and Parry talked to fans in and around his arena they discovered genuine affection for the owner. When they talked to Gillett they found an Oscar winner. The opening shot in a masterly performance being the revelation of his bankruptcy. He told of the pain he suffered as bailiffs took his dogs, of the shame he felt having to buy back his clothes, and all the time tears rolled down his cheeks.

Moores became very uncomfortable with the Gwyneth Paltrow act but Gillett used it to show he'd been at rock bottom and he wasn't going back any time soon. He now had the money again, he told them, because he had learnt his lessons and rebuilt his empire on sound principles. He told them to check out his business portfolio, and as he threw them the books and grabbed the Andrex, Moores and Parry believed they'd got a man of honesty and substance who wanted to buy Liverpool and hand it down through generations.

But they still wanted to go with Dubai, a wealthy sovereign

fund backed by a rich country, whose reputation would be on the line. So Parry told DIC about Gillett, in the hope that competition would kick them up the backside and make them seal the deal. He suggested that a trip to Dubai, based on the recent impressive Canada model, where Moores would get to meet all the top people, would impress the Liverpool chairman, and they agreed.

Except they couldn't organise a private jet to combat the chairman's nicotine-withdrawal problems and when he landed there, they failed to set up a meeting with the sheikh. One was planned but he went horse-riding that morning instead.

Moores wasn't impressed, believing rightly that if such a powerful man was behind this bid it could be done in a day. So far DIC had had eighteen months and there was still no concrete proposal on the table.

And then a breakthrough. DIC came up with an offer of £4,500 per share, and Moores had to make a decision. He was personally far more impressed with Gillett than the Arabs, but believed Sheikh Al Maktoum could be the sugar-daddy of his dreams. He had a gut feeling that if DIC bought Liverpool and the sheikh took his seat in the directors' box for a big European night he would be smitten by Anfield and driven to succeed.

On 4 December, the club announced they were in an exclusivity agreement with DIC to buy the club for £450 million. Amid a mountain of headlines about Sheikh-ups and Evertonian texts about DIC-heads, Liverpudlians were dreaming about blowing Jose Mourinho and Chelsea out of the water.

DIC officials, led by Sameer Al Ansari, met Rafa Benitez and Steven Gerrard who both gave them the thumbs up. Rick Parry said the takeover was 'about taking Liverpool FC to the next level and securing the future of the club for the next 100 years'.

Two days after the announcement there was a meeting between both sides' officials and lawyers where DIC were told they had exclusivity until the middle of the following month, but the deal really needed to be signed and sealed by the end of December. Not only did the manager need investment for the transfer window, but the club needed to place a £12 million steel order to ensure the new stadium stayed on schedule.

DIC were told they'd effectively had a year and a half's due diligence so there really was no excuse for not moving ahead swiftly. When that didn't happen and they were asked why, the answer was, 'It's OK, we're just having a dialogue with the banks.'

Which wasn't what Moores expected to hear from a sovereign investment fund with billions of dollars behind it. If that left him feeling jittery, what he read in the *Daily Telegraph* on 27 December under the headline 'Buyers plan to sell Liverpool in seven years', left him scouring his medical cabinet for tranquillisers. Respected sports journalist Mihir Bose wrote:

> Liverpool, who are being bought by an investment company effectively owned by the Dubai government, could be sold again in seven years' time, according to a confidential document.
>
> The document also reveals that Dubai International Capital are planning to borrow up to £300 million to finance their £450 million purchase of the club. DIC see their investment in Liverpool as purely a business deal built round the new stadium Liverpool are planning at Stanley Park. When they sell in seven years' time they are

hoping to make a huge profit, providing a return of around 25% on their investment for every year of ownership. There appear to be no plans to invest in new players.

Furthermore, DIC will not be the sole owners of Liverpool, unlike Roman Abramovich at Chelsea, the Glazers at Manchester United and Randy Lerner at Aston Villa. Although their deal to buy Liverpool is not yet signed and sealed, they are already looking for other investors to join them in a partnership. I understand that 30% of the 90% stake DIC are bidding for is being offered to City investors.

The seven-page document, which outlines the investment rationale, has been circulated to major City investors to attract them to join the consortium.

However, anyone reading the document can have no doubt that this is purely an investment decision. And with DIC seeking partners, there is also no knowing who else will be in the Liverpool boardroom.

One of the most revealing insights is when the document talks of how the financing will be done. A whole page is devoted to it and shows that three banks – Bank of Ireland, RBS and Bank of America – have been approached, with Bank of America the favourite.

The DIC document notes that the stadium, which will seat 61,000, will cost less per seat than Arsenal's Emirates Stadium. The document also provides a wonderful insight into DIC's thinking but is very different from the fans' expectations about this purchase – and would have been very different from the purchase of the club by Gillett.

Moores believed every word of the report, was horrified that he had agreed to sell to them and said to Parry, 'That's it, kick them out.' Al Ansari was equally horrified that the document had been leaked, but immediately rubbished the story with claims that due process determined the proposal had to be put through DIC's investment committee to win approval.

By the middle of January Parry was still telling the media the deal with DIC was almost done, but as the month dragged on it was being leaked that Gillett had capitalised on DIC's tardiness by putting in a bid which valued the shares at £500 more than the Arabs were willing to pay.

At this point the non-executive directors and major shareholders were getting anxious about DIC's credibility and wanted to see if Gillett could put a better bid on the table. Sources close to Moores say that Steve Morgan told him he believed Gillett was willing to bid more, and that as a shareholder he wanted maximum return on his investment.

The pressure on Moores to do the one thing in life he hated, confront a major decision head-on, was becoming unbearable. The steel order had still not been placed, which put the stadium in doubt, and there was no money for new players but Moores was insisting that he'd shaken hands on a deal with DIC, so, in his head, there was no going back.

By the end of January, with the DIC exclusivity deal no longer in place, major shareholders told Moores to forget about gentleman's agreements and consider any new and better offers or they would consider taking legal action against him.

In the middle of all the confusion Tom Hicks walked into town and nothing would be the same again. Moores met him and Gillett at Anfield for one hour, in which he claims to have looked them in the eyes and said: 'There's two things I want from you: a guarantee that there won't be any debt on the club and a guarantee that the new stadium will be built.'

Moores says they looked back into his eyes and gave personal assurances that there would be no debt on the club, because it was all family money, and that the stadium would be ready for the start of the 2009 season.

On 30 January, en route to Liverpool's game at West Ham, an impromptu board meeting was held in the Marriott Hotel in London's Docklands to consider the Americans' offer of £5,000 a share, despite DIC believing it was being held to rubber-stamp their own deal and set a date for the public announcement.

Moores and Parry told the board they had seen private schedules from bankers Rothschild which approved Hicks's and Gillett's family investments and justified their wealth. When asked about Hicks they were told that Gillett, who they now trusted implicitly, had assured them he was an honest guy who was good for his money and his word. Why else would he bring him in? The board then decided to ditch DIC and go with the Americans, but according to Parry, Moores was still saying he was unhappy about breaking his word and needed to be left alone for forty-eight hours to think through the biggest decision he would ever take.

The board moved on to West Ham where, waiting in the directors' box, was a DIC official keen to know how the Docklands meeting had gone. Cue much shuffling, coughing and staring at the pigeons on the stand roof opposite. DIC smelt a rat.

At ten a.m. the following day Moores rang Al Ansari to

explain that he hadn't been impressed with the feet-dragging and he'd been put under pressure from board members to consider another bid. He told him he hadn't made a decision either way and needed forty-eight hours to do so. An unimpressed Al Ansari told him he had until five p.m. that day to make up his mind or DIC would walk.

Moores was outraged at the threat, telling Al Ansari he had no right to bully the chairman of Liverpool Football Club in such a manner and refused to adhere to his ultimatum. At four p.m., an hour before their self-imposed deadline was due to expire, DIC announced their withdrawal from the bidding process.

Parry and Moores were baffled by DIC's behaviour, especially as the chairman had yet to make a decision on who he was going with. They began to wonder if the Arabs had been waiting for a face-saving excuse to pull out because the people who really mattered in Dubai were never truly behind the deal.

Al Ansari's official statement read: 'We are very disappointed. DIC is a serious investor with considerable resources. After a huge amount of work, we proposed a deal that would provide the club with the funds it needs.'

That was the diplomatic line. The *Daily Telegraph*'s quote from a DIC source more closely conveyed their Krakatoa-style reaction to what they deemed treachery: 'It has been an absolute shambles. Over the last few days it has been impossible to get a sensible answer out of them as to what's going on. The way DIC have been treated is staggering and to say they are unhappy would be way more than an understatement.'

Fans reacted with a mixture of shock, panic, anger, resignation and cynicism. On the website Red All Over The Land,

David Moores and Rick Parry were being lampooned as Laurel and Hardy.

Liverpudlians felt like they'd been led through the bling-drenched streets of Dubai, and told it was all theirs, only to reach the desert and find a mirage. They demanded answers: Why had they been told the DIC deal was not only the best one but virtually done and dusted? Why had they still been spun a vision of a golden future even when newspaper reports had tried to rubbish DIC's motives? Why had they met the manager and the captain? Why was Moores not saying anything? Was this yet another amateurish cock-up?

The *Echo*'s Liverpool reporter at the time, Chris Bascombe, who was probably the closest journalist to the story, was equally baffled. He confronted Parry on the night of the Docklands meeting to find out what was happening.

'He confirmed that Gillett had moved ahead of DIC in the pecking order and I thought "this is utter bollocks" because a week earlier Parry had dismissed rumours that Gillett was back at the table. Now they were inviting him in. It didn't add up.

'No one was saying anything. Moores wasn't explaining himself and the shareholders were quiet.

'I couldn't work out why Gillett had suddenly offered £5,000 a share when the offer below it was £4,500. It didn't make financial sense. You'd up it to £4,600 at first, wouldn't you?'

Parry stepped up to perform the mother of all U-turns, attempting to placate anger in an *Echo* front-page article under the headline 'Trust Us':

'The overriding message is "don't worry". Whatever decision is finally taken will be done so in the best interests of Liverpool Football Club... We had a duty as directors to consider a very interesting bid from George Gillett.'

As website wags took pleasure in pointing out, that calm attempt at reassurance from on high was slightly undermined by a photograph of Rick Parry on the front of the *Echo* looking remarkably like a stunned Harpo Marx.

When journalists pushed Parry on why Gillett was suddenly good for his money he told them a new element to the bid had made all the difference: Tom Hicks.

'I'd never heard of him,' said Bascombe. 'But when I put his name into my laptop search engine it immediately came up 'Hicks and Gillett'. I couldn't work it out. Then I remembered when Gillett came on the scene the previous summer someone told me he was working with Tom Hicks and when I'd tried to check him out an American journalist had said "he's an absolute disaster".'

Bascombe is sceptical about Liverpool's assertion that Hicks magically appeared on the scene: 'I believe they'd looked at Tom Hicks and thought PR-wise it's not good for him to be mentioned because Liverpool fans aren't necessarily going to like this brash, Republican Texan.

'But they were so desperate when they went with Gillett that PR-wise they had to make Hicks look good. So suddenly he's this big Wall Street player and powerful political figure, all of which proved to be garbage.'

Having covered the prolonged takeover story on a daily basis Bascombe says he sensed the turning point with DIC came when Moores and Parry weren't given cast-iron guarantees that they would remain in a job.

'Parry said, out of the blue one day, "There's been no

mention of any role for me and David, you know," and I remembered thinking he's starting to change his attitude here.' It is a charge both categorically deny.

When anger among Kopites surfaced over the DIC bid being rejected for a more lucrative one, which would give Moores £8 million more than the £80 million the Arabs would have paid him, he was said to be 'appalled and horrified'. But the chairman wasn't that appalled or horrified that he would explain to the fans why they had been led down the aisle with Dubai only to be jilted at the altar. This was turning into an episode of *Dallas*. Oil men, Texans, big hats, power struggles, back-stabbing and David Moores' shoulder pads. All it needed was Victoria Principal, but principles were in short supply.

And so, as we looked on that February day, DIC cast as mugs for letting this golden opportunity pass, the Americans seen as liberators, handing out nylons and chewing gum to a grateful public, all seemed once again right with the world.

We didn't even pay too much attention to the vague figures being bandied about.

They'd paid an initial £108 million for a 62 per cent shareholding, and after buying the remaining shares that price would rise to £174 million. They'd agreed to pay off the club debt of £44.8 million and vowed to put £215 million towards the new stadium.

No one was asking serious questions about where the money had come from, or why it was being lent on a one-year agreement, even though Hicks was thanking RBS for all their help. But then, as Parry had assured us, you only sell the family silver once, so even their most ardent critic gave them the benefit of the doubt that they had the guarantees locked in a safe.

Parry told anyone who asked that they had it in writing that this was not a Glazer-type deal, that they weren't borrowing against the club. But there was no such legal guarantee. The small print in the shareholders' document gave them the option, as owners, to borrow against the club at a future date. In other words, these strangers had simply been taken at their word.

Words like this, from Gillett, who weeks earlier was being dismissed – to borrow the famous lyrics of Roger Miller – as a man of means by no means: 'This isn't about making money,' he said at the takeover press conference. 'This is about winning and passion and tradition.'

When the man who'd allegedly brought the dollars to the table was asked if he'd ever even heard of Liverpool before this week, Hicks replied like someone who'd spent five minutes studying Wikipedia on his BlackBerry, during a mid-morning crap: 'I had obviously heard of Liverpool, yes. But when I had a chance to read about the 118 years of history, the eighteen championships, the bleak years of the 1930s and 40s, the revival in the 1960s and the tragedies of the 1980s, I was just awestruck by what this community had achieved.'

It was said the deal-clinching moment for David Moores came when he and his wife Marge had dinner with the Americans, and were bowled over by their charm. Moores said he realised then that he had found men of honour whom he could trust. Others said he felt far more comfortable dealing with down-to-earth folksy westerners than the rather aloof Arabs. Gillett was later to confide to a senior Liverpool figure that at the dinner, he and Hicks soon discovered who was in the driver's seat, and worked their charm on Marge.

On the day of the takeover Moores stayed away from his

beloved Anfield, choosing to watch the press conference on Sky, reportedly through very red eyes: 'It's very hard to think it won't be my club any more,' he said.

'Having said that, I'm handing it over to safe hands. This is not someone coming over just to make a quick buck. They are in it for the long term because they're involving their sons so they can plan for the future.'

Rick Parry said, 'This was probably the worst day in David's life.'

For now Rick. For now.

CHAPTER FOUR

'If Rafa said he wanted to buy Snoogy Doogy we
would back him'

— George Gillett

The blacked-out people carrier screeched up outside the 62
Castle Street hotel causing a stir in nearby Derby Square where
dozens of fans were drinking themselves into the mood for that
night's Champions League semi-final. Chelsea were back in town
for a repeat of Jose Mourinho's It Never Crossed The Line
thriller of two seasons previously, and despite being 1–0 down
from the first leg, optimism surged through red veins.

When a Men In Black security guard emerged from the hotel
to do a 360-degree glare in search of hit men or stalkers, the
crowd rose from the steps of the Victoria Monument and darted
through the Lord Street traffic to catch a glimpse of what looked
like a serious American celebrity.

Had Dr Dre finally turned up to show his devotion to the
Scouse cause? Would that other closet Kopite Samuel L. Jackson
emerge in a red beret? No. This guy was way past A-List.

'Tom, Tom, over here, mate,' screamed fans filming on mobile
phones.

'Well in, lad, go 'ead,' yelled others, breaking into an impromptu round of applause.

Hicks emerged blinking into the May sun in a dark suit with a red scarf round his neck, visibly taken aback by the wall of emotion outside the hotel door. As fans patted his broad shoulders he nervously brushed back his hair, posing for photos like an ageing crooner. When the crowd belted out a rendition of 'We Love You Liverpool, We Do', he raised his fist in the air, before swaggering triumphantly into his blacked-out car.

As it pulled away the applause and the singing rose to a crescendo. Three months into the honeymoon and Liverpudlians still loved Tom Hicks enough to give him their last Rolo.

Peter Hooton, lead singer of The Farm and lifelong Liverpool fan, was near Victoria Monument at the time and was aware that someone was getting mobbed.

'Once I found out it was Tom Hicks, I was embarrassed. I thought "imagine hugging a neo-Conservative with a John Wayne persona, who would have nuked Iraq given half the chance," so I found it cringeful to be honest. But you think "it's European Cup semi-final day, and well, that's just general euphoria." Fans weren't really looking into their background back then, they were just thinking, "well, these have got money; we're going to start competing with Chelsea in the transfer market."

'I didn't blame anyone for doing that. I just thought they were a bit naive for doing it because after a few months in charge the Yanks hadn't done anything other than put on a Liverpool tie and smile.'

Journalist Tony Barrett, then a feature writer on the *Echo*, witnessed a scene which surely had the fans who took pictures of their new hero later scouring their hands with bleach and dousing their SIM cards in battery acid:

'You know what, it felt right. Absolutely right. Although I don't agree with clapping people from the boardroom. But we were in the European Cup semi-final and these were the people who were going to build us our new stadium and buy all these new players. No misgivings about them had been made public. No-one had said these people are bad for Liverpool FC.

'You have to remember that Liverpool fans had always had a good rapport with their owners. We never sang a "sack the board" chant like Newcastle. Evertonians were far more cynical about their owners than we were because we always thought even if they got things wrong, their heart was in the right place. If I'd viewed that scene cynically I could have written it but I didn't have a shred of cynicism.'

Those at the club who had to deal with the Americans felt roughly the same way at the time. But looking back, some recall small doubts niggling away when they sat down with Hicks and Gillett and discussed football.

On the Monday before the takeover Rick Parry took the pair to meet Steven Gerrard and Jamie Carragher at the Lowry hotel in Manchester where they were away with the England squad. Steven Gerrard recalls being excited at the prospect of seeing them and buzzing with optimism afterwards: 'I thought it might be interesting to hear what they had to say and it was. They made promises and they were very convincing. They told me and Jamie what they did in America, about their businesses, etc. But to be honest I'd already Googled to find out about them so I had a rough idea.

'To hear from their mouths about their plans to improve the stadium and build a new team was at the time brilliant. During that first year I met them quite a lot because they were going to Anfield and were seen down at the training ground a lot.

'At first things went fine. They bought big players and I'll be honest, it was exciting. Especially the promise of the new stadium. Obviously it would have been a big wrench to leave Anfield but I thought it would be amazing to lead Liverpool out in a new stadium as captain.'

The impression they left their captain with was he was now a kid in a big sweet shop called Anfield. Or after naming rights, possibly the Willy Wonka Anfield. They said they were going to buy big players for the present and young players for the future, back Rafa and change the Academy. And they said they wanted feedback from him. That if their captain had anything that needed to be said he should let them know. He left them brimming with positivity.

'I thought this could be the time we go to the next step and really compete with Chelsea and United. And that was because of what I heard in that first meeting.'

Little did he know it would end up on the steps of the High Court. As for all the meetings that were promised, he would never have a face-to-face chat with Tom Hicks again.

Jamie Carragher recalls a stiff, awkward occasion riddled with small talk and pleasantries: 'No one grilled each other, we all just told each other what we wanted to hear. We told them it'd be great if they could do this and that, and they said it will be great when we do this and that. It was all "everything is going to be great".'

But he admits to slight reservations and fears that the board had made the wrong decision in ditching DIC for the Americans: 'I knew George Gillett had been interested for a while but it came out that he didn't have enough money and had to get Tom Hicks in for his cash.

'In the back of my mind I was thinking "this isn't right". One of them hasn't got the cash and the other doesn't really want to be here: this could end up going wrong. Also, I wasn't happy with joint bosses. We should have known better after having Roy Evans and Gerard Houllier as joint managers. I don't care what anyone says, there has to be a number one in everything. Eventually there's going to be a problem and they'll end up falling out.'

Surprisingly, Carragher had been given a warning about Hicks and Gillett from an unlikely source: Rio Ferdinand.

'Rio told me that the Glazers were terrified of the Dubai people taking over. They thought they'd have another Abramovich on their hands. The Glazers were really hoping Hicks and Gillett would beat them to it. Which made me think, "Hang on, have we made a mistake here?"'

Unlike David Moores, and many of the shareholders, the *Daily Telegraph*'s report about DIC's plan to sell the club after seven years hadn't bothered him.

'I guessed Hicks's and Gillett's plans were roughly the same. They just sold themselves to Liverpool more cleverly, saying they wanted it to be a family club who would pass it down to their next generation of sons. Good custodians of the club and all that. They cleverly appealed to Scouse romanticism. But I suppose in life if you're really desperate for something, when it comes along you're just delighted. If there is something in the background you're not sure of you just think "we'll be all right". And sadly, that was us.'

For more than a few reasons Carragher now looks back in anger: 'In a decision of such magnitude it should have been hook, line and sinker sorted, with nothing left to chance.

'This was a decision that those at the top knew was going to affect the club for ten, twenty years and obviously you'd have thought they really should have got it watertight. I think David Moores got so worried about selling it to the right people, in the end he worried too much.

'But what really annoys me is that the rest of us didn't see through them. Because Liverpool people aren't normally kidded. It's normally us who are kidding other people. We always think we're on the ball and sharp and that's one of the things that angered me later. I felt I'd been kidded by these Americans. There were times towards the end when I thought "I wish I could have that meeting with you again, because I'd love to tell you what I think."'

Gillett had no such misgivings about his meeting with the heart and soul of Liverpool FC, Gerrard and Carragher. 'They're special,' he said with a huge smile and a wistful sigh, before adding that Jamie had given him his first lesson in speaking the local dialect.

It wouldn't be the only time Gillett turned to Carragher for a Lern Yerself Scouse lesson. Months later, when he was showing Canadian friends around Melwood, he called the proud Bootle lad over and said: 'Jamie, Jamie do your Scouse.' Carragher, with the words Jesus, Effing and Christ written all over his red face, muttered a few noises and backed away, grimacing.

There were times when Carragher felt he was being used but could do little about it. After the Lowry meeting the Liverpool website put out quotes from him and Gerrard saying how bright the future looked under the Americans. Whenever new stadium plans were announced it would be the Jamie and Stevie show, with the local lads dragged out to big them up.

'It annoyed me the owners would always seek our approval, as though that would make it all right and the fans would buy it. But what else where we supposed to say? Yes, there was an element of us being used, but we were employees of the club and it felt like we were getting pulled in a lot of different directions.'

The captain and vice-captain weren't alone. On the day of the takeover, above a photo of the smiling families on the Anfield pitch, the *Echo* splashed the headline 'Rafa: We're In Good Hands'. In the story underneath the Spanish manager was quoted as saying: 'I am convinced they want the best for the club.'

But like his leading players he was very much toeing the party line. Benitez felt they were making all the right noises but sensed very quickly they had no knowledge or understanding of the game and weren't particularly bothered that they were flaunting their ignorance.

They would borrow phrases from ice hockey, baseball and gridiron to describe football situations, with one favourite of Gillett's driving Benitez to distraction. 'We'll see what we get in the draft' he would say when the manager inquired about his forthcoming transfer budget. Before one transfer window Gillett grabbed hold of Benitez's knee while he was in mid-flow and assured him: 'Roffa, I am going to give you £50 million of my money plus what we get in the draft.' You could have spotted the Spaniard's hackles rising in Madrid.

At the opening meeting they told Benitez they wanted Liverpool to be the best in the world and they wanted to give him the backing to realise that ambition. He told them it wasn't all about money. He didn't need a Roman Abramovich, or require a bottomless pit of funds, just a decent budget for a club of Liverpool's size, plus their support in overhauling the Academy, because he believed the lack of young talent coming through was at the root of the club's problems. They told him they were impressed with both him and his plan. Hence his public quote that the club was in safe hands. In private he was shrugging his shoulders, giving his trademark knowing grin and saying 'We'll see'.

With footballing honeymoons the new people tend to strike it lucky. The ridding of dead wood and the injection of fresh blood quite often stimulates a club. Liverpool in the spring of 2007 went through such a positive phase. It hadn't been a great season up to that point. After Benitez had won the Champions League in 2005, the FA Cup in 2006 and started the 2007 season with a clinical dismantling of Chelsea in the Charity Shield, hopes were high that he might take the final step on the road to sainthood by delivering the first Premier League title to Anfield.

Yet by the time the Americans arrived, the season was on a life-support machine. Five defeats in the first twelve games had killed title hopes and Arsenal had knocked them out of both FA and League Cups in January, meaning salvation rested on a trip to Barcelona in the last sixteen of the Champions League. Suddenly the critics were denouncing Istanbul as a fluke that belonged to some ancient saga.

But a fortnight later Liverpudlians were dancing down the Ramblas after storming the Nou Camp en route to making it past the 'world's best team' (copyright every journalist outside of Madrid) to face a PSV Eindhoven side they had already out-classed in the group stages. Many people were beginning to think the Yanks were a lucky charm. Benitez, though, could not be counted among their number.

Behind the scenes his frustration was growing. He saw quite a bit of Hicks and Gillett back then as they were frequently in town holding meetings. But whenever he brought up his summer budget and the necessity to start lining up deals before the season ended, nothing concrete was coming back. They would listen, sympathise, lay on the flattery and throw out the promises, but come the next meeting they would be at the very same point. Benitez felt he was getting more sense out of the flowers in the table vase. Nothing was moving apart from the signals in his head which were telling him he was being taken for a fool.

Benitez, paranoid at the best of times, was moving past thinking they didn't understand the urgency of Liverpool's needs to thinking they've got no intention of helping him. He was telling people that nothing had changed since the takeover, and he was right.

Cut through the hype and the sugar-coated words and David Moores is still there, bumbling along the way he always did (going to matches at home and in Europe for free and telling Rafa to 'see Rick' when he approached him with a problem), Parry is still there, doing what he always did (telling Rafa to 'leave it with me' whenever he raised an issue), no extra transfer money had been pledged, and no extra income was in sight because, despite a few elaborate plans, the sixty-day vow to make a pile of rubble in Stanley Park had turned into a pile of bollocks.

All the new owners appeared to have done was buy out the existing shareholders and gone home and waited for the team to win another Champions League, thus boosting the club's value. Actually it was worse than that. They hadn't bought out the shareholders, a bank loan had. And they wouldn't be paying the interest on that loan, the club's profits would. The *Guardian*'s David Conn was the first journalist to latch on to this after studying the offer document to shareholders. On 14 March, under the headline 'Americans borrow £298m to buy Liverpool: Club likely to foot annual £21.5m interest payments', he wrote:

> Thomas O Hicks and George Gillett Jr., the two American businessmen who are close to completing their takeover of Liverpool, have borrowed almost £300m from the Royal Bank of Scotland to finance the deal.
>
> The bank has loaned the money at 1.5% above the current standard lending rate, meaning that about £21.5m interest will be payable this year.
>
> The debt is not being taken on by the club in the way the Glazer family loaded Manchester United with £660m borrowings from their 2005 takeover, but professionals close to the deal said it was nevertheless likely that Liverpool would pay the interest, or pay Hicks and Gillett 'a big dividend' at the end of the year to enable them to do so.
>
> The terms of the loans are in the offer document sent

to all shareholders, revealing that the two men are borrowing £185m to pay for the £174m takeover itself and associated costs, with another £113m available as a 'revolving credit facility' to absorb Liverpool's debts and fund the club and preliminary work on the new 60,000-seat stadium. A further £200m will be borrowed to build the stadium but the way that will be done has not been worked out. The initial £298m loans are guaranteed by Hicks and Gillett personally.

The takeover is certain to go through after it was confirmed last week that over 80% of Liverpool shareholders had accepted the offer of £5,000 a share. Moores, the former 51.5% shareholder, will be paid £89.615 million for the 17,923 shares he bought for about £12 million.

Hicks and Gillett, who have said they intend to be custodians and hold Liverpool as a family asset, will own the club via a company structure based in the tax havens of the Cayman Islands and the US state of Delaware.

The ultimate holding company, Kop Investment LLC, is registered in Delaware, which has low corporation tax and no capital gains tax, and its principal office is at Hicks's corporate headquarters in Dallas, Texas. One professional involved with the deal said that this did not mean the two men foresaw a sale or flotation and were 'sheltering' those future gains from tax, but that it was simply 'a tax efficient' way to structure the deal.

Yet despite this story appearing in March, only five weeks after the takeover, hardly any fuss was made of it. Maybe that was because it appeared in the *Guardian*. Maybe it was because fans wanted to believe it was mischief-making, playing around with words to paint Hicks and Gillett as Glazers Mk II, when they hadn't actually taken a cent out of the club yet. Or maybe it was because nobody dared to believe it was true.

Nevertheless questions have to be asked of the shareholders. Not those minor ones, who inherited a handful of shares and had no say in the deal, but the major ones who willingly sold Liverpool short for that extra £500 a share. Moores only owned 51.6 per cent, yet he, along with Parry, has felt the full wrath of the fans for failing to see that they were blatantly putting their loan on the club. You'd have to presume the vast majority of these shareholders were intelligent people, many of them successful businessmen, to have been able to afford a financial stake in the club. So why, having read the offer document, didn't they speak out?

Why didn't they look at the details of the RBS agreement and realise Hicks and Gillett were only being given a one-year loan? In any businessman's head that should have set alarm bells ringing, as the bank was saying we only believe you're good for this huge loan for twelve months. Unlike DIC, who had a seven-year plan, these two were only allowed a one-year one, after which they would have to pay off what they owed to seek reinvestment.

If they were, as they claimed, custodians who wanted to hand the club down through generations of their families, why wasn't more of their own cash put in and a longer loan with lower interest rates negotiated?

City takeover adviser David Bick, chairman of Square1 Consulting, who has been involved in several major Premier League deals said: 'I looked at the offer document that was sent to shareholders and I couldn't believe my eyes. They'd bought it with one-year funding, which was effectively an overdraft. If you are borrowing that sort of money for this sort of asset you usually borrow for at least three years, more likely five or seven. You're not buying it on a twelve-month loan.

'The document alone should have said to the shareholders and Rick Parry "this is not right, they're buying this on an overdraft". It left them totally reliant on interest rates not going against them. No one envisaged the whole financial meltdown, but, even before it, this deal was never properly financed. It was fundamentally flawed from the off. The financial structure was wrong and everyone who looked at it said "this is lunacy".'

For shareholders to hand over the club to leveraged buyout men with unknown motives, who had been vouched for by banks who were so unsure they only gave a short-term loan, was a highly dangerous move. But then the more cynical among us were speculating that they were getting an extra £500 per share, plus they were given guaranteed ticket rights; meaning should Liverpool reach a major cup final, even if they hadn't been to a game that season they would receive tickets for the showcase occasion.

Three months later, when UEFA gave Liverpool a paltry allocation for the Champions League Final in Athens, this ruling meant thousands of season ticket holders, like myself and my son, who had been to every European home tie and travelled to away ones, were automatically denied a ticket.

It's easy to see why the major shareholders turned a blind eye to the small print in the offer document and grabbed their mini-lottery win, especially as they'd been assured from above that this was the right move. But it's hard to understand why, in the years that followed, when accusations of greed and stupidity were thrown at the chairman and Rick Parry for not seeing what was before their eyes in black and white, that these people escaped without a scintilla of abuse. Especially, as far as we know, with their ticket rights to big games still legally guaranteed.

If David Conn's article failed to ruffle any feathers, two months later the *Guardian* had another go at stripping the American emperors of their new clothes. This time they hit the bullseye. This time it came not through a journalist or a financial document but straight from the horse's mouth. Hicks had agreed to give reporter Lawrence Donegan an exclusive interview in Dallas as part of the Champions League Final build-up, during which he didn't so much let the cat out of the bag as toss it in the air and volley it across the Atlantic right over Ireland and straight down the Mersey.

He publicly admitted that the club's profits would be used to meet interest payments on the loan that had bought the club. In effect, he was owning up to doing a Glazer, which completely contradicted his denial of such a model at the takeover press conference.

'Hopefully the club will have extra cash flow so they can pay us a dividend to do that,' Hicks said when asked how the cost of the loan would be met. 'If they don't, then it will come from our pockets. But the club will have to have profits sufficient to pay those dividends.' And, as if to rub those naive Liverpudlian faces into the dirt, Hicks likened them in a cold, matter-of-fact way to breakfast-eaters, and their beloved club to a box of cereal:

'When I was in the leverage buyout business we bought Weetabix and we leveraged it up to make our return. You could say that anyone who was eating Weetabix was paying for our purchase of Weetabix. It was just business. It is the same for Liverpool; revenues come in from whatever source and go out to whatever source and, if there is money left over, it is profit,' he said.

It was an astonishingly frank admission but even more astounding was the fact that once again nobody picked up on it. Maybe this time because the *Guardian* published it on the eve of the Champions League Final, when every fan worth his salt was over in Athens – most trying to buy a ticket from a tout as the well-heeled former shareholders walked past the riot police and into the ground.

Something else that had been missed, or rather gone undetected as Liverpool sailed proudly towards what it felt would be its sixth Champions League title, was the fragile state of relations between key personnel. It wasn't just Benitez having reservations about the men he had to work with. Tensions were appearing between the Americans and Parry, and crucially between Hicks and Gillett.

A senior football executive, and Liverpool fan, who met both Americans individually in April 2007 said: 'There were lots of characteristics shown that as a Liverpool fan I didn't want to believe. It was only two months into their joint ownership of the club but George was talking about his view versus his partner's view. It was already 'I think this and my partner thinks that' kind of thing.

'When I later had lunch with Tom and some of his American associates I asked about the dynamics of their relationship. How his partnership with Gillett worked. Tom shrugged and said, "You'd better ask him," pointing at a senior figure from Inner Circle Sports Ventures, who had brought the two together for the deal.

'I was gobsmacked. Either they hadn't sorted out how their professional relationship was going to work, there wasn't a relationship, or there was a relationship and it wasn't working. The fundamental problem was, as I later discovered, that apart from the first two or three months in charge they absolutely loathed each other.'

Journalists were also amazed that a clearly negative vibe existed between Parry and Hicks, with Parry letting it be known that he didn't agree with everything the Texan said. And vice versa.

The Athens ticket fiasco blew into a storm when thousands of season ticket holders who had qualified for previous finals found they had lost out in a ballot. There were reports of groups of up to twenty season ticket holders (all of whom had booked flights and hotels) where none had got lucky in the ballot. Fans, many veterans of countless cup finals, smelt a rat lurking between the chief executive's office and the ticket office and demanded answers.

Parry did an interview with the *Echo* in which he was asked for a breakdown of the ticket allocation. He famously replied: 'I won't play the numbers game.' So the fans played the numbers game for him. Literally. Season ticket holder and IT expert Danny Nicolson did a forensic analysis of the allocation and through computer formulation worked out that only 9,579 fans had qualified for tickets out of the 16,779 Liverpool had received. Which meant 7,200 were being held back for former shareholders, sponsors, corporate clients and staff, or as sweeteners for fans when the tickets scandal hit the media.

Supporters were enraged. Not only were they missing out on seeing Liverpool in a Champions League Final, and being forced into the hands of touts, but no explanation was being offered as to why so many were being kept by the club for internal and corporate distribution.

So, for the first time in its 115-year existence, Liverpool supporters held a protest march on their own ground. Around 500 of them met at the Sandon pub, before the last game of the season against Charlton, with banners carrying such slogans as 'Parry – Any Spares? I Know You Have.'

It was a spontaneous response to the ticket scandal organised via the internet, but the problem was, Liverpool fans had never marched before and no one was quite sure what to do, or even who was going to tell them how to do it.

The general consensus is that a fan called 'Windows', who probably wasn't a relative of Bill Gates, but was anti-everyone and everything, came forward and channelled the anger towards Rick Parry. There were already accusations among fans about Parry advising Moores to go with the Americans to save his job, so when he dismissed the thousands who were unable to get Athens tickets with 'let's not play the numbers game' he virtually elected himself Public Enemy Number One.

'It was probably the first time since Hillsborough that Liverpool fans felt "we don't matter here",' said lifelong Red Paul Rice. 'And the whole thing about the numbers game was, "That's all we are to you isn't it? A number."'

While Parry took the rap for it, fans were starting to peek behind the curtains and wonder if that was what the owners thought of us too, because they were making absolutely no comment about the tickets.

They probably couldn't believe their luck. They probably thought to themselves, 'We can get away with anything with these dozy limeys because they'll believe anything we tell them.' This story was getting interesting on a personal level, and not just because I'd missed out in the ballot along with my son Phil, but because it was the first time I'd written anything critical about the Americans in the *Daily Mirror*.

Under the headline 'Hicks' clan final insult' I wrote: 'It probably wasn't the best of weeks for Liverpool's official website to tell thousands of season ticket holders who have been to all six Champions League home ties that they had not been selected in an electronic ballot for a ticket for the final.

'Especially when those same devastated fans, many of whom had already paid up to £800 for packages to Greece, could read a story below it headlined: 'Whole Hicks clan will be in Athens.'

'The article proudly boasted, on Texan Tom's behalf, that eight members of his family will have seats at the final.

'Bearing in mind his fan-card registers two Champions League games – Barcelona and Chelsea – whereas the disappointed fans have six, where's the justice in that?

'Oh, I see. He liked the brand so much, he bought the franchise.'

The hostile reaction to it took me by surprise. Some fans on the Liverpool Way website were disgusted with what they deemed a cheap shot and condemned me for having a go at Hicks and his family. One poster, called Section 31, went so far as to say 'I reckon Reade wrote that when he was pissed', which just shows how solid the backing was for the owners when the honeymoon was still in full swing. I'd love to tell you that I wrote it because I'd decided before anyone else that Hicks was the evil spawn of Kilroy and Rose West. In fact I'd love to tell you why I wrote it. But as Section 31 said, I was probably pissed at the time.

The protestors marched from the Sandon to the main stand car park chanting 'Parry, Parry, Parry, Tout, Tout, Tout' and a new song, unheard of before, which over the coming years would be sung at every protest, with different words but similar hostility, towards Hicks and Gillett: 'We don't care about Parry, he don't care about fans, all our tickets are in the wrong hands.'

Had those fans known the dark road the club was headed down and how many of those tickets had gone to former shareholders who had set them down that road, some of the protestors may have been aiming more than words at the men in suits shuffling through the directors' entrance.

Certain positives emerged from the fans' first-ever protest march. Parry vowed to look again at the distribution and insisted there would be no repeat in future, and those who took part actually enjoyed it and felt better for getting the anger off their chest. Tellingly, on the day after the protest, a member of the Hicks camp rang the *Echo* to brief against Parry, saying, 'Trust us, we'll make sure this never happens again.'

Athens was a grave disappointment on many levels. Despite the 17,000 ticket allocation, at least 40,000 fans tried to get into the Olympic Stadium, which was so unsuited for such an occasion it didn't have any turnstiles. Pandemonium reigned outside the ground, with police unable to control the numbers. Hundreds of fans with genuine tickets never reached their seats while thousands who showed forgeries, cigarette packets or fresh air reached someone else's.

On the pitch AC Milan gained revenge for the 2005 final, winning a highly forgettable game 2–1, thanks in no small part to a fluked handball by Filipo Inzhagi. Disappointingly, Liverpool had enjoyed more possession but lacked the adventure and cutting edge to beat an ageing Italian side that was there for the taking.

But the week of that final was relevant on another level. We caught, for the first time, a glimpse of the Madness of King George. In the build-up to the game Gillett's flattery went into overdrive. Watching Liverpool he said 'was like attending the greatest sports event you can ever go to … on steroids. Nothing can compare to that.' This from a man who'd owned basketball and ice-hockey teams, who until four months ago had never seen Liverpool play, and who kept using the wrong terminology to describe a football game.

As he showed on the morning of the final when Five Live's Nicky Campbell interviewed him from his Athens hotel room, and he predicted the score would be 'two to one'.

Why 'two to one'? Campbell asked Gillett, mocking the American jargon. Because, Gillett replied, he'd consulted a ouija board. 'It did come up two to one and we certainly hope it to be in our favour.'

Stunned silence. Was he joking, or was he serious? Three days later we would be asking the same question as he sat before the cameras, stuffing dollar notes in his jacket pocket saying: 'If Rafa said he wanted to buy Snoogy Doogy we would back him.'

To Jamie Carragher, and many others, the weirdness of Gillett, and thus the alien territory Liverpool found themselves in, was becoming apparent: 'It cracked me up when I saw him doing that with his cash. I'm like "Oh no, what's that about?" He just sat there chuckling away looking like one of the Muppets. It only needed Hicks next to him and we'd have had Waldorf and Statler.'

But the flakiest moment for many came when Gillett entered the Olympic Stadium before the final and paraded in front of the Liverpool fans like Caesar returning to Rome after conquering a foreign land, holding up his hands in a triumphant clinch, soaking in the adulation flowing back to him from a crowd so dense in some places it was three to a seat.

As I looked on from the stands I was thinking, 'Why is he glad-handing the fans when he hasn't had anything to do with Liverpool reaching this final? Why is he walking before us, acknowledging our gratitude like Bill Shankly after we'd won the League in 1973, when he's done nothing to deserve any love rolling down towards him?'

Peter Hooton was similarly bemused: 'I thought it was inappropriate for him to do that. It was showbiz, wasn't it? For him to be there, it was as though it was *his* achievement and it started to become obvious that him and Hicks were seduced by the adulation.

'They gave it all that spin: 'We love the passion of the fans … I've never seen anything like the Spion Kop' and anyone standing back from that with an ounce of healthy cynicism in them is thinking: 'What a load of rubbish.'

It turns out similar doubts and questions were going through Rafa Benitez's troubled head. The man who in the run-up to the final had been repeatedly referred to as a 'genius' and a 'brilliant tactician' by Hicks and Gillett, was tiring of being patronised.

A post-match meeting between the owners and Benitez had been scheduled for midnight at the Pentelikon hotel in Athens, where the team was staying. Win or lose they would sit down and finally hammer out plans for the summer transfer window, aware that their rivals who hadn't had to focus on the Champions League Final were already doing business. But it was cancelled due to the Americans flying straight home by private jet.

Benitez, already drained and deflated after losing football's biggest club final, was incandescent with rage. In meeting after meeting he'd had to put up with their false promises and said nothing. Now they had added insult to injury by cancelling the last chance they had to sort out a budget and targets before the summer holidays.

Inconsolable and depressed, he started to walk the streets of Athens, a trek which lasted all night, even when the rain began to fall. He saw no point sitting in the hotel bars with the players talking about what might have been, or with his staff about what might be next season, because he didn't know the answers. And there was no point going back to his room because due to a cock-up he didn't have one. The hotel Liverpool had booked became too small when partners of the players and staff turned up on the night of the game, so he let the wife of chief scout Eduardo share his room with his wife Montse.

Occasionally he would return to the hotel and leave again with one of his assistants who listened to him open his heart about his fears for the club and how the mistakes that were made last summer through indecision and lack of money would be made again. How this time he couldn't put up with it.

'I can't get hold of them,' he told a confidant. 'Which means I will have to go through Rick, who won't give me a straight answer and will be off on his holiday to Barbados. So how am I going to do business? I have to buy players and sell players. But there is no one running the club to do the business.'

On he walked, the turmoil growing in his mind, until break-fast. A few hours later, after some snatched sleep, sitting before the world's media who expected the usual post-match litany of hard-luck stories, he let out all the frustrations that had been building in his head. No one above him escaped. Not Parry, not Hicks not Gillett. All were told in a brutal, with-ering delivery, that their lack of structure, cohesion and backing for him was killing the club they kept telling the world they loved. The boil had been lanced. And nothing would be the same again.

'I'm tired of talking, talking. We talk and talk but we never finish,' he told the media. 'I'm worried about talking to players, for one or two months or even six months, and then losing them. I want things to be done.

'Now is the moment to take decisions and not just talk about doing things. If we don't change right now, understand how crucial this moment is, we will waste one month, two months, two or three targets and then we'll start having to sign third-choice players and we'll have to be only contenders to be in the top four. Nothing else.

'We need to react to make things easier. We can't work any harder, so if we want to progress, then we have to change these things.

'The owners know, clearly, they need to make big changes. We've been talking about these things. But maybe they need to understand this is the right moment. Not just waiting and talking.

'They need to invest in the squad. When you see Manchester United have paid £20 million for a midfielder and you know how far we are away, we need to spend money and improve the squad.

'It's clear we need lots of money. United can pay £20 million for a midfielder. OK, if we want to sign a striker? What will be the price if you want to sign a striker? If you go early, you might have an opportunity to sign someone. If you spend two or three weeks waiting, then talking and talking, either you can't sign the player or you'll have to pay more.

'We know how we need to improve if we're to compete in this market. Sometimes if you spend big money for a player it's still cheap because they are really good players.

'This is a crucial time if you want to do something. It's not about working in August – forget it. You'll lose your targets then.

'In cup competitions we can beat anyone. But we don't have enough quality in the squad for playing nine months on the same level as Manchester United and Chelsea in the Premiership.'

Bang. Over. Dozens of bloodshot, slack-jawed hacks who'd allowed their minds after the last game of a long season to drift to Mediterranean sunbeds, pinched themselves to see if they were having a bizarre dream where Rafa had morphed into Jerry Maguire and was screaming to be shown the money.

What he was really doing was attempting to live out the message on the Liverpudlian banner which had been hanging in

Athens Syntagma Square the previous day: 'History will be kind to me for I intend to write it – Rafa B.'

Five thousand miles away, Hicks and Gillett were sleeping, but an earthquake that started somewhere near the Acropolis would soon shake them from their slumber. The first shot in a very uncivil American war had been fired.

CHAPTER FIVE

'Are you sure you've sold to the right people, Mr Moores? ... How can you look me in the face and ask that?'

– Chris Bascombe and David Moores

We met in the house of a mutual friend on a cold, dark early-December night. I wasn't sure why Rafa Benitez wanted to see me but within minutes of staring at his pale, drawn features and listening to him bare his soul it was clear he was feeling besieged, betrayed and isolated. He was fighting for his professional life.

Hours after lobbing his Athens hand grenade, the PR wheels had started grinding into motion. A transatlantic conference call was hastily arranged after which the Americans claimed peace, love and understanding had been restored to Anfield.

It prompted Gillett's Snoogy Doogy pledge and a typically bizarre, boot-licking eulogy: 'Rafa's feeling is we need more depth because of the rigours of the schedule to be competitive. In every sport I participate in there is a difference between a league season and the play-offs. That's where the genius of the manager is so essential and that's where Tom and I have to defer to his background and genius.'

What play-offs?

As usual, Hicks was more blunt: 'We had a long call and agreed on actions to be taken with our own players and with possible new players and we are all comfortable with our plan.' When asked to comment on Benitez's Athens outburst his diplomatic reply was, 'He'd been very upset the day after the match.'

But that was all show. Privately they were seething. Especially Hicks, who classed Rafa's very public act of insubordination as a call-to-arms. His instinct was to throw on his Stetson, pull a Colt .45 out of his holster and pump Rafa full of lead. The problem was, with two European Cup finals reached in three years, and a fan base that still overwhelmingly saw him as the man who would bring back the title, he was about as unsackable as a panda in a Chinese zoo with a secret stash of Viagra.

Nevertheless, Hicks and Gillett made a decision to get rid of him as soon as he appeared vulnerable. Fortunately for them, that autumn the team's poor results and some of his own eccentric actions – and I'm not even referring to the new goatee beard – left Benitez increasingly exposed.

Paco Ayesteran, who had been his trusted number two throughout his managerial career and who was very popular with the players, had been put on extended gardening leave after a major fall-out with Benitez. The team made a poor start in the Champions League and, despite the arrival of Fernando Torres, were struggling in the Premier League.

Benitez's critics, both inside and outside Anfield, were becoming more vocal, especially over his caution and his rotation. When he kept a fit Fernando Torres on the bench for Birmingham's visit to Anfield, and drew 0–0, the rumblings of discontent were audible. When he substituted Steven Gerrard and Jamie Carragher with twenty minutes to go, in a 3–1 defeat to Reading, purely to keep them fresh for a trip to Marseille, the phone-ins, the letters pages and Fleet Street's back pages were filled with anti-Benitez ire.

If that wasn't bad enough for the manager, he was convinced the club was briefing reporters, sports editors and ex-players against him because they wanted him out. Hence the wish to put his side to the few supporters he felt he had left in the media.

'The truth is they're killing me. They're killing me,' he said, sitting on a couch, his coat still on and a leather briefcase between us, from which he would pull flow charts, fact sheets and dossiers to back up his arguments, or his statistics about how many minutes a player had played that season.

One chart he'd had made showed that statistically he was the third most successful Liverpool manager after Bob Paisley and Kenny Dalglish. It may have been statistically accurate, but the name Bill Shankly under Rafa's made me wince. I didn't need that dubious statistic pointed out to me, as in my heart no one who had stepped into Anfield since had been Shankly's equal.

I later learned he'd shown the same charts to senior players and it had drawn the same reaction. Clearly these were the gestures of a man desperately trying to cling on to his job.

He didn't see it that way, repeating throughout our two-hour conversation, 'I deal in facts. Only facts.' And the fact that Hicks and Gillett were now trying to kill him was true.

'I know they've talked to Jose Mourinho, Fabio Capello and Jurgen Klinsmann about my job, but what can I do?' he asked. At the time this wasn't public knowledge but the following month Hicks would admit to meeting one of those men with a view to replacing Benitez.

He spoke with pride about getting Liverpool to two European Cup finals: 'These people need to remember in a European sense we were the size of Atletico Madrid before we won the Champions League. Without that win we'd be nothing in Europe, nothing.'

He defended his transfer policy saying whoever he bought, even if it didn't work out, he nearly always got his money back. He talked of his frustrations working with Rick Parry, where every player he tried to sign would have to go through him, and Parry would delay for days. How he could get no work done unless Parry's secretary was there.

'I wanted Florent Malouda last summer but Parry wouldn't pay the signing-on fee, so he went to Chelsea. He brought in Ryan Babel and paid £2 million more than we wanted to. He paid too much for Jermaine Pennant and Yossi Benayoun and he made a big mistake with Javier Mascherano's contract because he allowed him a get-out clause, which ended up costing the club more money.'

He said he couldn't understand why the Americans kept Rick Parry on. He thought they were keeping him sweet for a reason but he didn't know why.

His frustration was tangible, his paranoia rampant. He was worried the fans might believe the poison that was being spread about him from the Americans and Parry, and would lose the faith: 'Some may believe it without knowing the facts.' His main frustration though was over money. 'Here is the truth: I am driving an old BMW while Ferguson and Mourinho are driving Ferraris. I have to swerve and cheat to beat them, and I can do that, but I need the money and the back-up to beat the Ferraris.'

Meanwhile, all he seemed to be getting from the Americans was flattery, which he saw through instantly: 'I don't like people telling me you are brilliant, you are great. I hate that. I know where I come from. I know my limitations. I wasn't a great footballer but I worked hard on the technical side. I am proud of what I have done but I know myself. I hate these sweet words. I like actions.'

His enthusiasm for the job and his love of Liverpool shone through. As did his honesty. He spoke of money going missing in the game and people being on the take. How he couldn't understand why people were doing this when they were so well-paid.

When I asked why he didn't just walk away from Liverpool if it was so much hassle, and take up one of the regular offers that were coming in from Real Madrid, he replied: 'I love the club too much and my wife loves living here. This is my home. Also, if I go, Reina, Arbeloa, Mascherano and Torres would all leave too. Xabi Alonso will go anyway because he wants to go back to Spain.'

I was struggling to reconcile the image of the cold, withdrawn perfectionist some of the players paint, and this passionate, emotional man pouring his heart out before me. I asked why his players said he didn't show them enough love and he said that most players don't need it, but some, like Steven Gerrard, do. He then said that throughout his managerial career he played bad cop while Paco was the good cop. It kept them on their toes. Certainly that was the Brian Clough/Peter Taylor model and at times the Bill Shankly/Bob Paisley way. But he'd effectively sacked Paco. Why? 'Paco needed to go. He betrayed me.'

I had a horrible knot in my stomach about what was happening at Liverpool and what was about to unfold. It felt very much like the war that was then raging at the top of the Labour government. As a national newspaper reporter I'd had similar briefings from Gordon Brown's people against Tony Blair, and vice versa, since the late 1990s.

Rafa's words simply backed up everything I was seeing, hearing and fearing: Anfield was riddled with empire-building, poisonous briefings, distrust, disloyalty and back-stabbing. It had become a nest of vipers.

But the people who mattered most, the fans, had yet to digest this. The full force of the Athens rant, and its implications, didn't register at the time with supporters scrapping with UEFA over who was to blame for the Champions League Final chaos.

Rick Parry was still Public Enemy Number One, over the farcical ticket allocation, not the Yanks. Indeed some felt sympathy for them over Rafa's outburst. What had they done wrong since arriving? Was this a diversionary tactic by the manager to draw attention away from losing a final he could, and should, have won?

Hicks and Gillett had an unlikely ally at the time in Jamie Carragher: 'I didn't see that Athens press conference coming. Nothing about Rafa before or after the game hinted he was going to say all that. At the time I wasn't too impressed. I couldn't see his point.

'I thought, 'Give them a chance, we only lost the Champions League final last night.' Having said that, it showed balls. There's a basic rule in life that you don't go into work and slag off your boss, but Rafa knew he was arguing from a position of strength after a European Cup Final and obviously thought he was doing it for the benefit of the club.

'And looking back I suppose you could say Benitez was right because they ended up giving him the money and suddenly we were buying players for around £20 million or more when we'd never gone above £15 million.'

The full implications of Rafa's outburst took a while to register with Steven Gerrard, who had fallen into a bout of self-critical analysis after the final defeat: 'To be honest I was worrying more about losing the Champions League final than what Rafa had said. His words didn't really sink in.'

It took two or three days for the full implication of what Benitez was saying to hit home to his captain. For the first couple of nights all he could think of was that another opportunity to win something big had been missed.

When the outburst sank in friends of his say he was delighted that his manager had spoken out because he was desperate for big-name players to arrive and that was only going to happen by stumping up the cash. The final had showed, despite outplaying AC Milan in patches, that the squad wasn't strong enough and Gerrard, like most fans, knew they were still trailing behind the biggest clubs in Europe.

But after the initial optimism that Rafa's words might force the new owners to dig deep, alarm bells started to go off in the Liverpool captain's head. For the first time he worried that he may be forced to take sides in a power struggle.

'The problem I had was I was caught in the middle. I had a good relationship with Rafa and he was telling me about his frustrations with the Americans, and the more I heard this the more I worried. The relationship between them wasn't as good as I thought it was before that final. I realised it was going to end in tears for someone.'

That the Americans flashed the cash in the first two transfer windows is indisputable. In the summer Fernando Torres, Ryan Babel, Lucas Leiva and Yossi Benayoun were signed for almost £45 million, and in the January Martin Skrtel and Javier Mascherano cost a further £24 million. Although Benitez would rightly point out that in the summer window alone, the sales of Craig Bellamy, Djibril Cisse, Luis Garcia, Mark Gonzalez and Florent Sinama Pongolle meant £24.5 million had been recouped. What also eventually became indisputable was that the banks, not the Yanks, were spending the cash, and that involved interest rates which would wipe out future transfer budgets.

To the more astute fans, however, Athens had registered. Benitez had been at Anfield for three seasons by then, and although they sensed he was driven, stubborn, liked to stir controversy and wouldn't suffer fools, they knew something was going badly wrong behind the scenes. No Liverpool manager had ever dared to do what he did in Athens. Surely, they thought, something must be drastically awry at the heart of the club's decision-making process for Benitez to have exploded so violently in public.

'This was the first time I had doubts about whether the Americans had any money because, after Athens, a friend of mine who is a mate of David Moores phoned and said, 'They've got no dosh, you know. There's no dough there. Anything they're going to do will mean debt on the club,' said Peter Hooton.

By the autumn of 2007, Hicks and Gillett were at war, united only in one aspect – sacking Benitez. The major fall-out came over plans for the new stadium and drove such a wedge between them that Gillett, who was also sensing major problems with the money markets, started to look for an exit strategy.

Only a few months earlier, in July, the Americans' popularity had hit an all-time high. Within one week, while the club was on tour in Hong Kong, they unveiled the record signing of Torres, and plans for a breathtaking 70,000-seater, £300 million stadium. It was a futuristic masterpiece of steel and glass which made plans for the previous one look like a tram-shed. An acoustic-friendly arena whose centrepiece would be a single-tier 18,000 capacity Kop. An environmentally friendly home with presidential-style underground bunkers plus changing rooms for Sunday League players and tennis courts. A stadium whose revenues would finally allow Liverpool to challenge Manchester United and Chelsea for the dominance in English football, regenerate the Anfield area and be ready for the kick-off of the 2010–11 season.

'It's spectacular and I can't wait for everybody to see it,' said Hicks. 'I think our fans will love it. It's very creative architecture, very contemporary but unique to Liverpool as it's all centred around the Kop.'

The club claimed that Hicks had immediately decided, in a typical Texan way, the old plans were neither big nor bold enough for Liverpool, and brought in Dallas-based architects HKS with a brief to build a stadium that would be a mind-blowing statement of the new owners' intent.

Not surprisingly, an *Echo* poll claimed 90.5 per cent of fans welcomed the new plans. But everything was not as rosy in the new Stanley Park garden as it seemed. Although Gillett gave his backing to the new stadium plans (he eventually backed everything Hicks told him to back), he was riddled with doubt about the cost. He could feel the cold winds of recession blowing across America, thought back to the painful days of bankruptcy when he'd over-borrowed at the wrong time, and was worried. Why extend the borrowing from £215 million to possibly £400 million with the markets so uncertain? His instinct was to stick with the original stadium and keep the costs down. Besides, he thought, who would lend that kind of money now?

In December, when the severity of the credit crunch kicked in and banks stopped lending, the super-duper stadium plans went into cold storage, only to be seen again in a frame in Hicks's Dallas mansion, as he spoke about what might have been.

What was clear at the beginning of their first full season in charge was that Hicks was sitting on the throne and calling the shots, while Gillett was gradually realising he'd made a monumental mistake with this partnership which needed to be rectified as soon as possible. Hicks would go on to win almost every battle between the two over the coming years, and would have won the stadium one if the credit crunch hadn't stood in his way.

But as we moved towards the winter of 2007, the future was moving out of Hicks's control. The global recession was pulverising his strategy. Borrowing had become nigh-on impossible, shattering any chances of delivering a new stadium for the foreseeable future. Without that, the £100 million naming rights and the increased match-day revenues, there was no pot of gold at the end of his Anfield rainbow.

Added to that, their businesses back home, many built on high-risk credit, suffered badly as the US banking system went into meltdown, meaning they couldn't free up cash to inject into Liverpool, even if they had wanted to.

It was in the midst of this growing confusion, which was yet to surface in public, that I bumped into David Moores. The opening of Jamie Carragher's Cafe Sports England on 7 October 2007 saw a healthy turnout from past and present players plus club officials. Healthy measures of wine were also on the bill.

'You were my predator,' yelled Moores as he spotted me. 'You hunted me down. You were in with Steve Morgan trying to get me out. You were always trying to bring me down. Didn't he hurt me, Marge?' he asked his wife, who by now was trying to usher him outside for a smoke. 'Well you got what you wanted, didn't you? Me gone.'

It escalated into a row as I pointed out he also got what he wanted, £88 million, but before it got nasty we were ushered away from each other. Not before Chris Bascombe tossed him a googly that almost made his reddening head burst:

'Are you sure you've sold to the right people?' Moores' eyes widened, his face hardened and he shot back a reply laden with disgust: 'How can you look me in the face and ask that?'

As Moores stared at his shaving mirror over the coming months and years, that question would be answered by the haunted face that stared back. He came to realise he hadn't.

Meanwhile, when Benitez was shaving around the goatee in his Wirral bathroom he was increasingly seeing eyes filled with anger. He not only had evidence that the owners were briefing against him, he had it confirmed from his contacts that they had spoken to Jurgen Klinsmann, and if he were to lose the Anfield Champions League game against Porto, thus failing to qualify for the knock-out stages, he could be sacked. As communication lines with the absentee landlords closed down he felt he was being backed into a corner. Where they intend to kill him.

In mid-November he tried to get approval for bringing in two players during the January transfer window – one on a free. His transatlantic emails went unanswered until one flew back from a clearly riled Hicks telling him to focus on coaching and training the players he already had.

Which would have been a red rag to most bullish managers. To a proud and bristling Benitez it was a red flag. Throw into the mix the fact that Hicks had typed his command in capital letters, making Rafa feel like a child having his legs slapped, and we're talking about a red wall being built around the bull. A wall he was always likely to leap over at the first opportunity.

To the assembled journalists it was just another routine Melwood press conference on the eve of the league game at Newcastle. But it became apparent, when Benitez didn't show up on time, or even thirty minutes later, that something was wrong.

The reporters knew he was in the building, and a quick walk-about saw him locked in his office having an animated discussion with the club's Head of Press, Ian Cotton.

Thirty-five minutes after he should have arrived he took his seat before the media and conducted the most bizarre managerial press conference in the club's history:

'How much will you have to spend in January?'
'As always I am focused on training and coaching my team.'

'Are there assurances you'll have what you want?'
'As always I am focused on training and coaching my team.'

'So what is the long-term plan?'
'My plan is training and coaching the team.'

'Is there anything upsetting you?'
'As always I am focused on training and coaching my team.'

'Do you have anything to say?'
'As always I am focused on training and coaching my team.'

'Even off the record?'
'No.'

'It's clear something is up.'
'You have my answer.'

'You're very different from normal.'
'You have my answer.'

'You said after the story linking you with the Bayern Munich
    manager's job that you were happy to stay here a long time.
    Is that still the case?'
'As always I am focused on training and coaching my team.'

'You're not normally late. You were obviously preoccupied by
    something.'
'Because as always I was focusing on the training session.'

'Is there anything you'd like to say?'

'As always I am focused on training and coaching my team.'

'You always say you're focused on that but usually give off-the-record answers to enquiries. How come it's suddenly changed?'

'No off-the-record stuff. Nothing. I'm just focused on training and coaching as always.'

'You suggested you were open to the possibility of the England job. Is that something we should treat seriously?'

'It's your decision. You never know what will happen in the future.'

'Were you serious when you answered it?'

'I was serious.'

'One day you're looking to stay here a long time, the next you're talking about the England job. That's a contradiction.'

'The future is the future. Now, as always, I am focused on training and coaching my team, so I cannot say anything else. Just to keep preparing for the next game.'

'So what you're saying suggests perhaps the future here is in question?'

'I am focused on training and coaching my team.'

'So who knows?'

'As always I am focused on training and coaching my team.'

'Are you being allowed to do that as you wish?'
'I am focused on training and coaching my team.'

'Does everyone at the club share that opinion?'
'As always I am focused on training and coaching my team.'

This time there was no collective apoplexy in America. If anything the performance played into their hands as they could use it as evidence of a disloyal and eccentric manager who was talking about taking the England job. The owners' response was speedy, curt and questioning of Benitez's professionalism: 'We made a significant investment in the squad during the summer and desperately want this team to succeed. There are some very important games coming up and all of us need to focus on winning those games and getting the best out of the players we already have. We'll leave any talk of buying or selling players until we come across to Liverpool in December and sit down with the manager.'

Two days later, after Liverpool won 3–0 at Newcastle, they issued another joint statement, this time claiming they had 'nothing to say' about a report that Benitez was about to be sacked for his latest outburst, and replaced by Jose Mourinho.

Ten months after Liverpudlians accepted Hicks and Gillett with open arms, the beast within was stirred. The rumour about them wanting Rafa out wasn't a rumour but a fact, the gossip about Rafa having his hands tied over transfers was more than gossip, and the fears that these people were not what they seemed took hold.

The press conference performance left Jamie Carragher gobsmacked: 'I couldn't believe it. I was getting text messages saying "wait until you see this on Sky". I have to say at first I admired the manager's balls. Not many people would attack their boss so openly. I thought it was funny, but then I thought, can't you just do it in private?

'The Americans are probably thinking "hang on we've just spent nearly £50 million and you're moaning at us again for more money."'

At this point Carragher is beginning to tire of the constant bickering: 'Everyone was trying to be too clever, playing politics with no regard for the damage they were doing to the club.

'I thought the manager and owners mightn't like each other, but can't they just let us play football? You don't want your manager at a press conference playing stupid games, by going on and on about concentrating on coaching and training. We know you're not getting on but just leave it alone for the sake of the team.'

To Carragher, the blame isn't all one way: 'I blame both Rafa and the owners for what was going on. Him saying things before a game like focus on coaching and them hitting back through briefings or in videos.

'It was as though they were all playing their own games instead of worrying about the most important thing, which was Liverpool winning on a Saturday.'

Before the game against Porto, three days after Hicks and Gillett refused to deny a story calling for Rafa's head, 2,000 fans gathered outside the Sandon pub, the club's birthplace, and marched the short distance to the ground in support of Benitez.

It wasn't an anti-American, Yanks Out rally, more a shot across their bows and a statement of loyalty to Benitez. A firm reminder of Bill Shankly's philosophy that the manager manages and the men in the boardroom only get involved when it comes to writing the cheques. But underneath the politeness the anger was simmering away.

The protestors handed out leaflets, one of which read: 'We may not agree with some player selections or tactics but this man is the nearest we are ever going to get to Shanks or Sir Bob.'

At the front of the march they carried the famous Rafa-Tollah, a gilt-framed photo of the Spaniard, and held banners pledging support for the man who had given them the best night of their lives. One had a Spanish flag painted on it, along with Benitez's face superimposed on a picture of Che Guevara's and the phrase 'No Pasaran'. They shall not pass.

Another proclaimed 'En Rafa Confiamos'. In Rafa We Trust. Just in case the Americans' grasp of Spanish was less than perfect there was one written in English but dripping pure Scouse: 'You're the Custodians. It's Our Club. Rafa Stays.'

The fans had been told by journalists that the situation was now becoming serious and that the club was engaged in a civil war which was only going to get more vicious as time went on. They were being urged to grab a stick and be prepared to draw a line in the sand.

Before, during and after the game all sides of the ground echoed to the sound of 'Rafa, Raf-ael, Raf-ael Benitez' and the manager applauded all four stands before the game started. He couldn't resist his own little shot at the board, jabbing his fingers towards the directors' box then pointing it at the chanting fans. His first words to the media after the game, with the fans still singing 'Rafa's going nowhere' in the streets and pubs around Anfield, were to thank them 'with all my heart'.

A few days later, when the enormity of the show of solidarity sank in, he would give his most generous assessment of the fans, and an insight into why, when things became increasingly tough for him over the coming years, he would never abandon them.

'Where have you ever heard in your life, anywhere in football, this kind of support for a manager?' Benitez asked reporters.

'Both before the game, on the internet and during the game it was the same. Why? I am not Bill Shankly. I'm sure he was a fantastic motivator. I have just tried to be a good professional. What happened the other day was different class. Am I surprised? From the very beginning the fans have been good to me. I have enjoyed every day here. Some people have said to me because I was fighting for the club on different issues the people of Liverpool like this. The people here like fighters. Maybe that's an area where there is a connection between us. It is a very, very powerful connection.'

Benitez's critics always claimed he was a lucky manager, abandoning Napoleon's take on fortuitous generals, and using his luck as another club with which to beat him. There is no doubting the fact that when he needed to dig deep and pull off results which kept him alive he could. And so it was proving that November.

Although they had rarely been outstanding in the League they went into December unbeaten and in sight of leaders Manchester United. The Kop was bouncing to the sight of a new goal-scoring legend, Fernando Torres, and they had managed to claw their way back to European survival by slaughtering Besiktas 8–0 and hammering Porto 4–1.

Win in Marseille (which they did with ease) and, as far as the fans were concerned, it was panic over. That's certainly what David Moores and Rick Parry thought heading out to the south of France on 11 December. Until George Gillett summoned them to his hotel suite and handed them a document to sign which blew away any pretence that Liverpool had been bought with family money. Their worst fears were confirmed and their fiercest critics proved correct. They had indeed sold the family silver to a pair of shysters.

Gillett asked the pair to sign up to a whitewash procedure. Until the mid-eighties it was illegal to buy a company with that company's money. But the law was relaxed in 1985 to permit leveraged buyouts allowing companies to be bought using money borrowed against it.

A whitewash procedure (which was made illegal in October 2008) would have allowed Hicks and Gillett to move their acquisition debt directly on to Liverpool FC's books, as long as all of their directors gave written guarantees stating that for the next twelve months they could repay all of their creditors. Moores and Parry felt Liverpool's income was already being used to fund the Americans' takeover, contrary to what they had stated at their initial Anfield press conference. So they refused point-blank and harsh words were spoken.

Gillett became emotional and apologetic, blaming the credit crunch and asking them to see it his way. He reiterated that he fully intended not to put his debt on to the club but the banks had got the jitters and wanted greater security against their loans. He swore his intention had been to sell off other assets to repay the acquisition debts, but that wasn't possible now, and the banks were demanding they use the club as collateral.

Moores and Parry walked out in disgust and Gillett informed his absent partner. They would never attend a board meeting or be asked to approve anything again. Five days later, when Hicks turns up at Anfield for the Man United game and pivotal talks with Benitez, the two geared themselves up for a Texan toasting. But instead of being hauled through the boardroom window into the car park Hicks slowly sidled up to them in the directors' suite and whispered: 'I hear there's a bit of a local issue with the debt.' As the two nodded Hicks just laughed and walked away, saying nothing. Local issues and local people, 3,000 miles away from Dallas, meant little to Thomas Ollis Hicks.

The United game was a downbeat affair, with a lone Tevez strike separating the sides. Talk before and after the game was of what would happen at the big clear-the-air powwow between Rafa and the owners. For the first time though, Hicks and Gillett sensed an apathy towards them, bordering on suspicion.

When the PA announcer George Sephton told the crowd that one of Hicks's sons had proposed to his girlfriend the day before in the centre of the pitch, and that she'd said yes, the glad tidings were hardly acknowledged.

The meeting lasted three hours and was described as 'meaningful, positive' and other such press release phrases. Benitez said they patched up their differences, which he put down to communicating long-distance with people when his English is not the best. In reality Benitez had been told he had to sell before he could buy in January and that any further public outbursts aimed at undermining them would be dealt with severely.

He asked if they'd spoken to Klinsmann and they told him

that they had, but it had only been about consultancy work. It wasn't their fault, they told Benitez, if others had mischievously put two and two together and arrived at five. That night Gillett spoke at the Former Players' Association Christmas dinner and reassured them that Benitez's position had never been under threat. 'Rafa is the one we want as manager and we intend to keep him on,' he said to prolonged applause.

Former Liverpool striker John Aldridge attended the dinner and he was impressed: 'At the time I thought, fair play to him, he's turned up at the do, he might be a decent fella.' Looking back, he views the evening in a different light.

'He was playing us. Trying to flatter and impress us. He gave a speech saying he would back the manager and back us ex-players. He basically said what he thought we wanted to hear. In hindsight it was simply everything you'd expect from someone who conned the fans out of their hopes and dreams. My dad was a con man, honestly. And a brilliant one. But those two were in a different league. He'd have seen through them straight away, mind, because he could recognise others who were good at conning.

'But I didn't. I'd met Gillett and Hicks in the Anfield press box at one of the early games and although something was always ticking away in the back of my mind about them, I didn't see through them the way my dad would have. But we wanted to believe them, didn't we? Even though we sensed they knew nothing and cared nothing about Liverpool Football Club and were only turning up at Anfield every now and again to show their faces and sing "Walk On". We needed the new stadium and we were just hoping and praying they would deliver it.'

*

When Tony Barrett accepted the job of Liverpool FC correspondent on the *Echo* at the start of the 2007–8 season, he realised a lifetime ambition. As a staunch Kopite what could be a better way to earn a wage than reporting on the day-to-day happenings at a club you'd worshipped all of your life? The reality could not have been more different,

'I can't think of a job I could have done at that time which could have been harder because I was effectively reporting on a civil war. Usually when you get a new job you have to start from scratch and create your own contacts, but they were coming to me. Everyone, and I mean everyone: owners, directors, manager and players, were coming to me trying to get their side across.'

The Klinsmann story first appeared in the *Sun* on 10 December, with a German source confirming he'd been approached. But because the *Sun* is as widely read on Merseyside as Grouse Shooters' Monthly, and has far less credibility, nobody paid any attention.

The story wouldn't go away though and the fans, who were trying to decipher the power struggle at their club, were looking for answers. By the middle of January, with speculation reaching fever pitch, Tony Barrett took it on himself to go straight to the top for the definitive answer:

'I thought, "Why not directly ask Hicks the question?" because I was guessing he would be naive enough to go for it.

'He'd built his career on image and spin and I think he believed that he was bulletproof. What his ego wouldn't allow him to understand was that he was in a sport which he just didn't get, and in a place like Liverpool which he certainly didn't get.

'So I rang and said, "Tom, there's so much misinformation. The national press are saying you're trying to get rid of Rafa Benitez, but I can't believe that."

'He then went into a big speech. He was in the car on his way to his daughter's volleyball match and we had this big conversation in which he admitted speaking to Klinsmann but only as an insurance policy in case Benitez left. And he added, by the way, it was George's idea.

'"By speaking about going to Real Madrid, Rafa was playing us," he said, "and we had to do it."'

Barrett was now operating very nicely in cunning bastard mode: 'I said, "Tom that's perfectly understandable. If the manager's messing you about you're perfectly within your rights to speak to another one, and I think you should put that to the fans."

'And he went for it. The thing is he was going a bit deaf and he couldn't understand what I was saying. Everything I said I had to repeat and he'd come back with "I love your Scouse accent" but he had his PR head fixed on so tightly I think he'd have said anything just to get me to like him.

'"The fans need to know this, Tom", I said. "Yeah, you're right," he replied. So I persuaded him to let me email back to him everything he'd just said and give me the OK.'

Barrett turned his phone off and stared at it, struggling to comprehend what he'd just heard. He'd been told by one of the owners what both of them had been denying for months. That they tried to replace a manager who had been to two European Cup finals in three years with someone who had no experience of club management. Mid-season. As Barrett thought through the magnitude of his exclusive, it popped up in front of him, on his email inbox, approved by Hicks:

AN EPIC SWINDLE

In November, when it appeared we were in danger of not advancing in the Champions League, weren't playing well in our Premier League matches, and Rafa and we were having communication issues over the January transfer window, George and I met with Jurgen Klinsmann to learn as much as we could about English and European football.

He's a very impressive man. We attempted to negotiate an option, as an insurance policy, to have him become our manager in the event Rafa decided to leave our club for Real Madrid or other clubs that were rumored in the UK press, or in case our communication spiraled out of control for some reason.

After George and I had our long and productive meeting with Rafa following the Man United match, we put all of our issues behind us and received Rafa's commitment that he wanted to stay with Liverpool.

We never reached agreement on an option with Jurgen, and we are both pleased for him that he has a great opportunity to return to Germany and coach a great club team. Rafa has both of our support, and our communication has greatly improved.

Foster, Rick Parry and Rafa now have regular meetings at Melwood on Monday mornings. The two families always try to have a telephonic meeting on Monday afternoons, so we all are on the same page. We all want to win more games!

p.s. We are learning how to bridge my Texan and your Scouser (and my half deaf hearing!) My family loves the Scouse accent ... I'm the one that struggles. Hope we get everyone settled.

Tony Barrett was hauled into work at six a.m. the next day and by lunchtime the *Echo*, bearing a front-page splash headline of 'Hicks: We Lined Up Klinsmann' hit the streets.

Suddenly two Americans were less welcome in Liverpool than they would have been in Osama bin Laden's Tora Bora cave.

CHAPTER SIX

'Get out of our club, get out of our club, you lying
bastards, get out of our club'

– The Kop

The Sandon is a big, unremarkable, working-class pub on a
bleak, semi-derelict road. Unremarkable, that is, except for one
remarkable fact. On 15 March 1892, in one of its snugs,
Liverpool Football Club, the love-child of local fourteen-year-
old floozie Everton, came screaming and kicking into the world.

Back in those pre-Boer war days the Sandon was where the
players would change into their knickerbockers, and directors
and fans would take porter and ale before ambling to a patch
of grass, a goalie's clearance away, called Anfield. What better
venue then, for the descendants of those moustachioed Vic-
torian pioneers to gather 116 years later to formulate a way
of reclaiming that same club?

If the Klinsmann story lit the dynamite that had been placed
around Anfield a year earlier, news that Hicks and Gillett were
attempting to refinance their initial loans by putting £350 million debt on the club saw the explosion. The FA Cup third
round replay with Luton became a show of anti-Americanism,

with the soon-to-be-familiar chant, 'They don't care about Rafa, they don't care about fans, Liverpool Football Club is in the wrong hands' being belted out from sections of the Kop.

A banner 'Dubai SOS – Yanks Out' was unveiled which referred to the fact a Dubai-based consortium had re-emerged as serious buyers. Gillett, who had severed all but the most formal of relations with his partner after he went public over Klinsmann, wanted to sell his 50 per cent share to them, and get out of the place.

Hicks, however, believed he possessed a precious diamond coveted by Sheikh Al Maktoum, and was holding out for his juiciest-ever piece of quick-buck making. He was bullishly claiming to be going nowhere, putting it out that he wasn't even talking to the Arabs – he'd been talking to them for four months since pheasant shooting with Amanda Staveley in York-shire – and that his family just adored being custodians at this wonderful, storied club – BBC radio journalist Gary Richardson blew that out of the water when he told his *Sportsweek* listeners he had overheard a very close relative of Hicks say in the Anfield boardroom: 'I can't wait to get rid of this club, I'm sick and tired of it.'

Any scales that had clung to fans' eyes during the past year had well and truly fallen away. As Liverpool's Capital of Cul-ture Year burst into life, the locals were inviting foreigners to come and enjoy The World In One City. Well, all foreigners except two: Messrs Hicks and Gillett. All one half of Liverpool wanted to invite them to was a lynching party.

Reclaim The Kop (RTK), the group behind the pro-Benitez Porto rally, called for a mass demonstration at the Aston Villa game on 21 January. Author Kevin Sampson, who founded the

RTK with another veteran Red, John Mackin, told the media: 'The fans want George Gillett and Tom Hicks out unconditionally. It's as simple as that. They are no good for us and no good for the club.

'As the world is currently seeing, Liverpool is the most welcoming city and its people are the most generous hosts you're going to find anywhere. But cross us and that's that. We are enemies for life. Ask Kelvin MacKenzie, Margaret Thatcher or Boris Johnson. These two Americans tried to capitalise on our goodwill and our unswerving love for this club. But they underestimated us and badly underestimated our love for Rafa. The moment they admitted they had been plotting to oust Benitez, they may have well started saddling the horses. The fans despise them as passionately as they do any rival. At the moment, it's worse. If they had a shred of common sense, they would take the money on offer from Dubai Investment Capital and gallop out of town.'

The media observed the anger on Merseyside and spotted a big story moving from the back pages to the front. To Liverpool fans the Anfield Civil War was a harrowing saga turning fan against fan and ripping the heart and soul out of their club. To the national media it was an enthralling power battle between a George Bush ally and an Arab sheikh, with a shower of revolting Scousers caught in the crossfire.

On 21 January a demonstration was planned for the home game with Aston Villa, and London sent its finest colour writers up to ignore the football and concentrate on the rebellious mob. That cold Monday night was a poignant and emotion-charged Anfield occasion for all the wrong reasons, but it was important and historic nonetheless.

This was not the type of heart-pumping occasion of raw passion and glorious abandon we'd seen against St Etienne, Inter Milan and Chelsea, which had made open-mouthed viewers across the world categorise Anfield as one of sport's great amphitheatres. It was not even a night of Kopite solidarity. Rows broke out, even the odd scuffle, as some of the older generation told younger ones who released screams of hate from twisted faces that it wasn't part of their job description to distract Liverpool players from going about their sacred duty of winning.

I experienced that generational gap in reverse as I went to the toilet, still chanting about 'lying bastards' and their need to get out of our club, when a steward in his thirties without a hint of irony said, 'Oi, keep the fuckin' language down will you, mate?'

'What fuckin' language?' I replied.

'That fuckin' language.'

'Would that be the same fuckin' language you're fuckin' using?'

'Yes it fuckin' would, but I'm not fuckin' shoutin' it at the top of my voice at the fuckin' pitch, am I?'

'Neither am fuckin' I. I'm fuckin' shouting it at the fuckin' directors' box, which is my fuckin' right so fuckin' well fuck off.'

It was a revelatory moment which took me back to being a nine-year-old and the school colour-blind nurse telling me the news that I was red-green deficient, which meant that when I grew up I could never be a train driver or an airline pilot.

I may have been fifty, but I knew as I went for that leak that even if I'd fancied those big yellow coats and watching the game through the back of my head, when I grew up I could never be a steward.

We'd never seen anything like this kind of demonstration before. Standing in the middle of all this anti-Americanism made me feel at times like Hanoi Jane Fonda. I even had an army jacket on. But it wasn't all Yanks Out. There were banners proclaiming: 'Taxi For Hicks', 'If It Ain't Broke Don't Hicks It' and 'One DIC Is Better Than Two'.

As the game started the chant of 'They don't care about Rafa, they don't care about fans' segued into 'Rafa, Rafael, Rafa, Rafael, Rafa, Rafael, Rafael Benitez' and on it went for eight long minutes without a break, with its object of desire occasionally standing up in the dugout to give an approving wave back to the Kop.

From then until the end of the 2–2 draw, it would be sporadically repeated along with that other new soon-to-be classic: 'Get out of our club, get out of our club, you lying bastards, get out of our club.'

By the way, special mention must go to the Villa fans in the Anfield Road End for filling the Kop's silences with chants for their own American owner Randy Lerner and 'You-You-You-Ess-Ay.' Ah, if only Doug Ellis had taken up George Gillett's offer, none of this would have happened, I thought.

Photographers didn't miss the chance to capture the three empty directors' box seats beside Rick Parry and David Moores where Gillett, Hicks and Foster Gillett usually sat. They were over in America negotiating separately with the banks to strengthen their grip on the club, even if their primary motive was to put them in a stronger position to deal with Dubai.

The hate-filled, anti-American songs and banners, the personal attacks and the blunt demands that they get out of their own club, barely registered. Back in Dallas nothing could be heard. This wasn't yet a noise to be dealt with. It wasn't even a whisper. But the Bill Shankly boys were coming down the road.

Peter Hooton was conscious of a group called Liverpool Supporters Network, who were trying to bring websites and fanzines together to unite against the Americans. He contacted the men behind it, Andy Heaton and Dave Usher, and proposed that instead of everyone being a website warrior in their bedroom, they held a face-to-face meeting, and worked out a proper line of attack.

'They were under the impression that this would be a group of fifteen to twenty people from fanzines and websites sitting around and agreeing on a policy,' said Peter. 'I, on the other hand, thought it was going to be a mass meeting for anyone who wanted to come, so there was misunderstanding at first.

'We went onto a loop of about fifteen to twenty people and we began to get emails, a couple of days before the scheduled meeting on 31 January, saying: "Look, this is going to be chaos because it's getting too big. It's going to be like a mob and we're not going to get anywhere. We need a small, controlled group."'

The idea of a mass meeting appealed to Hooton, but he feared it could get out of control and descend into a futile gesture if it wasn't properly run. So he brought in Paul Rice, who was a former chair of the Broadgreen Labour Party. Hooton's thinking was that if you could control a meeting of the Broadgreen Labour Party back in the days of Militant, then you could control a herd of bulls in the red flag department of the Chinese Red Army gift shop.

'I didn't mind at all,' said Rice. 'After the Klinsmann story became clear I remember thinking, "Something's going to have to be done here. Someone's going to have to stand up to these."'

He felt he needed the Americans' financial situations analysed and clarified, so he contacted Dave Elder, a New York financial expert, asked him to pick the bones out of Hicks's and Gillett's dealings and send him a fool's translation. Which he did.

'We circulated it at the meeting and basically it began to explain how they had structured their debt and how it was starting to come back on to the club,' said Rice. 'And I think that was the first time we'd actually realised the severity of the situation and had been able to put it in front of the masses. It was the first time we'd been able to explain what a leverage buyout was. And that was the thing that broadened it out from suspicion and anger about Rafa into something much more fundamental. We now found ourselves having to say: "We've got to do something about this; it's no good taking the piss out of the likes of Newcastle and Manchester City because we've got a real crisis here."

'The meeting, actually, wasn't that difficult to chair because what we had was a body of information that people hadn't seen or didn't know about. So when we started talking, in very simple terms, about how much debt was on the club, it confirmed people's worst fears but also crystallised the issues. When we then went on to cover such areas as how the fans were treated at the ticket office, suspicions over local fans being overlooked, etc., it became obvious there was a broader need for action other than just that against Hicks and Gillett.

'Yes, the Americans were the ongoing target, but there was actually an appetite out there to do something much wider and that's really how the idea of a supporters' union came up, rather than a single-issue protest group.'

As 350 fans packed the back hall of the Sandon, the air crackled with anticipation. Every major fan group was there: Reclaim The Kop, The Urchins, the fanzines, the websites and the forums. It was like the coming together of the Five Families in The Godfather.

The intention was to build the union from as wide a base as possible. Hooton, Heaton and Usher made sure that everyone who organised a coach, ran a forum or a website, or was involved in the supporters' club was invited, and that the microphone would be passed to anyone with the balls to speak.

'What fascinated me was the broad spectrum of people,' said Paul Rice. 'It struck me that, as well as a lot of people our age, who you would have expected to be ready to take a stand, there were all these young lads, who, and perhaps we didn't realise this, had been disenfranchised completely. Whereas, at their age, the likes of us and the lads we've gone the match with over the years could go to the games, these lads were like the Sandon Wall Babies: they couldn't get into the ground, so they watched it here on the telly in the pub. And yet they still had the passion.'

Like most fans, inside and outside the Sandon that night, Tony Barrett's views on the takeover had undergone a sea-change. As a devoted fan and a local lad, plus a journalist with a responsibility to see through the PR mist and deliver the truth to the fans, he was understandably beating himself up.

'I'm thinking, "How badly have I got this wrong?" Well I got it so wrong that I realised I had to try to put it right. I had a guilty conscience. I had to give the fans as much backing as my job would allow. Fair play to the 350 who turned up that night because they knew there was something badly wrong within Liverpool when others were refusing to recognise it. They were fighting for their club when no one else was. Those who didn't like the idea of fans acting like this said they were militants, and maybe some of them were. But what's wrong with that? Everything they said back then was spot on, and Liverpool owes the Spirit Of Shankly a debt of gratitude for taking a stand.'

At this point it wasn't the Spirit, but the Sons Of Shankly they were calling themselves, after playwright Nicky Allt's inspired suggestion met with warm approval – although when it was pointed out they'd be allowing in members with breasts and the Glenbuck Messiah had only sired daughters it was changed to Spirit Of Shankly, keeping the politically correct lobby happy and maintaining the SOS message. Allt it was who had organised the Sandon venue, became the union's first chairman and, in those early months, was a key player in attracting membership and media attention.

Sons, or spirits, you could argue about, but Shankly needed to be in the title. He was everything every Liverpudlian who hadn't been around in the mid-1950s, and many who had, identified with. With his own unique brand of wit, his inimitable frankness, his deeply felt socialist beliefs and his unshakeable love for his adopted city and its people, Shankly was the spirit of Liverpool FC.

As powerful brands go, his was up there with Coca-Cola, Disney and Jesus Christ.

'There was a strong parallel going on between Shankly and Benitez which was crucial to what we were about,' said Paul

Rice. 'Fans, whether they liked Rafa or not, and even at that early stage there were people who were not keen on him, felt that the role of the manager was being compromised like it had never been since Shankly arrived and told the board, 'If you won't let me be the manager I ain't coming.'

Peter Hooton explained: 'Shankly initially refused the Liverpool manager's job because he couldn't pick the team and he only came back when they said, "OK, you've got authority over the team." So it was inevitable that we would have some link to Shankly.'

With a name agreed and broad aims established, word had to get out about the formation of a new fans' alliance. A website was set up and a leaflet produced, which looked at today, seems remarkably like a page out of a 1960s programme. The paper was rough, the red ink so light it was almost pink, the typeface the same one used in headlines on the old Kop magazine and the Liver Bird looks like it was plucked off Ron Yeats' cloth badge. But underneath a thumbnail picture of Shankly, arms widespread on the steps of St George's Hall, were words that Liverpool fans should never have had to write or read:

'An alliance of supporters and all major Liverpool fanzines and websites have come together to force the owners, the poisonous, dishonest Tom Hicks and George Gillett out of OUR club.

'They want to buy our club with our money. Let's not give it to them. Boycott ALL forms of official LFC merchandise, food and drink, starting TODAY. Buy a fanzine instead of a programme. Go to a stall rather than the club shop.'

At the foot of the leaflet was a quote from Shankly. Or rather a pair of bullets coming out of a double-barrelled shotgun aimed at the faraway cowboys:

'At a football club there's a holy trinity – the players, the manager and the supporters. Directors don't come into it. They are only there to sign the cheques.'

The words were fine, but to stand even the slimmest of chances of taking on the might of corporate America, SOS needed to convince a significant chunk of the fan base to join them.

The decision was taken to form a body based on the trade union workplace model, giving all members one vote and forcing anyone who wanted to be on the steering committee to stand in a democratic election.

'We were very conscious that the first meeting only had a Liverpool audience and we wanted to reach out to the club's broader fan base,' said Paul Rice. 'We all knew people from other parts of the world who were coming to support the club and who bought into its values. There are others who just come to take photographs and are tourists but there are as many people from the rest of England, Norway and Ireland who understand what the club is about and are more Scouse than Scousers in that respect. And we wanted to get them involved.'

'We were also conscious that we needed to be organised,' said Peter Hooton. 'For a long time I'd been watching documentaries about Boca Juniors and Lazio. Unfortunately Lazio fans are from a political persuasion that I don't agree with, but they were organised. I remember watching those documentaries thinking, if only Liverpool fans could be organised maybe we wouldn't have to put up with what we have put up with for years. We needed a catalyst to take us there, and inadvertently that catalyst was Tom Hicks, George Gillett and what they were trying to do to our club.'

I love being paid to write a weekly football column on a national newspaper, which I've been doing since 1997. Short of being the man who picks up the laundry in the female dressing room on the *Hollyoaks* set or the valet whose job it is to put the paste on Prince Charles's tooth-brush (just so I'd have one shot at putting haemorrhoid cream on and watching him crumple to the floor weeping), I can't think of a better job.

But there come points when big decisions have to be made. The first one was 'Do I declare my club loyalty?' It was a decision made redundant by the sheer volume of anti-Manchester United sentiment I was pouring on to the page which was matched only by the amount of pro-Liverpool bias.

I was outed quicker than a Lib-Dem MP by a gay masseur, and before I knew it 'Brian Reade is a Scouse Cunt' websites were springing up all over the net, complete in one United case with a cartoon of Italians pushing my garden wall on top of me with the caption: 'How do YOU like it, you murdering twat.' Nice.

I actually believe, and not just because I was quickly sussed, that every football journalist, analyst, pundit and commentator should be open about their club loyalties. We make our MPs declare their outside interests, so why not the people whose outpourings really make the public want to kick the lining out of their cat?

Yet even for those of us who have placed our tribal affections into the public domain there come hard decisions. I'd reached one with the Spirit Of Shankly. Do I join, and if so, how active do I become?

The first one, as a slappable young toad on *The Apprentice* might say, was a no-brainer. Not only did the union need and deserve all the support it could get, to not join would have made me feel like a scab. But if you become part of the organising committee, a media spokesman or take a lead on the marches, you compromise yourself. I doubt I'd have been sacked by the *Daily Mirror*, but I would never have been able to write articles or go on radio and TV to praise their actions. So I took a backseat, armed with a laptop.

'A fortnight ago something astonishing happened,' I wrote in the *Mirror* in March 2008:

> More than 600 Liverpool fans met to form a supporters union called The Spirit of Shankly (SOS), aimed at forcing out the club's owners. And on Wednesday representatives of Dubai Investment Capital held a meeting with them to discuss ways of grabbing power from George Bush's side-kick, Tom Hicks (or as he used to be called in Hollywood – Tom Mix, King of Cowboys).
>
> Let me run that past you again. Representatives of Sheikh Mohammed Al Maktoum, one of the world's richest men, swopped thoughts with a three-week-old fans' group on how to bring down a billionaire adviser to the most powerful man on earth.
>
> This remarkable scenario came about because these fans realised they'd been taken for patsies. That American speculators had spun bullshit to them about their passion for their club. That they planned to milk it for all they could without putting in a dime of their own.

And the grass roots fury has spawned more Liverpudlian
groups than Merseybeat.

That mass meeting I referred to was held in the Olympia The-
atre on West Derby Road, a huge Grade II listed ballroom which
first entered Liverpool legend in 1905 as a purpose-built indoor
circus.

The ideal setting, therefore, to perform an act of escapology
which would free us from the grip of clowns. The only warmth
in the icy room came from wrapping ourselves in the nostalgic
red-blooded banners which had been draped in stadiums
around Europe on all those nights of glory, which now hung
from the balcony. Below them, on the old Locarno dance floor
where our mums once jitterbugged with GI Joes, hundreds of
solemn-looking men mooched about in dark coats, certain
about why they were here, but unsure of the path they were
about to tread.

We picked up leaflets laid out neatly on rows of seats, sat
down and stared up at a stage where a dozen fans who made
up the steering committee, some well-known others not so,
nodded, shrugged, grimaced and finger-jabbed. They told us
why they were here, and why they believed we should be here.
They let anyone who wanted to have their say, have it – thanks
to Peter Hooton doing something he never does as singer in
The Farm: pass around the microphone – before unveiling the
union's list of aims and objectives:

IMMEDIATE AIM: To rid the club of Tom Hicks and
George Gillett.

CONSTANT AIMS: To represent the best interests of our

members and by extension the best interests of the supporters of Liverpool Football Club on both the local and international level. To hold whoever owns the football club to account.

SHORT-TERM AIMS: To institute a functioning structure for the Spirit Of Shankly. To create long-lasting relationships with all aspects of Liverpool FC's supporting community. To improve the quality of service for Liverpool FC's supporters. To improve the standard and value of travel arrangements for Liverpool FC's supporters.

MEDIUM-TERM AIMS: To work with any relevant agencies to improve the area of Anfield. To build links with grass-roots supporter groups both home and abroad.

LONG-TERM AIM: To bring about supporter representation at boardroom level.

ULTIMATE AIM: Supporter ownership of Liverpool Football Club.

The words 'so, a piece of piss then,' fluttered through my cynical head as I joined in with the rousing round of applause. And as we quickly voted unanimously to approve those aims (mainly so we could get a few pre-match pints in before that afternoon's FA Cup fourth round game with Barnsley) I'm sure hundreds of my new fellow members were as sceptical as me.

But you know what, it didn't matter. Something important was being built that day. Something that needed to be built and something that may outlast most of us who were present. Nobody had seen the need to build it, not up to a month before, but the plans, the tools and the cement had been thrust at us by two cowboys who were still in bed 3,000 miles away.

The occasion could have had the feel of a 1980s Socialist Workers' Party student union sit-in over South African wine being stocked in the campus Spar, or an anarchists' Kill The Rich convention, but it didn't. It felt real, grown-up and sincere. And what those fellow fans asked us to help them achieve seemed achievable. Not all of it, not this year, and maybe not in our lifetimes, but some of it and some time soon.

Before we headed for a mile-long march on Anfield, a message was read out from Karen Gill, Bill Shankly's granddaughter, who had been contacted at her home in Athens, told about the union and asked if she thought the family would approve of using the Shankly name. Her reply, as always, was to give unconditional support. Karen is a marvellous woman who has inherited many of her grandad's traits, not least his fight and his passion, as witnessed in this truly inspirational message of support she gave the union:

I would like to thank each and every one of you for honouring my grandfather's name by calling this union Spirit Of Shankly. For me though it's more than just honouring his name. In these times of corporate gluttony I am truly heartened to discover that there are still so many people who embody my grandad's spirit. It's an Olympic spirit – passionate, pure and true. It's a dream of greatness and glory which comes from dedication, hard work and integrity. In this dream money is only a means to an end, it's not the end itself. My grandad had a dream for Liverpool Football Club and you are all helping to keep that dream alive. It's the people with dreams who achieve things in the end because they have a vision which drives them on. We know Bill Shankly 'made the people happy' but I know that you would have all made him happy were he alive to see this legendary support today. I speak on behalf of the Shankly family when I say that we are wholeheartedly behind The Spirit Of Shankly.

Say it in an Ayrshire rasp and it could almost be a blessing from beyond the grave.

Liverpool fans have taken a lot of stick over the years, and still do to this day, for a perceived mawkishness and an unearned sense of entitlement. Especially in the long years since we last won the league, because in certain eyes that should make us feel as mediocre about ourselves and our club as some of the football we've had to endure.

'You think you're special, you think you're unique, you actually believe you are God's Chosen Tribe' are charges I've had hurled at me not just from Everton, United and Chelsea fans, but from one of those clubs' chairmen. And in many ways they have a point. I've felt as embarrassed hearing some Liverpudlians spout over-sentimental guff as you may feel reading the next paragraph.

Rightly or wrongly, Shankly made us this way. He instilled the idea that we were the most special part of the most special club in the world. Just as he did with his players he imbued in us a sense of superiority bordering on invincibility and a will to not suffer fools easily, especially if they interfered with the fortunes of our beloved team.

I was probably one of the lucky few in the Olympia that day who had actually spent some time with Shankly and asked him about his philosophy, his beliefs and his motivation. I was a seventeen-year-old schoolkid in 1975, he had retired a year earlier as manager, but was still turning up at Melwood whenever the players weren't there to breathe in the grass and the liniment, and do a little jogging around the kingdom he had built up from a patch of wasteland.

He'd agreed to let me interview him for the school magazine but really I was there to gawp at the only god I believed in. He talked about many things, about the great players and nights he'd had and the reasons he'd walked out on the club, but what left the most profound impression was when he spoke about his socialist beliefs. He told me with a glint in his piercing eyes and a jut of his Cagney chin, that if he was ever put in charge of Liverpool's street-cleaning and refuse operation he'd make it the cleanest city in the world.

He would achieve that status by insisting every worker in his department, including him, earned the same money, but he'd also demand big bonuses for all of his men if they achieved their aims. Which they would because he would motivate them to succeed by convincing them of the prize to be gained by having an unquenchable pride in your work, your city and your people.

Sod studying A-Levels to get into university, I wanted to pick up a brush, join his army, get out on to the streets around Melwood and start straight away.

Shankly's socialism wasn't party-political or driven by dogma, it was instinctive. It had seeped into his soul as part of a big family during a poor upbringing in a Scottish west-coast pit-town. It was of his essence. It defined how he treated everyone he came into contact with, especially the working-class fans who handed over what spare cash they had, every other Saturday on their half-day off, to the Anfield gatemen.

He would drum into every Liverpool player he signed, from Kevin Lewis to Kevin Keegan, that those fans weren't the most important people at a football club, they were the *only* people. And while they are paying your wages never treat them with anything but the utmost respect and never, ever cheat them. Not an inch.

I thought of those words as I stared at his image on the stage in that big, cold room. And I thought back to the words Tom Hicks had used before the Athens Champions League Final, to define his relationship with Liverpool fans: 'I bought Weetabix and leveraged it up to make my return. You could say that anyone who was eating Weetabix was paying for our purchase of Weetabix. It was just business. It is the same with Liverpool.'

I realised in that moment why that meeting and that union were vital to the survival of the club that Shankly had built. In the years that followed I would come to realise that for all the pain, debt and disgrace Hicks and Gillett piled on Liverpool, one good thing came out of their time in charge. They reminded us of who we were and where we'd come from. They made us realise what was special about the club that Shankly built and why we needed to fight for it.

So on we marched, this band of very unmerry men, down West Derby Road, holding up three buses and obstructing pram-pushing mums who were trying to get back home from Aldi before their baby's next feed. Down through the side streets and into the sea of fans pouring down Walton Breck Road towards the ground, chanting 'What do we want? Yanks Out. When do we want it? Now.' Mainly at bemused out-of-town Weetabix-buyers in replica shirts, clutching bags heavy with official merchandise they'd just bought from the shop to help pay off Tom and George's bank loans.

One of them, a big blond man of Viking descent, photographed me on his phone and gave me the thumbs up. I probably appeared on some Norwegian Facebook page, chanting like a tragic, grey-haired old hippy at an anti-Vietnam rally, with curried chip paper glued to my knees. Not how I saw myself acting at fifty when, as a ten-year-old I marched down the same pavements with a wooden stool under my arm dreaming of nothing more than an Alun Evans hat-trick. Ain't life full of surprises.

Amanda Staveley is one of those women who ticks the fantasy boxes of every throbbing male. The former model has the sparkling, perfectly proportioned face of an all-American Miss Universe winner but with the elusive class of an English rose. She comes from land-owning Yorkshire stock and had a boarding school, then Cambridge, education, yet maintained the warmth of a down-to-earth Northerner who hugs strangers and calls them 'love'.

She's tall and athletic, could run 100 metres in 12.6 seconds at fourteen, and would have been an Olympic sprinter if she hadn't snapped her Achilles tendon. She has the charm and cunning of an old-colonial diplomat plus the brains of a double-first nuclear physicist. But best of all, when that jet-propelled golf trolley His Royal Randiness Prince Andrew became utterly smitten with her and proposed marriage, she said words to the effect 'You're all right, love. Rather than be Fergie the Second I'd prefer to be a successful private equity financier who makes millions off her own bat, and has a life.'

And millions, many of them, was what she made. Partly through being a workaholic, but mostly through cultivating a twelve-year friendship with Middle East royal families during which time she soaked herself in their culture and won their trust. Staveley it was who earned £10 million from Sheikh Mansour for delivering him Manchester City, and Staveley it was who Sheikh Al Maktoum turned to when he became troubled and baffled as to why Liverpool had ditched DIC at the last minute in favour of the Americans. In the autumn of 2007 she set about finding the answers for him, which didn't tax her brain too much. It's simple, she told him. They had moved slower than a comatose slug on a duvet day.

Two things then happened. Virtually every professional figure involved in the first bid found their position within DIC reassessed, and he told Staveley to buy him Liverpool. Even if it meant having to pay an extra couple of hundred million. This was a wrong that had to be righted.

So into battle she went, charged with prising the jewel of Anfield out of American clutches, not for DIC this time but for an Al Maktoum-backed Middle Eastern fund, which was potentially better for Liverpool as it meant the club would be his own personal responsibility, and not answerable to some dithering investment committee.

She threw herself at the task in a typically driven manner. Anyone who could be worked on was worked on, day and night – and as some journalists can testify by producing their phone bill, halfway through the night if she felt she hadn't quite hammered home her point. She told reporters with Liverpool connections that Al Maktoum was set on buying the club. He knew it was in the wrong hands and unless it was taken out of those hands it would only be damaged further. One *Echo* man said: 'She identified early on the need to get the local paper on board and pulled it off brilliantly. But to be honest, none of us fell for the line that she, or Al Maktoum, genuinely had the club's interests at heart. Staveley was very impressive but she reeked of money. Like the Yanks, that was her only reason for being in Liverpool.'

No sooner had the Spirit Of Shankly been formed than they appeared on her radar. Her people spoke to their people and their people met her people, and it was quickly decided they should get together to work out how best to end the American occupation. Bar-owner, restaurateur and Liverpool fan Rob Guttman laid on a private room and set up a table for dinner in his Albert Dock Circo restaurant. Meeting and greeting Spirit Of Shankly members Paul Rice, Andy Heaton and Neil Atkinson, on their arrival, was Staveley.

After the niceties and the starters they got down to business. Staveley told them that powerful people right at the top of Dubai had seen the mess the Americans were making at Anfield and noted the pleas from fans to be rescued. They also realised the mistakes DIC had made first time around. But this isn't DIC who have come back in for Liverpool, she said, this is the Sovereign Fund and Sheikh Al Maktoum is very serious about doing business. Indeed he feels, as a matter of honour because he allowed Hicks and Gillett in, that he has a certain responsibility to Liverpool fans.

He knows how important the fans are going to be if he takes over the club and he wants you to be involved, Staveley told the SOS lads before playing her ace: the new structure would have an operating board below an executive board and the sheikh would like a fan on that board.

She looked round for nods of approval, the banging of glasses on the tablecloth, maybe the odd chorus of 'You'll Never Walk Alone', but instead got a slap around her finely chiselled chops. Blank looks. Welcome to Liverpool, love.

'I think at this point we were supposed to roll over and get our tummies tickled,' said Paul Rice.

'But we went, woh, hang one a minute. We're not having a token person on any board. If the Spirit Of Shankly is going to be on your board we're going to want to have some clout. We'd want something that would lead to moving beyond the sheikh's involvement so that we could build up our own position to the point where, hopefully, we could buy the club ourselves. So anyone on that board would have to have full voting rights. You're not going to get away with sticking a fan on there who would be getting turfed out every time there was a financial decision to be made.'

Staveley and her Dubai team looked on slack-jawed. 'I think she was partly taken aback and partly quite in admiration of the fact that we didn't just roll over,' said Rice.

Let me run that past you again. Representatives of Sheikh Mohammed Al Maktoum, one of the world's richest men, sought approval from representatives of 350 fans who'd met in the back room of the Sandon a few weeks earlier, for their plan to bring down a billionaire adviser to the most powerful man on earth. All for their benefit.

And they were told to do one.

Shankly would indeed have been proud of the Spirit he'd left behind.

CHAPTER SEVEN

'If you look at what has happened under Rick's leadership it's been a disaster'

– Tom Hicks

As the chants from the main stand car park grew more raucous an agitated Tom Hicks paced around the crammed boardroom. Spotting a senior club figure whom he considered an ally, he sidled up and said, 'What the hell's going on out there? What are these marches all about?' The figure replied that it was an alien sight to him because in the forty years he'd been coming to Anfield and the sixty years his father had been, there had never been any protests or marches.

'So why now?' said Hicks.

'You know why,' he was told.

'No I don't,' he answered. 'Tell me.'

So he did.

'You can't have it both ways, Tom. When I asked you why you bought Liverpool and not some cheaper club you said one of the reasons you wanted it was the fans. Because they're so engaging and so loyal. You can't expect them to be those things then sit back and take it up the arse when you're giving it to them with both barrels. That's why they're out there and they've got every right to be.'

Hicks didn't like what he heard, muttered 'gimme a break' and sauntered away with the noise ringing in his ears.

The great Texan bluffer took a massive gamble when he went public on the pursuit of Jurgen Klinsmann. He calculated that in playing the honesty card through their local paper, and spinning it so it appeared it was Gillett's idea which he foolishly went along with before realising his partner was making a terrible mistake, that all would be well.

He played the odds in his head and believed that fans would view Big Bad Gillett as the enemy and Uncle Tom as the saviour. Which served his ends at this point, because by January 2008 he had broken off all communication with Gillett, who was negotiating with Amanda Staveley to sell his share of the club. By briefing journalists to say he wasn't interested in selling his share – he was, but he valued the club at a ludicrous £1 billion – and by painting Gillett as the man who stabbed Rafa in the back, he hoped the fans would believe he'd been the good guy all along. The one who was trying to hold it all together.

It was a classic Hicks tactic. As one man who observed their working relationship at Anfield at close quarters described it: 'Gillett's philosophy was: "I'm the owner. I hire the management team and let them do their work." Hicks had to be in charge. He had to run everything. And he did so through a policy of divide and rule. He constantly played one person off against the other, so he ended up making all the major decisions.'

This divisive, control-freak strategy was revealed within the first hour of walking into Anfield in February 2007. As preparations were being drawn up for the press conference, the media man who was managing the event, Mike Lee, read out the running order. He told Rick Parry to go first and explain the situation, then introduce George Gillett because he'd been involved in the deal for six months, who would then hand over to the new guy on the scene, Tom Hicks.

Before Lee had finished his sentence Hicks piped up with: 'I'm going second.' All eyes turned to Gillett who just looked at him, shrugged, pulled a face that said 'OK' and stared at the floor.

He was laying down a marker. Pissing on this new territory like an alpha male lion and leaving his scent to warn off rivals. Letting everyone know that he was the one with the cash and thus the one in charge. Gillett was never left in any doubt about the reality of their partnership. The Wisconsin Kid was forced to bring in Hicks because stumping up the cash to buy a club the size of Liverpool was out of his league. Without the Texan's bankers vouching for his paper wealth Gillett would probably have ended up buying Leicester City.

It wasn't just Gillett that Hicks bullied into a corner at Liverpool. Anyone who challenged him was swatted away. Take the proposed new stadium. The New Anfield (insert name of £100 million naming rights sponsor) Bowl was his baby, the one that would lay him a golden egg, and no one messed with it.

As early as the first week Hicks had decided to ditch the original stadium plans and get his Dallas architects to design him something bigger and better. A meeting was scheduled in Liverpool's Malmaison Hotel for the Saturday morning where Martin Jennings, the stadium's project manager, would talk the new owners through the plans.

Jennings, an unassuming, down-to-earth, non-football man, had heard the promise that a spade would be in the ground in sixty days and that the steel order was about to be placed, so guessed they wanted a detailed briefing on where exactly they were up to. As he opened his comments Hicks interrupted him to announce he was dropping all the assurances he gave the previous board: 'We ain't building that stadium,' he said. 'It's not big enough.'

When he was asked on what criteria it wasn't big enough he replied: 'Man United's is bigger.'

As it was explained to him that United have always had bigger attendances than Liverpool, he brushed it aside saying: 'Well, we're going to have it bigger. I'm going to get new designs done.'

Jennings told him he wouldn't need to do that as the current architects had allowed for an option to expand their stadium to a 70,000 capacity and it could be redesigned, not only quickly but relatively inexpensively.

Hicks snapped back: 'Are you fucking listening to me?' Jennings asked what he meant. 'Are you with us or against us?' Jennings said he was with him but was merely pointing out that if he wanted a 70,000-seater stadium the plans were in place to build it.

To which Gillett rode in on cue, adopting the same aggressive language as his partner: 'Martin, we ain't building that fucking stadium.' They didn't build that stadium. Or the new one.

Hicks's divide-and-rule policy may have worked in America, and it may have worked in the Anfield Civil War to isolate first Benitez, then Gillett, then Parry, but it had backfired spectacularly with the fans.

Many of them didn't read his sugar-coated Klinsmann quotes in the *Echo*, they just saw the headline which told them that two men who knew nothing about football had gone behind their Champions League-winning manager's back to offer the job to a German novice. That was enough. Fans and players now questioned not only the Americans' wealth and motives but their judgement and decency:

'I didn't agree with the fans who slagged the owners off for approaching a manager behind the other one's back,' said Jamie Carragher, 'because it always goes on. Do we really believe the club didn't speak to Rafa before sacking Houllier?

'And although I was totally behind Rafa I could see why the owners were unhappy with him. They'd both undermined each other. But I totally disagreed with their decision. We were near the top of the table, and Rafa's record was second-to-none, plus Klinsmann was too inexperienced as a manager at club level. Liverpool don't get rid of managers mid-season. Especially one who has just been to two Champions League finals in three years. It was a big mistake which showed they didn't understand Liverpool or English football properly.'

As the bloody civil war spilt from the boardroom, to the dugout and on to the streets around Anfield, the briefing and spinning from all sides made the viciousness of the Westminster media machine look tamer than the Women's Institute press office.

Hicks's PR people were explaining the Klinsmann debacle thus:

Tom can be a bit of a soft pussy at times and goes with the flow to keep everyone happy [I kid you not]. *He'd never heard of Klinsmann but George had met him at Richard Steadman's clinic in Vail, Colorado, where he has his skiing resort. The German was having an operation, Gillett took him for dinner a few times to pick his brains about football, and they became big buddies. When Rafa's threats and tantrums were getting out of hand, Gillett rang Hicks and told him to do his research on Klinsmann. Which he did. Purely to find out who he was and what all the fuss was about. Then George suggested he meet him and, purely to keep his partner sweet, Tom said, 'OK. Sure. What do I know?'*

In the meantime, Gillett and Parry had set up a meeting with Klinsmann in New York which Tom reluctantly flew to. By the time he got there the other two had been speaking to the German for three hours, and he didn't know what they'd said to each other. Tom spent another couple of hours with him, they had a pleasant chat, he seemed a nice guy, they said they'd keep in touch in case Rafa threw his toys all the way out of his pram to Madrid, and that was that.

According to Hicks's PR machine, devious George was pulling the strings, pushing the agenda, saying 'we gotta hire this guy, we gotta have him on board' and Tom was still doing a bored teenager impression, making a W for 'whatever' with his fingers behind everyone's back.

In the end, say the spinners, Tom decided Rafa was going nowhere, Klinsmann went to Bayern Munich, and when the *Echo* asked him for the truth, as a brother of the Sigma Phi Epsilon fraternity, he followed its three guiding principles of 'virtue, diligence and brotherly love' and fessed up.

To summarise: 'It was Gillett's idea. I was led astray. I made a mistake, and put it right when I realised, so forgive me.'

But that's not how someone very close to the story remembers it. He reckons once Hicks met Klinsmann the Texan was desperate to make him the next Liverpool manager. And he's got the documents to back it up. His version is that when he checked out Klinsmann and discovered he lived in California on Newport Beach, Hicks invited him and his wife Debbie to a Thanksgiving dinner at his second home in La Jolla, near San Diego.

As they talked over turkey, Hicks liked what he was hearing and, in typical style, took the bull by the horns. The idea of working at Anfield was put to Klinsmann – with conditions such as Benitez could still be at Anfield for a while but don't worry about it – and the German was asked to think it over.

It's at this point that the agent of a Liverpool player was asked to sound out his client about the prospect of having Klinsmann as his manager. The player couldn't believe what he was hearing and told his agent to transmit back words to that effect. Gillett then realised they were getting ahead of themselves and got cold feet. Although he too wanted Benitez out, he wasn't sure it was the right time to sack him or whether they were going about it the right way. He could sense a horrific backlash awaiting them on the other side of the Atlantic and asked Hicks to slow down.

This was typical Gillett behaviour. He would take a shine to a stranger, tell them they should be working for him, arrange for that person to see one of his managerial team, then when the manager reports doubts, Gillett agrees and drops him. This was how he expected the Hicks and Klinsmann meeting to go but he was left unpleasantly surprised.

The deal then stalled. Klinsmann began to harbour misgivings, lost interest and went back to Germany as Bayern Munich coach, leaving Hicks furious.

'Shame on us all,' he wrote in an email to Gillett and Rick Parry.

'The idea that Tom Hicks was an innocent party in the Klinsmann saga is a joke,' said a former senior Liverpool figure. 'The opposite is true. I know for a fact that he kept in touch with him, because when we were doing the deal for Martin Skrtel in the January he emailed Klinsmann to ask if we were spending too much.'

Gillett was astounded that Hicks had volunteered his version of the Klinsmann saga to the *Echo*, and any lingering life in the Americans' relationship was now snuffed out. Gillett's son Foster, who was installed in Melwood at the start of the season to liaise with Benitez, headed home and was rarely seen again.

That had been a curious move. Players and staff say Foster was a likeable enough young man, he just didn't seem to know why he was there or what he was supposed to be doing. His nickname was '24/7' because that's when he told everyone at the club he would be available. Although no one remembers ever having to disturb him from whatever he was getting up to at night to solve a problem.

Foster was very much a chip off his father's block. He went out of his way to make people like him, through flattery, and telling them what he thought they wanted to hear. But the most anyone remembers about him is sitting at lunch and answering all his questions about football.

One man who remembers slightly more about Foster is the

former chairman of Wigan Warriors rugby league club, Maurice Lindsay. Most people at Anfield felt sorry for Foster being stuck thousands of miles away from home and went out of their way to make him feel wanted. Liverpool's stadium manager, Ged Poynton, a big rugby league fan, took Foster to watch St Helens play Wigan and he was instantly smitten by these muddy monsters and their oval balls. In the boardroom he fell into conversation with Lindsay who told him that Wigan was up for sale at the right price.

Foster then set his heart on buying the club. He came up with a few proposals and Wigan began to believe they may have had a buyer. However, when he did his disappearing act after the Klinsmann debacle, it wasn't just Liverpool that ended up being left in the dark.

Suddenly a senior member of the Anfield set-up was receiving phone calls from Lindsay saying, 'Where's Foster gone? I can't get hold of him because he's not answering my calls.' The Anfield figure told Lindsay that if he tracked him down, could he ask him to give someone at Liverpool a ring.

Hicks's son, Tommy Jr., was the only other member of the combined clans to make any sort of impression in Liverpool. Like Foster, Tommy was a little rich kid who wanted to be clasped to Scouse bosoms, but who failed spectacularly.

A week after the Spirit Of Shankly's call to arms in the Olympia, Tom Jr. committed what was either the bravest act by an American since Rambo wiped out an entire squad of Burmese soldiers just to rescue some happy-clappy missionaries, or the most stupid one since Republican bigwigs mistook a cretinous, moose-hunting MILF called Palin for a potential vice-president.

Following a 3–2 home win against Middlesbrough, Tom decided to pay a visit to the packed Sandon pub to meet the fans. He jumped out of his silver people carrier, surrounded by a team of burly black-clad minders, had a cigarette and took photos of the historic birthplace of Liverpool FC. He stubbed out the fag and told his bodyguards he was going in for a drink, which made them assume the kind of body language you'd see on CIA agents if President Obama went on walkabout in Kabul.

He strolled into the packed middle-bar and ordered a pint of lager for himself and soft drinks for his security guards. If a 6ft 4in clean-cut boy in a sharp, handmade suit, surrounded by Men In Black hadn't already stood out in the Sandon on a match day, the Texan accent did the trick.

Necks strained, heads turned, word spread quicker than a bush fire through the pub's rooms and the doors were suddenly jammed with disbelieving fans catching a glimpse of the devil's spawn.

At first everything went OK. Maybe it was the shock of seeing him in the flesh in their midst, or an outbreak of respect for having the balls to walk into their manor as though everything was fine between them. Questions were thrown at him about why he was there, what had happened to the stadium, was his dad going to sack Rafa and when would his dad sell to the sheikh?

One fan gave him a Paxmanesque interrogation for almost five minutes and Tom answered politely, but as more people pushed into the bar, anger replaced shock, and the mood began to turn nasty. Songs about Liverpool Football Club being in the wrong hands started, and grew louder. Venomous insults were hurled in his direction, the minders became increasingly

twitchy, and as the bar rocked to the tune of 'You lying bastard get out of our pub' Tom wore a look that said: 'I've seen
what happens next in every saloon scene in every Western. I
just pray they ain't carrying guns.'

A pint of lager was thrown over him (Carling, I think, which
to be fair isn't a bad drop in the Sandon) and in an act not
seen in Anfield since the days of El Hadji Diouf, a stream of
spit flew in his direction. The bodyguards then formed a ring
around him and forced themselves, inch by inch, out through
the door and into the people carrier. As meet and greets go it
wasn't the most successful one in history. In fact I've followed
Ian Paisley around Catholic areas of Edinburgh on the morning
of a Papal visit, as his followers waved Protestant Bibles and
muttered things about the anti-Christ, and seen less hostility.

Kopite and scriptwriter Roy Boulter, who saw the entire incident, said: 'It's just another example of how these people failed
to understand English football culture and more specifically
Liverpool fan culture. How they just didn't get how hated they
were.

'Coming when it did, after we'd held a mass meeting in that
same pub to share our sense of outrage and disgust over what
his family were doing to the club, it almost smacked of defi-
ance. To brazenly stroll into a pub packed with die-hard fans
surrounded by a team of minders was almost laying down a
statement of 'Come on then, gobshites, let's see how hard you
are.'

Tony Barrett, who was present throughout and wrote an eye-
witness piece in the *Echo*, took criticism from Evertonian readers
for not fully condemning the fan who spat at Hicks. At the
time he agreed with them, saying after rereading his piece that

he should have been harder with his own fans because that kind of cowardly behaviour is unacceptable. Today he's not so sure:

'Knowing what I know now, about what they did to the club, I think that's the least he deserved, and he was very lucky that's all he got. Because these fans were the life-blood of the club. They went everywhere for their team and his family deliberately brought it to its knees for their own ends. And if all he got was spat at that's the least he deserved. Also, if you're surrounded by security men there's no such thing as Queensberry Rules. Looking back I don't regret not condemning it because I believe he got away lightly.'

Hicks Jr. released a statement saying he had only wanted to meet the fans, he'd had several conversations with some and he 'looked forward to following them up the next time I am in Liverpool.' He never did.

The Sandon owner, Gemma Hindley, offered a formal invitation for Tom Jr. to return to the pub with his father to have a proper meeting with the fans. They never did.

But then Tom senior was pretty busy back then plotting a new phase of divide-and-rule having seen Rick Parry side with Gillett. Since Parry and Moores refused to do the whitewash and back his plan to put all the debt on the club, the Texan sharpshooter was merely clicking the spurs on his Liver Bird-encrusted cowboy boots, biding his time before slaying them.

What he needed though was a fresh, powerful alliance. A major player to hold close to his chest who he could use to destabilise his enemies. Bizarrely, he chose a man he'd despised so much he had been trying to sack him for the past eight months. The stubborn, outspoken, bloody-minded obstacle to his strategy of putting as little money as he could into Liverpool and exiting with the handsomest of profits, Rafa Benitez. Hicks felt that by becoming Rafa's cheerleader-in-chief, his version of the Klinsmann saga would be believed, and he'd win the fans back onside.

Benitez, no stranger himself to the world of realpolitik, signed up to this alliance of mutually loathing bedfellows mainly because he was completely isolated and needed all the help he could muster to survive.

He knew they were both culpable of gifting his job to Klinsmann, just as he knew Parry was involved in the talks. He had tried to get answers from Parry but was told: 'I'm sick of being blamed for everything so I'm staying out of this.' He tried to get answers out of George Gillett but was stonewalled. He rang up Foster Gillett but he wasn't answering his phone. Maybe he thought it was the Wigan Warriors.

So Benitez stuck a wet finger into the storm that was blowing around Anfield, captured the wind direction, decided his enemies' enemy was his friend, pulled back the Texas Rangers bedspread and jumped into the sack with Uncle Tom.

He phoned certain friendly journalists asking them to call their dogs off Hicks and turn them on Parry and Gillett. From now on, he said, I only deal with one owner. His reasoning, he claimed, was not self-serving. Hicks was promising to give him a contract extension and cut Parry's balls off, which, in Benitez's eyes, was the only way the club could be saved.

The Spaniard refuses to admit he ever aligned himself with either owner, instead claiming he was stuck in the middle of a raging civil war and, in order to do his job properly, he needed a line of communication with at least one of the owners. Preferably the one who called the shots.

He was finding it impossible to move forward. The only time he would hear from either Hicks or Gillett was when he sent one of them an email and the other demanded to know why it hadn't been mailed to them. They would follow that demand up with another one telling him that the next time he sent an email he should do so just to them.

When Hicks began to respond more to his demands, and when he told him that Gillett wanted out of the club, Benitez chose to go with the one he thought was more powerful and less crazy.

Gillett certainly did want out, and had done for many months. When Moores and Parry refused to do the whitewash he knew if the club loan was to be refinanced in February he would have to dip into his own pocket and supply written guarantees before the banks agreed. As the chill winds of recession began to blow across the world, he thought back to the bailiffs dragging away his yelping dogs as they kicked him out of his house, and suffered a serious dose of the jitters.

Hicks, like Gillett, realised when the credit crunch kicked in that buying Liverpool with all that debt had been a mistake. But in Hicks's eyes only a partial one. He still viewed them as a rough diamond that could yield untold riches once the stadium was built and football clubs took control of their own TV rights. So he refused to give it up without making a whacking profit, especially when he believed he had a sheikh poised with his pen over a blank cheque.

Hicks initially met Amanda Staveley at a pheasant shoot in Yorkshire in October 2007. She told him that Sheikh Al

Maktoum was considering whether to come back in for the club and Hicks told her the valuation was now £1 billion, but they could give him £150 million for a 15 per cent stake if they fancied it. Unsurprisingly that was rejected out of hand, but she returned with an offer of just over £500 million to buy the whole club in early 2008.

Hicks, who was close to securing a new refinancing deal, told them the figure was way too low. He also told Gillett, who verbally agreed with DIC in March 2008 to sell his 50 per cent stake for just over £250 million if their overall bid failed, that he was wasting his time.

He had power of veto over his partner's 50 per cent and he would use it because there was no way he was ceding equal partnership to the Arabs. If anyone was buying Gillett's stake, he told him, it was Tom O. Hicks. Indeed, his only compromise on Gillett selling to Al Maktoum was if he could take 1 per cent of his partner's stake, with 49 per cent going to the sheikh.

In other words, they would put their hundreds of millions in but he would call the shots. The talks between the two camps lasted, on and off, for almost a year and a half until the sheikh walked away for good in early 2009, with those close to the bid saying Hicks's attitude had been so brash and obstructive he would never return.

Amanda Staveley arrived at the conclusion that a deal with the Americans, particularly Hicks, would never be reached because whenever she came close to an agreement, they saw it as a point of weakness and demanded more.

David Bick, whose Square1 Consulting firm was advising the Middle Eastern consortium, said: 'The Americans were constantly playing the game and were impossible to deal with.

Their thinking was that just because somebody else wanted to buy the club, keep asking them for more.

'Hicks never seemed to get the picture. He still kept sending people over to the Middle East behind the Maktoum group's back to strike deals but they knew who they were seeing and when they were seeing them. They didn't understand there are a lot of connections in the Middle East. They just hacked off so many people there.'

Some journalists go even further, claiming when word of Hicks's brusque approach to business spread through Arab circles the chances of another serious Middle East investor coming in vanished.

A senior Anfield figure at the time said: 'There is a way of doing business in the Middle East based on respect. They were flashing into town, virtually going through the Yellow Pages to find rich businessmen and speaking to anyone who would listen. The Hicks family approach was like American foreign policy in the Middle East. Very random.'

Tony Evans, *The Times* football editor, who dealt closely with Al Maktoum's representatives, said: 'They managed to alienate not just a city like Liverpool but an entire world region, and that takes some genius. Bearing in mind who Tom Hicks was dealing with, his business technique was the equivalent of sending the US Marines into Grenada. Go in, unleash maximum force, and get it over with.'

Such a shock-and-awe policy backfired as word began to spread across the seriously rich families in the Middle East.

'Whenever a story came into *The Times* linking a Middle Eastern group with them we ignored it because we knew that no one was seriously dealing with them,' said Evans.

'It was very interesting when a Kuwaiti takeover deal got within hours of being done, only to fall apart inexplicably. There was a strong suggestion that the Arabs were deliberately leading Hicks on before pulling out at the last minute at the behest of Dubai. What is indisputable is that Liverpool could have been sold much earlier to rich Middle Eastern interests if it hadn't been for Tom Hicks's unpalatable approach.'

The irony of Hicks's stubborn refusal to take this generous offer was not lost on Liverpool fans in 2010 when the club was prised off him at a reputed personal loss of £70 million. Had he accepted the Al Maktoum bid he would have walked away with £100 million profit from less than twelve month's work, and spared himself another two and a half years worry, effort, stress, abuse and misery. So, life's not all bad, is it?

At the time the fall-out with Staveley and Al Maktoum was no big deal to Hicks. Unless they were going to make him an offer he couldn't refuse, he wouldn't be flogging the club to Dubai. And it had nothing to do with Israeli passport-holder Yossi Benayoun being ineligible for pre-season tours of the United Arab Emirates.

No, he'd managed to secure a new £350 million bank loan, with RBS and Wachovia, at interest rates of 7–8 per cent, meaning £30–£40 million would have to be found every year out of club revenues just to pay it down. While Liverpool were still in the Champions League that wouldn't be a problem, and as Rafa's men brushed Inter Milan aside to make the quarter-finals, the prospect of more brand-enhancing glory lay ahead. Why the rush, or the need, to sell, thought Hicks.

One significance of the new deal was that the details of the takeover were no longer shrouded in confusion. It was out there for all to digest: Hicks and Gillett had borrowed £185 million to buy the club the previous February and were lent a further £113 million by the RBS for twelve months. They refinanced that total loan of £298 million, and with interest and further work on the stadium, the new loan came to £350 million. Because Moores and Parry had refused the whitewash Hicks and Gillett had to pledge £40 million between them as well as personal guarantees and letters of credit.

Which, in layman's terms, meant that Liverpool FC, or Kop Football Holdings, was just another company registered in the low-tax US state of Delaware, via the Cayman Islands. It would be paying the interest on Hicks's and Gillett's loans out of its own cash flow and only if it failed to make enough one year (which was not likely to happen) would the Americans need to use their own money. So while the American duo stayed in charge, the club would be paying up to £40 million annual interest, year after year, on the cost of being taken over. Any difference between this deal and the Glazer one, scale aside, was clearly negligible.

One interesting aspect of the new loan arrangement was that Gillett had refused to put his name to it. He wasn't quoted on the statement, only Hicks, further confirming their partnership's terminal fracture. This was a club in such paralysis they didn't hold a board meeting for two years.

And in case anyone had failed to notice that a civil war was raging at Anfield, Hicks took it upon himself to lay it bare before the world, with one of the most dramatic letters ever leaked in the club's history, followed by one of the most shameful PR stunts.

Less than forty-eight hours after Liverpool dramatically beat Arsenal 4–2 at Anfield to reach the Champions League semi-final (in April 2008), Hicks sent a three-page letter to Rick Parry, demanding his resignation. Parry, who was in London at a league management meeting when the letter dropped on to his office desk, began to receive texts from family members telling him the contents of Hicks's missive were all over Sky News. Fans' groups also claimed they were texted extracts of the letter from somebody in the Hicks camp.

Parry, to his credit, maintained some dignity when he was besieged by reporters as he left the meeting, telling them he was too busy concentrating on doing his job to respond. Indeed the texts from his family as he waited for the league management meeting to start brought out a whole new side in him. During the roll call each club was supposed to respond with the word: 'Here.' When Liverpool was called, a straight-faced Parry responded: 'Just about here.' The meeting erupted with laughter, not so much at the quality of the gag but at the realisation of who was cracking it.

Sadly for Liverpool fans there was little to laugh about. They were still basking in the glow of a glorious comeback against Arsenal after a Theo Walcott solo goal looked to have killed the dream of another Champions League semi-final, when Hicks's leaked letter lashed a bucket of cold water over their heads.

Once again their club was big news off the sports pages for all the wrong reasons, with the *Daily Mirror* demanding a front-page comment piece from me under the splash headline 'Another Kop Out':

They gave the Anfield faithful less than two days to bask in euphoria..

Barely 40 hours after pulling off a stunning Champions League triumph over Arsenal, one half of the Barnum and Bailey circus act who own the club woke up in Texas and chose to remind Liverpudlians of their horrible reality.

That their beloved club's future lies in the hands of ruthless sharks who care nothing about them or the Reds' reputation, whose sole motivation is to screw every cent out of Anfield and bring down any opponent who tries to stop them.

Tom Hicks yesterday demanded chief executive Rick Parry's resignation. Hicks believes Parry is siding with co-owner George Gillett in the club's increasingly bitter boardroom battle. The latest twist came on the day representatives of Dubai's sheikh Al Maktoum said it will wait for the ridiculous saga to be resolved before pursuing its interest in the club.

The fans weren't to know it at the time, but when George Bush's pal Hicks and his sidekick Gillett swaggered into Liverpool last February promising the earth, they were taking them for patsies.

Their club was simply another underperforming brand which could be bought with a bank loan, its customers fleeced to pay the interest, and eventually sold on at profit. Only when the American credit crunch put pressure on their borrowing plans were their true intentions revealed.

And for six months the club has been engaged in a bloody civil war, with virtually every senior figure washing filthy linen in public, forming shifting alliances and briefing against each other.

Only on the pitch and on the terraces on nights like Wednesday, when that unique communion between fans and players produced another historic victory, has Liverpool FC been recognisable.

So it was no surprise to hear yesterday that the chief executive had learned via Sky Sports that his resignation was demanded.

Such a joke has the club become, the buddy of the most powerful man on earth couldn't even sack him. Because he doesn't have enough plotters in his camp.

There won't be too many fans weeping over Rick Parry's plight. It was he and former chairman David Moores who jilted DIC at the last minute to sell to the Yanks for a bigger return.

But fans will despair for their manager, Rafa Benitez, and their players, who once again face questions about ownership when they should be thinking about football.

And they will despair for their club. The most successful in British football history and not long ago one of the most respected sporting institutions in the world.

And wonder how it was ever allowed to become such a laughing stock.

In an echo of Rafa Benitez's famous 'focus on coaching and training' response, Parry released a public statement saying: 'It is my intention to remain focused on the job of serving Liverpool Football Club to the best of my abilities.'

In private he did three things. He took legal advice from a

top lawyer, gained assurances from Gillett that Hicks couldn't sack him because he did not have the required boardroom majority, and wrote a letter back to Hicks.

In it he thanked him for his letter and the offer of a generous pay-off should he wish to walk, reminded him that what the club needed more than anything was unity, and told him his personal criticisms had made 'interesting reading' but he would only resign if the entire board asked him to. Until that day he was remaining Liverpool's chief executive.

Which only served to stir the beast in Hicks into even uglier action. His favourite Sky News reporter, and a camera crew, were summoned to his Dallas mansion for the most repulsive PR stunt ever pulled by anyone connected with Liverpool.

As he sat in his favourite armchair, his facial expression as fake as the gas-flamed fire burning behind him, making wistful glances and measured frowns at camera, opening out his hands in gestures of innocence, complaining in a slow, self-pitying tone about an abusive partner, media manipulation and a world that failed to understand his noble motives, déjà vu kicked in.

This was Princess Diana at the peak of her manipulative powers. This was her famous 'there were three people in my marriage' interview with *Panorama*. For Martin Bashir read Sky's Alan Myers. For Charles and Camilla, read Gillett and Parry. For the People's Princess read the People's Cowboy.

And like Diana it ended up in a car crash because there wasn't a Red on the planet who didn't stare at that comical face beneath the tragic comb-over and feel a vomit-surge violently make its way up their windpipe.

Reciting a script that was undoubtedly honed by his PR people, in the kind of homely setting Perry Como shot his

Christmas TV Specials in, Hicks went straight for Parry's jugular: 'If you look at what has happened under Rick's leadership it's been a disaster, to fall so far behind other top clubs.

'The new stadium should have been built three or four years ago. We have two sponsors, maybe three, when we should have twelve to fifteen.

'We are not doing anything in Asia the way Man U is and Barcelona is. We've got the top brand in the world of football, we just don't know how to commercialise it.

'In the very first meeting George and I had with Rafa a year ago he told us about a number of players we have missed out on and his inability to communicate with Parry when he needs to.

'The manager isn't in charge of contracts, he just hands them over to the CEO and too many times nothing happens.

'Rick needs to resign from Liverpool. He has put his heart into it but it's time for a change.

'A football club has to grow and that's how you have success. You certainly have to have the ability to work with your general manager and I think Rick has proven he can't do that.

'We need change and we've got a great group of guys ready to go.'

Liverpool's dirty washing was not so much being hung out in public as draped over the Shankly Gates and the Kop crossbar as the club's owner passed around snacks for the grateful camera crew.

'I can't force George to accept but I can make him an attractive offer soon. George and I started this as friends. Fifty-fifty is a difficult business proposition but we had a good honeymoon.

'Over time we had serious issues, with the stadium design being the biggest one. I wanted to make the change with Rick Parry and the chief financial officer for some time now but George doesn't because he likes his relationship with Parry.

'I'm working on the money to make Liverpool's finances more sound. If I'm the majority owner I can put more capital in. I know of investors who want to be a minority investor with me.

'My goal is to take the debt off the club, except the normal working capital needs, and get the permanent financing in place for the stadium.'

Read the beginning of that sentence again, 'My goal is to take the debt off the club,' then remind yourself who created the debt in the first place, who tried to force Moores and Parry into whitewashing every penny of debt on to the club, and who had just taken out a £350 million loan at interest rates of 7–8 per cent against the club.

'If I were to buy George out the first thing I would do is offer Rafa a one-year extension to make sure he is going to be here up to when we get the stadium.

'Hopefully we could have some success and then extend him again. Rafa and the players have their heads down. They are playing great. We communicate regularly.

'I know he feels comfortable with the way things are going. I think we will continue to have success. I think Rafa has unique skills, he motivates the team and we have some great players who are learning how to play with each other.'

This from a man who, only months earlier, had told Parry and Gillett 'shame on us' for not hiring Klinsmann as Benitez's successor.

'They've stirred the pot of Liverpool to create dissension and it kind of worked because it made the fans think "Gee, Dubai have a lot of money, if they were to buy us we could buy all these players". But I know for a fact from talking to Dubai that's not why they approached, they are smart businessmen.

'DIC are masters of British tabloid spin. They have got a girl called Amanda Staveley on point for them and she's got a consultant called David Bick and going back to December they've continually put out disinformation.'

This from a man who already had PR firm Financial Dynamics and Kekst and Co. working for him and was about to sign up Freud Communications to take on the impossible task of spinning his image in a positive light.

'The fans gave George and me such a heroes' welcome when we arrived. I think they were so concerned at what's happened to Liverpool for ten to twenty years and they thought we were going to fix it. We didn't fix it and I think that's what's made them angry. As long as Hicks and Gillett don't change – and I'm telling you Hicks is going to change – the fans feel like we let them down and I think to that degree we have.

'The fans don't like the fact that we've borrowed too much money on the club but I'm going to fix that. My family loves Liverpool, that's the only sad thing right now that we don't feel we can go there as a family until we get this sorted out.

'All six of my kids really love the city, my wife does and I do and I'm really looking forward to this all settling down.'

And with that we cut to a close-up of him in an LFC casual shirt, clutching a Liverpool mug, which has been so recently taken out of the box you could almost taste the white polystyrene, watching on a big screen Liverpool's 3–1 win over Blackburn. On the settee next to him sat two of his sons in replica shirts. The younger one, with a scarf round his neck, is so bored he yawns and stares at the floor. As the final whistle sounds on the Liverpool win, he turns to his sons and says: 'Well, Everton won't like that,' and their disinterested faces scream back: 'Can we take off these stupid clothes you made us wear for the cameras and put *The Simpsons* back on?'

On many levels it was the most sickening stunt ever pulled by a Liverpool employee, at a time when fans were hoping for solidarity at the club ahead of another epic Champions League semi-final with Chelsea. Once again he had tried to win the fans over through cynically manipulating the media but all he had done was lose even more of them.

The Spirit Of Shankly responded: 'Why should any statement from him have any credibility? It's time he shut his mouth, took the handsome profit he has been offered and got out of Liverpool. The football club needs a clean sweep, but he has to go first because he has no respect for football or this club. The man cannot be trusted. The situation with Rick Parry is really an irrelevance. He is good for one thing only and that is his vote at board meetings to keep Hicks at bay.'

Les Lawson, secretary of Official Liverpool Supporters' Club described it as 'horrendous' and 'a living nightmare'.

For many fans the betrayal went far deeper, down to a depth you just don't plumb. At least some of the video had been shot on 15 April 2008, the nineteenth anniversary of the Hillsborough tragedy. To claim that Rick Parry had been a 'disaster', even if he was unaware of the weight of that word and his grotesque insensitivity in using it on that day, showed how he would never, ever understand the football club he owned.

Clearly when the Texan Googled Liverpool, he got bored before the bit about ninety-six fans dying, and switched off. Exactly sixteen years previously, the then Liverpool manager, Graeme Souness, had appeared on the front page of the *Sun* kissing his girlfriend under the headline 'LOVERPOOL' on the third anniversary of Hillsborough, and all hell broke loose.

That newspaper was still reviled for claiming Liverpudlians had urinated on and stolen from the dead at Hillsborough, and as far as many fans were concerned there was Souness hoovering up blood money to help it win back circulation on Merseyside, with no regard for the bereaved. On 15 April 1992, Souness instantly became, in the eyes of many fans, a non-person. Sixteen years later so did Hicks.

Had I been one of his PR gurus I'd have told him to ring Souness for some words of advice. I'm sure he'd have given him a couple based on his own experience. Words beginning and ending with the letter 'f'.

CHAPTER EIGHT

'When George said, "Trust me, Tom's a decent guy,"
we thought, "Well, you obviously know him far better
than we do." That's essentially what we relied on'
                                              – Rick Parry

There wasn't a person working on the same floor as Ian Ayre who failed to feel the quake. Not an employee in Liverpool FC's Old Hall Street offices whose jaw didn't hit their desk at the tsunami of abuse that exploded from George Gillett's mouth in the direction of the club's commercial director:

'You fucking bastard, you've been trying to sell my fucking club from under me. This is not the fucking way to do it. I'm going to make sure this is the last fucking day you work for this club …' and on and on he swore and threatened for three minutes, veins popping out of his skull, sweat dripping from his brow, pasting a man who'd been in his job less than a year, but who was already turning around the club's finances, all over his office walls.

Here was a microcosm of the Anfield Civil War. A vicious retaliation blow aimed at Hicks, via Ayre, which would force the Texan to strike back at Gillett by demanding Parry's 'disastrous' head on a platter. The blood-letting really was becoming that public now, the bare-knuckle fighting that out of control, and prisoners no longer being taken.

Ian Ayre is a lifelong Red from Litherland, who had earned his spurs as a fan through an impressive European awaydays CV, and his right to run the club's commercial affairs through a hugely successful business career in Asia and, closer to home, as Huddersfield Town's chief executive and chairman.

Most Liverpool fans cite Ayre as the only decent thing Hicks and Gillett brought to the club. After headhunting him soon after they arrived he took up his 'dream job' in August 2007 and almost immediately pumped life into the flat-lining commercial department. His biggest coup was landing Standard Chartered as the club's main sponsor in a deal potentially worth £81 million over four years. In other words, he was a sharp, streetwise Scouser, who'd been around the block, proved he could do it, knew his own worth and was nobody's fool.

A couple of weeks before Hicks's infamous video, he summoned Ayre, along with financial director Philip Nash, to do a PowerPoint presentation about the club to a large group of investors at Merrill Lynch's London HQ. The aim was to persuade the twenty or so moneymen to come in with Hicks to buy out Gillett's stake.

Ayre and Nash travelled down, did the job, left without speaking to any of the prospective investors, jumped the train back to Lime Street and thought no more of it. Until two days later when Gillett, along with son Foster, and Parry, stormed into Ayre's office and unleashed the tirade of profanities.

Throughout the three-minute attack an embarrassed Parry stared at his shoes while Foster fiddled with the top of a Coke bottle. Ayre took the kicking in his stride and when it was over asked everyone in the room if they had anything to add. When there was silence he told Gillett that when one of the owners, and 50 per cent shareholders in the club, asked him to do something, he felt obliged to do it.

He didn't know the exact reason he was doing the presentation, who he was doing it to, or whether Hicks had or hadn't told Gillett he was doing it. Why should he? He was doing his job and he'd have done the same if it had been Gillett who had asked him. So if you're going to have a go at me, he told Gillett, have a go at me for doing something wrong. Otherwise, if you've got nothing else to say to me then I've got nothing else to say to you.

Gillett was tongue-tied as he stood there in trademark suit and walking boots, pulse-rate dropping, breathing slowing, veins ceasing to throb. He was conscious that everyone outside the office had heard the conversation and was unsure where to go, so asked Ayre: 'OK, anyway, what's going on in our club?'

From that day on Gillett viewed Ayre as Tom Hicks's man and put their relations in deep-freeze. Sources close to Ayre believe Gillett then told Hicks he wanted the commercial director fired for trying to sell his share of the club behind his back but was told 'no chance'. Hicks then rang Ayre and told him never to give a damn about the Wisconsin Kid because he couldn't sack him without his approval.

And then our very own J.R. Ewing decided to serve up a cold dish of Dallas revenge. He'd had Parry in his sights for a while. His refusal to do the whitewash, his siding with Gillett, his inability to squeeze enough money out of the brand, a radio interview in which he'd been critical of Hicks and a demeanour that plainly spoke of making a horrendous mistake the day he advised Moores to sell, had left the Texan waiting to pounce.

When he'd heard that Parry had accompanied Gillett to the Ian Ayre pasting, he had his moment. According to Parry he didn't even know why Gillett wanted him with him when he took on Ayre, but the co-owner insisted he accompanied him. From then on his fate was sealed.

It was a case of tit-for-tat. You try to take out one of my men and I'll sure as hell take out one of yours. In this ugly civil war Parry was merely collateral damage, but he was also, in Hicks's eyes, a means of strengthening his power base. It was divide-and-rule time again. If he called for Parry's head, as many fans had been since the botched DIC sale plus the Athens tickets fiasco, and as Rafa Benitez had been for more than a year over his transfer dithering, he would look informed, decisive, the good guy with Liverpool's interest at heart.

Hence the letter and the video and the credibility of a once-proud club gurgling down the drains into an open sewer.

Tony Barrett, who was still on the *Echo* at the time, watched the Sky interview with utter disgust: 'I thought, that's not an interview, that's a PR script and I was embarrassed that Hicks was in any way linked with Liverpool FC. I thought what has the club come to when it would do that to someone?

'Some of the things he said about Rick Parry would have chimed with the fans but he was using a club employee who, whatever you think about him, is a Liverpool fan who loves the club. Parry would never have done that to anyone publicly and he didn't deserve anything like that.

'The thing was, Hicks knew the fans had turned on Parry after Athens. His role with Klinsmann, Rafa's complaints and the fact he brought them two in didn't help. So it was an open goal. But he managed to miss it. And Parry saw it as a badge of honour that Hicks thought so badly of him.'

Gillett responded by saying he was 'staggered' by his co-owner's version of events and accused him of destabilising the club. 'I am saddened at this latest outburst,' he said. 'Here we are, a few days away from a vital Champions League semi-final, and Tom has once again created turmoil with his public comments.

'Tom needs to understand that I will not sell my shares to him. He should stop. He knows that Rick Parry has my support and that airing his comments in this way will not change my position.

'Any decision to remove him would need the approval of the full Liverpool board, which, it should be remembered, consists of six people: myself, Foster, David Moores, Rick himself, Tom Hicks and Tom Jr.'

Parry stood up for himself publicly, by branding Hicks's behaviour 'offensive to the players, the manager and the fans. In the week when we had another great European triumph there's more dirty linen being washed.' He reiterated that he had no intention of resigning, while making a plea for 'leadership at the top' at a time when there is 'a severe lack of unity' at the club. Honorary Life President David Moores took another drag on a ciggie and said nothing.

Meanwhile, Rafa Benitez, although believing a lot of what Hicks had said about Parry to be true, and enjoying a rare moment of *schadenfreude*, couldn't comprehend the very brutal and public way it was delivered. In Rafa's head, if Hicks didn't think Parry could do his job then why didn't he fly over to

Liverpool and sack him instead of issuing threats on TV from his Dallas fireside? The answer, of course, was that he couldn't sack him because of Gillett. It was merely a show of force and bluster.

This was the most curious dynamic of them all. Here was Benitez, one of the world's highest-rated coaches, who had won two Spanish leagues, the Champions League, UEFA Cup and FA Cup, forming an alliance with a man who knew nothing about football, who hated him and had tried to sack him. A man he knew was wooing him with the offer of a contract extension to keep him close to him as a sign of credibility in his ongoing battle to take overall control of the club.

Yet rather than fly back home to Real Madrid, who regularly pestered his agent with offers, he chose to live with the indignity of such a soiled relationship. His critics would say the Machiavellian scenario appealed to his darker tendencies; his supporters would say it showed how deeply he cared for the club. That's certainly how most fans viewed it, allowing him his alliance with their most detested enemy because he needed the man with the power to back him and allow him to get on with his work.

Benitez knew Hicks had never forgiven him for the Athens outburst but he also knew he was such a political animal that it wouldn't matter. He thought at least with Hicks he could have dialogue. There would be angry replies sent to emails, and ugly stand-offs, but he would eventually get a reply which allowed him to plan.

Once Gillett realised he was in the Hicks camp he ceased contact with his manager, meaning the only way Benitez could get anything out of him was through Rick Parry. But what hair he had left he didn't feel like pulling out. So he would only recognise Gillett's presence at the club by cc-ing him into his emails to Tom Hicks.

Peter Hooton called it 'a confederacy of fools' and he was spot on. The club was so utterly dysfunctional that every major player was exploiting everyone else, forming pragmatic alliances with enemies to stay alive. If only Kopites had been enamoured with, rather than repulsed by, the trend to wear jesters' hats, Anfield would have been a living recreation of a medieval court.

Ladies and gentlemen, roll up, roll up, for the one and only Anfield Civil War four-a-side tournament. In the Lone Star State corner, Tom Hicks, Tom Jr., Rafa Benitez and Ian Ayre. In the Badger State corner (that's Wisconsin to all you non-pub quiz bores), George Gillett, Foster Gillett, Rick Parry, David Moores. Nobody a winner.

As one of the players in the four-a-side tournament admits today: 'Yes there was civil war. No doubt. But what used to crucify me was how unnecessary it was. Hicks and Gillett could have dealt with their own issues outside the club and not harmed it.

'That was the real tragedy and their downfall. Apart from being a magnificent football club Liverpool was a great business which made a lot of money. They were supposed to be these successful businessmen but they were too busy fighting each other to focus on that.

'Throughout it all, neither of them were thinking like anyone else at Liverpool. There was no recognition that they'd done anything wrong. Both blamed the other right to the end.

'Tom's problem was that in corporate jousting everything is fair game but when you start messing around with sports clubs you're dealing with things that affect people's lives. I don't think he could ever get his head around that, which was why he totally lost the plot.

'Even after the club had been sold he didn't believe he'd made a mistake. He thought he'd bought an absolute gem which he could eventually turn around.'

Stories like the Great Attempted Ian Ayre Massacre rarely made it outside journalist circles or the rumour factory, but the extent of the fear and loathing that existed within the Anfield hierarchy was visible even to those who crossed roads with labradors.

Take the directors' box five days after Hicks's Diana interview when Chelsea turned up for yet another Champions League semi-final. Tom Hicks took his seat near the front, although it was touch and go whether he would show, after Merseyside Police officially warned him to stay away for his own safety. Four rows behind Hicks, looking distinctly sheepish and isolated were David Moores and Rick Parry. To the extreme right of the box sat Foster Gillett with the Dubai delegation, including Sameer Al Ansari and Amanda Staveley (much to the delight of Sven Goran Eriksson).

What a splendid show of unity on this great Champions League occasion. I doubt there was another family in Europe, apart from Josef Fritzl's, which was more screwed up.

Further to the right of the Dubai gathering, in the press box, national journalists were laughing at the photograph in that night's *Echo*, of Spirit Of Shankly members putting spades into Stanley Park. The group had organised an event called The Big Dig, 440 days after fans were told at the takeover press conference that a shovel would be in the ground in sixty days.

Forty SOS members, wearing high-visibility jackets and hard hats, dug up part of the park with shovels. 'There must be a perfectly reasonable explanation why the owners have not carried out their promises,' said organiser Neil Atkinson. 'They didn't manage to get the stadium started, so we are doing them a favour.'

Mental instability was not confined to the directors' box on that Champions League semi-final night. For ninety-three minutes all was going to plan. Liverpool were 1–0 ahead and looking like taking a crucial lead down to Stamford Bridge where a Torres shimmy-and-poke, or a Gerrard curler, would have left Chelsea needing three goals to win.

The Kop was bouncing, 'You'll Never Walk Alone' filled the spring night air, the prospect of a trip to Moscow and victory over Manchester United making it the sweetest night ever was in our sights. Until John Arne Riise inexplicably popped up to head into his own net, and left us all floored.

Almost on cue, a middle-aged man lifted himself out of his main stand seat to leave, and yelled at Hicks, 'Happy now, you fuckin' tosser? See what you've done?' You couldn't script that. As much as all Liverpudlians wanted to blame the resident cowboys for every failing, as much as they ached to run them out of town, only a madman could have believed it was Tom Hicks who had stooped in the Kop penalty area to score for Chelsea – not least because he had a comb-over worse than Gregor Fisher's in the Hamlet photo-booth advert, meaning he would never have been able to nut it that sweetly.

But we could all identify with the pain of Angry Main Stand Man. We were becoming so drained and stressed, we weren't thinking in a sane manner. No one was flying over the cuckoo's nest. How did we get here?

It was almost reassuringly appropriate that when Rick Parry agreed to a meeting, we should have it in a nondescript service station off the M56.

That was always, as Rick would put it, The Liverpool Way. That's how Bill Shankly signed his future England captains for peanuts. After a meeting of Ford Cortinas over strong tea and Spam sandwiches by the side of a motorway. No fuss, no fancy setting, just somewhere quiet and ordinary away from prying lenses, where they could fade into the background. This was the 2010 version. Lattes in a Costa Coffee, weeks after the NESV takeover, halfway between Liverpool and Chester.

I wanted the much-castigated former chief executive's version of events. I wanted to put to him the widely held belief that whatever we thought about the motives or morality of Hicks and Gillett, they were global speculators who spotted a chance to turn a quick profit at a failing business. And to those American eyes Liverpool FC had been so badly run it was as ripe for picking as a lush field of Mississippi cotton in the fall.

What truly angered Liverpool fans, who were put through a totally avoidable 44-month trauma, was not so much what the Americans did or didn't do, but the fact they were allowed to stroll into Anfield in the first place and give us all such a royal shafting.

We needed answers. I told Parry that he must have had many sleepless nights over the past years, as the scale of his mistake sank in, and asked how much he regretted allowing Hicks and Gillett to take over Liverpool.

'I don't think anyone looks back with anything other than regret but hindsight is much easier than foresight,' he replied. 'I wish David had decided not to sell because no one cared more for the club than he did. We could have borrowed the money to build the stadium, which would have cost less than £250 million, and been in it by 2009. But the credit crunch was just around the corner and we'd have been borrowed up to the hilt. If we'd had a bad year on the pitch, there'd have been no headroom to buy players. This wasn't a risk David was prepared to take and I can understand why.

'The one thing you can't criticise Hicks and Gillett for, at least until the summer of 2009, is a lack of investment in players. They put in place the personal guarantees and letters of credit that enabled us to keep on strengthening the squad.'

Yes, I told him, but it wasn't their money, was it? It was our money, the club's money, the fans' money. I put it to him that Liverpool was ripe for a predator attack because it was so badly run. It was there for the taking, wasn't it?

'I don't accept that at all,' he replied.

So why did Rafa Benitez constantly complain to me and other journalists that he could never get deals done because you held things up?

'Look at all the evidence of the players we did sign – which is a substantial number. The evidence doesn't support the claim. No one has ever equated buying quickly with buying well in football. Tell me who we missed out on?'

I could, but I would simply be regurgitating a list Rafa had long ago trailed, and Parry was bound to have an answer in every case. Instead I told him it was patently obvious that Hicks and Gillett acquired Liverpool on the cheap, and one of the main reasons for that was that the club wasn't performing off the pitch as well as it could have done.

'Not at all,' argued Parry. 'The price reflected the need for new owners to take the risk on developing the new stadium. In 1999 we finished seventh in the Premier League and we had to focus on getting things right on the pitch. Our philosophy was to focus on the core, i.e. football, and bring in partners who had more expertise than us in other areas.'

But you were outsourcing all of our profit areas, letting other firms like Heathcotes, Granada and George Davies milk our fame and our fans, I said.

'Bringing in Compass/Heathcotes and George Davies made a big impact on the quality of what we offered as well as increasing our profits in those areas. Arguably Granada didn't perform too well commercially but they injected £42 million into the club at a vital time. This was invested 100 per cent in the playing squad and provided the platform for our success in 2001 and the subsequent regular Champions League participation.'

What about the countless horror stories about the online store always being out of stock?

'Forget the anecdotes. Our retail turnover increased from £5 million to £25 million and George Davies gave us an operation to be proud of. He did a great job.'

So how come there's been such a big jump in commercial revenues since you left?

'The big jump has been from second in the Premier League to seventh. It's not fair for me to comment on commercial performance without being aware of the numbers. But I'd love to see a line-by-line comparison of revenues and costs. And factor in the loss of Champions League revenue since our whole philosophy was to drive revenues through success on the pitch. We were great believers in the virtuous circle.'

The general consensus, I told him, was that you couldn't cope with all the various departments. When you took on the job there was no structure in place. It was run with a small-club mentality. Your problem was you had a weak chairman who didn't want to be involved in the day-to-day running of the business and rather than take on a tier of senior management to share the load, it all went through you. You had total control of everything from the manager's buys to the ticket office and the club shop and it just became too big a job, didn't it?

'I wasn't running the online shop or the ticket office. We had loyal and competent people doing that. But one of the reasons we wanted new owners was to help expand our operations. There is always scope to improve. DIC were exciting because Dubai had made a great job of transforming a country brand and provided a gateway to the Far East. And Hicks and Gillett had extensive experience of running US sports teams. We wanted to draw upon their knowledge and their contacts.'

Rick Parry is a lifelong Liverpool fan who went to Ellesmere Port Grammar School and the University of Liverpool, where he graduated in maths before moving into chartered accountancy and management consultancy.

In 1991 he became involved in the planning of the new Premier League, and the following year was appointed its chief executive, brokering lucrative TV deals which would eventually make it the biggest football cash cow on the planet.

As Liverpool's veteran chief executive Peter Robinson neared retirement he singled out Parry as his natural successor, and in July 1998, David Moores made him an offer he couldn't refuse. A few years later, with Liverpool falling behind its rivals and Moores deciding to sell up and bring in new investment, Parry was the man charged with selling the family silver. The stuff you only sell once. And he ended up selling to men who cared so little about the club they were eventually prepared to see it go into administration so long as they could turn a profit.

Why was the deal done so quickly with the Americans, and why were they allowed to do virtually no due diligence when DIC had spent eighteen months doing theirs, I asked.

'Gillett had been looking at the books since September, so had had five months.'

OK, but did you judge Tom Hicks's character purely on George Gillett's word?

'Effectively, yes. It's the easiest thing in world to ask "shouldn't you have taken your time and done your due diligence on Hicks?" but we'd known George Gillett for six months, got to know him quite well and thought we'd got a decent feel for him. So when George said "trust me, Tom's a decent guy" we thought, well you obviously know him far better than we do, you've decided to give him 50 per cent of the club so you must have done your checks. That's essentially what we relied on.'

But surely, if you'd done your job properly and checked him out thoroughly, you might have found things you didn't like, and said no?

'I honestly don't know because I've spoken to people in baseball and ice hockey who to this day say that from an official league perspective Tom Hicks was a model owner. They never had any issues with him.'

Come on, Rick, half of America knew him simply as this big, leveraged buyout king, didn't they?

'We asked him all about that and he said, "Hicks, Muse, Tate and Furst used to be my day job. This is what I do with my family money. This isn't Hicks, Muse, Tate and Furst. This is me, Tom Hicks. It's completely different." So what do you do? Take the answers at face value or say we don't believe you? On what basis do you say that, when he had bankers like Rothschild vouching for him?'

Yes, but Rothschild's were his and Gillett's bankers. Of course they're going to vouch for him. So long as they know they'll get their money back they'll vouch for anyone. Isn't that how they earn their profits and bonuses?

'Yes but they have a responsibility to ensure their clients are good for their money. There's a statement to this effect in the offer document.'

I take him back to February 2007. You've lost DIC, the fans are desperate, you've gone to the *Echo* and said 'Trust Us'. Did you feel you had to put something in place quickly otherwise you were right back at square one, meaning you really wanted to believe that Hicks and Gillett were trustworthy and their offer was a good one?

'Yes. I'm naturally more of a believing person than a disbelieving one. You wouldn't be in football if you were an ultimate cynic. We did want to believe them and George had made a very good impression. He was a nice, plausible guy. We'd seen him in his own environment and everything stacked up. There were never any issues that said this is a wrong 'un.

'And don't forget this had been a close-run thing in the December. It wasn't as if Gillett had come up on the rails from nowhere. In reality we were reverting to Plan B. What David also had was incredibly senior people warning him about DIC. About having to go back to an investment committee to get decisions made. What's it going to be like if you want to sign a player? Will you have to wait ten weeks for a decision?'

What about the allegations that you only went with the Americans to feather your own nest, I ask. Did Hicks and Gillett offer you a job whereas DIC didn't, and did that sway things?

'I find it pretty offensive that people suggest I favoured Hicks and Gillett because I had a good offer from them, not least because they know there isn't a shred of evidence to support this. It is just not true. I had three conversations with prospective bidders – Steve Morgan, DIC and George Gillett – and on each occasion I said that there could be no discussion about my position until after the deal was done. Feel free to check that with them.

'With DIC the deal was effectively done in early December and I sat down in January with Sameer Al Ansari to discuss my package. Remember I'd got to know DIC over an eighteen-month period. DIC invest in companies rather than manage them and it was always clear that they would need a CEO.

'There was no discussion at all with Hicks and Gillett until April. I have no doubt I would have been better off financially with DIC. Nobody can ever say with justification that I chose any option for the club because it suited me. Ever.'

So how soon did it become clear that these two weren't really partners but two strangers who loathed each other?

'It soon became clear that they had very different philosophies on how the club should be run. One was hands-off, the other hands-on; one courted publicity, the other didn't.'

How did you feel watching that video when Hicks called you a disaster?

'I've never watched it and I never will. My response was that someone had to focus on doing what was right for the club so I kept my head down and got on with it. It's almost impossible to build a winning culture when you've got people at the top pulling in different directions but we had to try to concentrate on getting things right on the pitch. It's pretty remarkable that we came so close to winning the Premier League in 2009, given all the distractions.'

What struck me in our long meeting, of which these exchanges are only a small part, was his repeated references to The Liverpool Way, a phrase I believe became a convenience to hide behind. I asked Parry if the constant harking back to The Liverpool Way disguised a failure to modernise and stay in the real world?

'Not at all. Given The Liverpool Way stems from the Shankly era, it can never be an excuse for failure. It is as relevant today as it was then. It is about being respected for the way you do things, whether that be playing the game or carrying out complex negotiations. And it is about treating others with respect. I will always hold my head up and say I'm proud that I tried to do things The Liverpool Way.'

There are many who have been around since the days of Shankly, myself included, who disagree. I respect where it came from and I know what the phrase aspires to, but in reality any trace of what it was disappeared when Graeme Souness tore down the Boot Room. Since then it has been used too often as a cop-out in the face of change. It defined a certain time but time moves on, and it's no coincidence that Liverpool haven't won a league title since the wrecking-ball swung through the Boot Room walls.

Rafa Benitez spoke about it being an albatross around his neck. A myth that held the club back because people kept looking at the past through rose-tinted glasses, rather than forward with the blinkers off.

It wasn't only people employed by the club. Many older fans used and abused that phrase too. To them The Liverpool Way was the magic ingredient in a world-beating formula. Like the secret part of the Coca-Cola recipe, it would be handed down from generation to generation to maintain world-beating success. The problem was, unlike Coca-Cola, the genie had long escaped from Liverpool's bottle.

Some of the extreme Liverpool Way-ists reminded me of God Squad nutters who march around Arkansas schools with sandwich boards around their necks screaming 'Kill All Faggots' when they suspect the sixth grade teacher is gay. Hypnotised robots bending quotes from the Bible to prove God decreed that all homosexuals should be stoned to death.

Liverpool Way-ists usually recite their mantra in a context that says 'Shankly would never have approved of that.' But, like the Bible, you can twist the Gospel According to Shanks to make it say anything that you want it to say.

Just as Parry did in February 2007 when he said Shankly would have approved of the way George Gillett pulled off a 'masterstroke' by bringing Tom Hicks in to conclude the takeover.

Would he really? Does that make Shankly a fool then? Or does it make Parry one for assuming personal knowledge of what a man he never knew would be thinking had he lived another twenty-six years?

Maybe it's time Liverpudlians ceased assuming what Shankly or Paisley would have thought thirty or forty years ago, and did their own thinking, because that's what they did. Which was why they were so forward-looking and so successful. To be fair to Parry and Moores, a deep strain of Scouse cynicism has rebelled against progress since the 1980s. We weren't United or Chelsea. We were Liverpool and we didn't want to be tainted with anything as common as money.

If we're honest, we even found the bumbling incompetence of the old regimes funny to the point of being almost quaint. We were crap when it came to commercial activities but our activity on the pitch made us an awesome trophy-winning machine. It's what set us apart. We operated the right way, the old-fashioned way in this old atmospheric ground in this old working-class area of a proper footballing city.

Yet Anfield, the district, perfectly symbolised the club. It had been allowed to rot and was neglected. Bad decision-making, a lack of foresight and weak leadership had frozen it in time, so it looked like it hadn't moved on since the days when Thatcher put her iron boot through the old industrial landscapes.

The players, fans and managers, the worldwide appeal based on seventies and eighties success, were papering over the cracks. Istanbul was a magnificent, almost heaven-sent reminder of what we had been and could become again. But the reality of what we were was that the club was incapable of capitalising on a moment the biggest PR budget in the world could not buy.

That's why we fannied round for two years before falling into the lap of the American sharks. If we couldn't capitalise on Istanbul, and sell ourselves after that momentous triumph which showcased everything special about Liverpool, something was seriously lacking at the top of the club.

A senior Liverpool figure involved in the sale to NESV had some sympathy with Parry and Moores: 'It's not as easy as you think to flush people out. They want to buy something, you're questioning their ability to buy it and the banks are telling you that they're good for their money. It's easy to be wise after the event.

'So I don't blame them for selling to Hicks and Gillett. What they're more culpable of is allowing the club to get into such a state they had to sell it. Because if they'd managed the business properly they wouldn't have had to.

'Moores didn't have the revenue streams to secure the loan. The club was only making a £13 million profit in 2007 when it could easily have been making £40 million.

'That would have been enough for banks to lend them the cash to build the stadium, and once that was up and the revenue grew further, there would have been no need to sell at all. Liverpool could, and should, have stayed in local hands.'

In the February of 2009, ten months after Hicks's 'disaster' video had effectively left Parry limping around Anfield like a wounded soldier, he decided it was impossible to carry on. Transfer deals, like Robbie Keane's back to Spurs, and meetings with prospective buyers, were going ahead with him more or less out of the loop.

Drafts of the manager's new five-year contract made it clear that power was being switched from him to Benitez, and although Gillett was giving him 'over my dead body' reassurances about not signing it, he was becoming so marginalised as he sought his own exit, they were an irrelevance.

Plus it was looking increasingly likely that Hicks was going to ride out the credit crunch and come out the other side with his hands still on Liverpool.

Rick Parry still tried to do his job but had stopped enjoying it. The negativity had ground him down and as he surveyed a relationship between the owners which was never going to work he realised that neither could he. He had to get out before his professional reputation fell off a cliff.

The final straw came at a home game when Hicks sat beaming in the middle of the directors' box while Gillett had been pushed into the overflow. Parry began to suspect that his ally, Gillett, had given up the battle. If he had he knew he was toast because without his support, Hicks would crush him.

Parry asked Gillett for a favour. If I'm reading this right, he said, and you're about to disappear, then please get me out of here. A week later Hicks rang his chief executive and told him the owners had decided it was time for a change. Severance terms were agreed on 23 February 2009, Parry's fifty-fourth birthday. He would remain at the club until the end of the season and he would leave with a £3 million pay-off, thanks to David Moores' insistence that such a figure was put in writing when the club was sold.

'My position became untenable,' Parry told me. 'Hicks and Gillett made efforts to sell in late 2008 but by February 2009 it became clear they would be around for a while. The structure we had was dysfunctional and something had to give. Tom Hicks certainly didn't want me around. If by leaving it would help the club to progress then I was certainly prepared to go. Although I certainly didn't want to.'

In other words, the only job he had ever wanted became

impossible, so he walked away while he felt he still had some credibility left.

Tom Hicks released a short statement saying: 'We're very grateful to Rick. He will always be a friend of the club.' How ironic was that? An enemy of the club who had never heard of Liverpool until three years before, and would never want to hear of it again if someone would pay him enough to walk away, telling a lifelong fan, who as chief executive had overseen teams win every trophy apart from the league, that he would always be looked on kindly at Anfield.

It was madness. But it was madness partly of Rick Parry's own making.

Few, if any, people who worked with Parry believe he was motivated by greed or power. They just say he took on too much, failed to delegate, and was out of his depth when it came to selling the club. He is not so much in denial today about the catastrophic sale to the Americans, he just refuses to see it as the major failure of his eleven years at Anfield.

'Leaving aside the change of ownership, I have two major regrets. First and foremost, we didn't win the Premier League. This was the key target when I arrived and we failed. Second places don't count. I'll hold my hands up and accept my share of responsibility. And the second is not delivering the new stadium,' he said.

Argue that both those failings can be directly linked to the sale to the Americans and he counters that Hicks and Gillett were simply the means who failed to deliver the end. That The Liverpool Way says we only exist to win trophies and that is what we failed to do under them. He asks rhetorically that if

Liverpool had won the League and built the stadium, would the fans have been that upset with them?

That's a bit of an 'if my auntie had bollocks she'd be my uncle' theory, I tell him, because the reality is none of that happened. For that, says Parry, blame no one but Hicks and Gillett because they failed to deliver what they promised.

Parry's work these days takes him over to the east coast of America, and ironically he played a part in advising Boston-based NESV to buy the club. He is still a huge Liverpool fan who tries to get to as many games as he can. Away games that is. He hasn't been back to Anfield since they beat Spurs 3–1 on 24 May 2009, the final game of his final season.

As he was leaving, the man who was about to replace him, Christian Purslow, looked him in the eyes, shook his hand, and told him he'd always be welcome at the club. So far he hasn't put that offer to the test.

He doesn't want to be in the way, he says. He doesn't want to walk past a shadow.

CHAPTER NINE

'Jeez, you're not very big for all that money we spent
on you, are you?'

– George Gillett to Robbie Keane

As George Gillett digested the words he was reading on the
page in front of him the blood drained slowly from his face.
It couldn't be true, could it? Surely there was a misprint in this
report about Steven Gerrard marrying his long-term partner
Alex which completely changed its meaning. Maybe it was a
practical joke those wacky English liked playing on each other.
He read it again and again, but it still came out the same. There
was only one option open to him. He had to make the call.

His hand reached for the phone and he dialled his co-owner's
number – in the May of 2007 Gillett and Hicks were hardly
bosom buddies but they were still talking to each other.

'Tom, have you heard the news about Steven Gerrard?' He
hadn't.

'Well there's something you need to know.' He wanted to
know it.

'Our team captain is gay.'

After a silence, a bemused Hicks asked for the evidence and

when his co-owner read it to him, in between guffaws, he explained that in England the term 'partner' can refer to a member of the opposite sex. Their captain wasn't tackling for the other side, neither was he taking part in a civil partnership ceremony. Alex was a woman. He could relax.

Gillett thanked his partner (not in a sexual sense obviously) and as a wave of relief washed over him, he decided to arrange a gift for the happy heterosexual couple.

So he rang Rick Parry's secretary and asked for Gerrard's home address.

'Why?' he was asked.

'Because I've heard he's getting married and I would like to send him a gift.'

'Don't worry about it, the club will be sending flowers,' he was told.

'Yes, but I'd like to send him a separate gift on behalf of my family,' he replied.

'That won't be necessary as it's not really the Liverpool Way,' was the final word on the matter.

Gillett was left stunned. 'This is what we're up against,' he told a senior club figure. 'If the owner can't achieve the simple objective of trying to get his captain's address, what chance have we got of doing the things that really matter?'

That story perfectly encapsulates two of the reasons Rafa Benitez spent most of his time at Melwood headbutting the wall. Whenever he tried to sign a player, make changes to the coaching structure or find out how much money he would have to spend, he would come up against a bureaucratic nightmare, dithering, deliberate stonewalling, and that old favourite The Liverpool Way. Plus, for the last two and a half years of his reign he came up against The Madness of King George.

'I'll give you £50 million, Roffa, plus whatever we get in the draft' was his favourite response when it came to asking Gillett about his transfer budget. But even that was topped when Benitez emailed the owners a few months before one window, telling them the squad needed strengthening so asking what sort of funds he would be given.

(Even though at this point Benitez was really only dealing with Hicks, he had to cc Gillett into every email because he had once contacted one of them with a request at a time when they weren't talking, word of the request got back to the other one who accused the manager of treason.)

Hicks's answer was short and sweet, telling him it was too early to give a figure because there were developments going on with the banks, but as soon as he got one, he'd let him know. In other words shut up and get on with your job.

Gillett's was short and mad, telling him he'd seen a new, innovative running machine that was all the rage in America, and perhaps if he got one of these it would help the players improve. In other words: Nurse, the screens!

As one person Rafa showed his Gillett emails to remarked: 'They looked like they'd been sent from the funny farm.' The irony of that was Gillett confided in more than one journalist that he thought Benitez had serious mental problems. He even coined a name to describe his condition. Roffa, he would say, is a 'serial transactionist'. Thank you, Doctor Dolittle.

But as the man who gave Snoogy Doogy to the world often showed, there were more symptoms on display to diagnose a madness in King George. A former club official tells how he was on true eccentric form on the trip to Florence in late 2009.

The singer Sting was at the game as a guest of the Fiorentina board and Gillett couldn't take his eyes off him at half-time. When he was asked if he was a fan of the former Police lead singer and thus a bit overawed by his presence, he replied, 'No, no. There's just one thing that intrigues me about him. How does a guy get to be called Sting?'

Ten minutes into the second half, Gillett rose from his seat and disappeared inside the stadium. When he was gone for five minutes people started to look at each other, slightly worried in case something had happened to him. And then he reappeared, his arms full of Cornettos, Magnums and choc ices, and proceeded to dish them out to everyone in the directors' box. At ten p.m. at night with winter around the corner.

Senior players tell how he would strike up a conversation about skiing, then tell them: 'I've got a great ski resort in Colorado, it's one of the best in the world. You've got to come over with your family and do some skiing.' Apart from the fact that footballers contractually aren't allowed to ski, and virtually all of them would rather be on the golf course, they didn't want to hear he had the best ski resort in the world. They wanted to know how much of its profits would be diverted into that summer's transfer budget.

On the morning of the famous 1–0 Premier League victory at Chelsea in October 2008, the players were in their hotel restaurant queuing for food, when Gillett came bouncing through the door shouting, 'Hi, guys.'

As he approached the queue he told one of the players he wanted to meet the new £20 million signing. 'Hey, where's Keano, where's Keano? I gotta see this Keano that I've heard so much about.'

Keane, who was in front of him in the queue, turned round and said, 'Hello, I'm Keano.' To which Gillett replied: 'Jeez, you're not very big for all that money we spent on you, are you?' Keane just shuffled off looking baffled and embarrassed.

His interest in Keane may have had something to do with his role in the farcical summer transfer business which heralded the Irishman's arrival at Anfield. Before the window opened Benitez had told Rick Parry his primary target was Aston Villa's Gareth Barry.

Keane was letting it be known he wanted to move to the team he supported as a boy, and Parry told Rafa he could buy both if he wanted them. Benitez agreed but said they had to get Barry first because if they couldn't sign him, he wouldn't want Keane. He'd formulated a system in his head and without Barry, Keane wouldn't fit into it. According to Benitez, Parry said he had to do the Keane deal straight away but told him not to worry as there would be enough left in the kitty to buy Barry. It didn't quite pan out like that.

Once Keane was signed the Americans refused to match Aston Villa's valuation and Benitez was told to forget Barry. An incensed Rafa went public, telling journalists he wouldn't be signing Barry, even though he was told he could sign him, because the club had no spare money. Gillett, sensing Benitez was trying once again to deflect failure in the transfer market on to the owners, sent him an angry email saying they did have the money, but had decided not to sign Barry because he was too old for the price Villa were asking. As Benitez was fond of pointing out back then, Barry was twenty-seven, Keane was twenty-eight, and Barry would have cost the club less.

Five months later, when Benitez was trying to sell Keane back to Spurs, Gillett had changed his tune on the little Irishman he was so eager to meet. He breezed into Rafa's Melwood office one December morning with his usual greeting, 'Hi, guys, what's happening?' to be told they had reached an agreement to sell Keane back to Spurs. 'No kidding? That's fantastic business, guys, well done,' he declared.

It would be, Gillett was told, if they could get hold of Rick Parry, but he had gone off radar. Without him doing the necessary paperwork there was no deal. With that news Gillett raced out of the room yelling, 'Where is he, where is he?' before spotting a secretary and demanding: 'Get me Rick on the phone now, we need to do this business.'

A senior figure tells of the comical nature of one of the early board meetings (they ceased to hold any after the autumn of 2007). Halfway through it a bored Gillett stood up and announced: 'OK, Foster and I are leaving now because we're going to Melwood to catch the players training.'

There was an embarrassed silence as the pair left, then a few nods and whispers, and a decision was taken to move the meeting from Anfield to Melwood. So they all climbed into cars and zoomed off in pursuit of the two Gilletts. Which is surreal enough in itself, but was made even more so when they reconvened the meeting in the Melwood dining room, only for Gillett to constantly leap up and wave at players. As the figure put it: 'If I'd have been smarter and worked out what was happening, I'd have got off there and then.'

Whenever he was in Vail, Colorado, and heard there was a

footballer visiting the clinic of renowned knee-surgeon Richard Steadman, (which was 100 metres from his home) Gillett would go round, get pally with the player and attempt to hang around with them throughout their stay, in order to pick their brains and soak up information, and gossip, about this new sport he'd bought in to. He met Michael Owen there, the summer before he bought Liverpool, and it was in Steadman's clinic where he struck up his friendship with Klinsmann. When he discovered that Kop legend Robbie Fowler was in town, he was round like a shot.

At one point, he phoned someone at Anfield, and said, 'You'll never guess who I'm with out here in Colorado. Let me put him on to you.' When Robbie said hello, the Anfield man said, 'Are you as embarrassed about this as I am?' Robbie replied: 'Far more embarrassed' and was told: 'OK, just turn the phone off, hand it back to him and pretend you lost me.'

That same Anfield man has cringeful memories of his conversations with Gillett: 'George would always big you up, tell you what a great job you were doing, then tell you something about someone else which was really bad. He'd always have dirt on players or former players, and he always had dirt on Tom.'

'He'd say things like, "He's going bust in three weeks." He slagged so many people off it made you wonder "what is he going to be saying about me when I walk out the door?" He portrayed himself as warm, sincere and affable, but underneath it all he wasn't. If he wanted to impress someone he'd be all over them saying, "You should come and work for us, you're just what we're looking for." I've seen this first-hand.'

'He once phoned me up and said, "You gotta meet this guy and give him a job." So I met him, decided he was a complete flake and left it at that. A few weeks later he asked me if I'd met him, I said, "Yeah, and he's a complete flake," and he nodded and said, "Yeah, I thought that too.'"

Businessmen talk of the Gilletts leaving behind a trail of broken dreams. Just as Foster had made noises about buying Wigan Warriors before vanishing, George talked of his great ideas to Phillip Jones, the managing director of Halliwell Jones, the BMW dealership which supplies Liverpool with cars.

He told him about the dealerships he had in Canada and proposed they did deals together. He came up with quite a few ambitious plans, which left Jones sceptical but nonetheless keen to hear them through. That was until he could no longer get through to Gillett, his messages went unanswered and his phone seemed permanently off the hook.

The dynamic between Gillett and his co-owner was the most fractured of all and it did more damage to the club than any of the other false and forced relationships at Anfield. As the first press conference showed, when Hicks told Gillett he was going to speak ahead of him and he caved in to the demand, this was not a partnership of equals. Hicks was in charge; Gillett had power of veto but very little else. It was similar to Britain's so-called special relationship with the USA. We help them do their killing and their shafting, they take the plaudits and the profits and in return they patronise us by telling us how special we are.

The difference being Hicks wasn't telling Gillett how special he was, only how junior he was and how bereft of power he was without the clout of the Texan paper billionaire. Gillett would bad-mouth Hicks to the rest of the Anfield board and come out with big promises to stand up to him and stop him pulling off his latest outrageous stunt, but time after time he would cave in. A classic example came in the spring of 2009 with Rafa Benitez's proposed new five-year contract. He swore to a senior Liverpool figure who shared his antipathy towards the Spaniard that he would never sign it. Three days later it came back signed.

Whatever happened, Hicks always seemed to come out on top. That same figure relates a comical story to that effect.

Seven minutes before the kick-off of the 2007 Champions League game against Barcelona he was standing next to Gillett in the Anfield boardroom, when he suddenly demanded a scarf. He was asked if he was cold and he replied that he wasn't. He just wanted to show the world how much he loved the club. The senior figure told him, 'This is Liverpool. You don't wear big scarves, especially if you're a director.'

He was slightly peeved because he'd set his heart on wearing his colours on such a big night, but he agreed and thanked him for the advice. Then he took his seat in the directors' box, only to find, standing next to him with the biggest, reddest, shiniest Liverpool scarf resting on his shoulders, Tom Hicks and a cameraman clicking away at the pair of them. Hicks with scarf, Gillett without. He wasn't happy.

Hicks, on the other hand, never sought anyone's advice. He would just do his own thing and not give a monkey's cuss about tradition, taste, or anyone else's sensibilities. How else do you explain him walking into the Anfield boardroom one match day and hitching up his suit trousers to reveal a brand new pair of cowboy boots bearing the Liver Bird crest? Worse still, he told the disbelieving directors, shareholders and guests whom he'd summoned to admire his leather masterpieces, that if they wanted a pair he could get them a good price.

When the owners rowed it wasn't a pretty sight as Hicks swatted Gillett like a mosquito. Someone who witnessed several arguments described them as being heated but never physical. No hiking boots on cowboy boots action to report, I'm afraid. A typical scenario would be Hicks dismissing his junior partner with a put-down and Gillett playing the injured victim asking 'What have I ever done to you?' to which the Texan would reply 'What have you ever done?'

An Anfield insider who saw one row unfold said: 'Hicks looked at him like he was a sad little man. He made reference to the meat-packing deal which brought them together and said: 'When you were a minor shareholder you acted like you were in control. Now you have parity you're insufferable.'

But, to misquote C.J. from *Reggie Perrin*, Gillett didn't get to be where he was today without having some impressive traits. One of his finest is an extraordinary capacity to digest a huge amount of complex detail and regurgitate it with a conviction that convinces listeners he knows everything about his subject.

It was that skill that convinced Moores and Parry that 'he got The Liverpool Way', when what he'd got was a five-star crib-sheet and recited it without error in a seemingly spontaneous manner.

Choose the ten stand-out facts about Liverpool's history from Rome to Istanbul, Heysel to Hillsborough, Liddell to Dalglish, throw in the ten greatest reasons for supporting Liverpool and he not only had them all stored up, but he could rattle them off with more conviction than the reddest sage in the Albert pub.

Journalists saw him as a flattering fantasist who was desperate to be liked, someone who wanted to be thought of as a favourite uncle but who, underneath, was a calculating machine. He was happy to dish out harsh opinions and leak information that was favourable to him, but he would rarely go on the record. He dealt in nods and winks, nudging you towards asking questions about his enemies.

He once told *The Times'* business reporter Alex Frean that there was a senior journalist on her newspaper receiving financial inducements to write nasty lies about him. As Frean could only think of one person who was constantly critical of him, the newspaper's football editor, she asked if he was talking about Tony Evans. He gave a 'you may say that but I couldn't possibly comment' look and when she told Evans about it he said: 'As if I would ever need paying to write nasty things about him.'

Another *Times* journalist, Tony Barrett (formerly of the *Echo*) recalls an impromptu, off-the-record meeting with him at the Academy in September 2009:

'He stood there in his trademark hob-nailed boots and told me how much money he'd put in to the club, how much more he was going to put in, how he was going to revolutionise the stadium, how the club was being let down by Tom Hicks and Rafa, blah, blah, blah. It was his standard liturgy of nonsense.'

He accused the reporter of writing falsehoods about how much interest he and Hicks were paying and said this truly hurt him because Barrett was a wonderful writer. When he asked the *Times* man what issues he had with him and Hicks he was told 'You're ruining the club.' Which sent him off on a Walter Mitty tangent, accusing Barrett of listening too much to Benitez, who was the real destroyer of the club: 'The disturbing thing was I think he actually believed all the rubbish he was spouting. Every time I spoke to him what he said was so divorced from reality as to be laughable. I think the fact he chose never to go on the record proved he knew he was talking bollocks. He gave out figures about Rafa's spending which were completely ridiculous, and his theme never changed. It was always Rafa is destroying the club and so is Tom Hicks but I'm going to make it all right. I reached the same conclusion that most British journalists did: He's barking.'

It wasn't just British journalists who were left baffled by some of his answers though. When he finally chose to break his silence on his unworkable relationship with Hicks, he did so on a Toronto sports radio station, Fan 590. Throughout the lengthy interview in March 2008 he couldn't bear to mention his partner by name. Not once did he say Tom or Mr Hicks, just 'him' and 'others within the ownership group' (like there were more than the two of them).

It was a classic example of how he played the victim – the affable pensioner who'd been mugged by the brutal Texan. The popular uncle figure among Liverpudlians who had become tainted by association with Hicks, not through anything he'd done or said. He talked of 'him' being the root cause of fans' animosity whereas he was so popular he'd been invited on pre-match benders in pubs around Anfield (presumably just as one of those pubs was about to become a mysterious arson target).

'I've had several conversations with fans who represent important blog sites and so forth and they are inviting me to come to the famous pubs to be their guest and see how they sing their songs, or get ready to sing their songs. And there's none of the hostility that seems to have been directed at others within the ownership group,' he said without falling off his chair in a fit of laughter, apologising for having a warped sense of humour and asking the station's producer if he could go again.

'We've gotten as many as 2,000 emails a week here and I would say that 95 per cent of them have been directed at some of the comments made by my partner and 5 per cent have been aimed at both of us, saying "Go home Americans."

'The thing that angers them the most is the prospect that I might sell even one share of stock to my partner. They don't want him to have controlling interest of this club. They don't want him to have any ownership of the club, based on what they're saying and sending to me.

'So as a result of that it has been a difficult time for my wife, based on the amount that I travel, because we've received calls in the middle of the night, threatening our lives, death threats. I would come to the office and the threats would come to the office and Foster and Lauren, my son and daughter-in-law, have received a number of them as well.

'We're very private people but my phone number is in the phone book, and I'm not shy and if I make a mistake then I'm prepared to take the hit for that. But private numbers and mobile phone numbers are apparently on some blog sites and we've received some calls.

'And again it's interesting that calls aren't against my wife and my son and my daughter-in-law as much as they're against us selling to our partner. So we're rethinking that. Frankly I don't think it's fair for me to put my family in that kind of danger and, instead of thinking about selling, I don't know, maybe we will think about buying.'

So he's a very private person who puts his number in the

public phone book. Fans ring him in the middle of the night to issue death threats, only they're not death threats but a mixture of invites to pubs for singing practice, and pleas not to sell his share to Hicks. And despite being desperate to get out of the club, petrified about the credit crunch making him bankrupt again, and having no spare funds and no legal way of forcing his partner to sell his 50 per cent share, he's thinking of buying Hicks out.

This interview was also worth listening to on another level. To hear how, after fourteen months in charge of a football club, he had truly mastered the sport's terminology:

'Our loss to Man U last Sunday 3–0 was a heartbreaker because we played eleven on ten. We had Mascherano thrown off when it's unclear what happened, but clearly they sent out a referee with a no-tolerance programme and we happened to make the wrong comment to the referee at the wrong time.' Go soccerball owner, go!

What was also worth hearing was Tom Hicks's priceless response to the interview. When his PR people were asked for his reaction a statement was released which read: 'Mr Hicks will be making no comment as he would prefer to allow the team to get on with the important games over the next few weeks'. Less than a fortnight later, just before the Champions League semi-final, Hicks was leaking the fact he'd just sent Rick Parry a letter demanding his resignation for being a disaster.

To be fair to Gillett he was never loathed by Liverpudlians as much as Hicks was. They knew Gillett soon realised he had made a mistake buying Liverpool with Hicks and would willingly have sold his share to Dubai if he could. They also knew he grew to hate Hicks as much as them, which was one of the reasons he wouldn't sell him his 50 per cent. Towards the end he was definitely viewed as the lesser of the two evils.

There is also evidence to suggest he did view buying the club as more than buying Weetabix. He did take on board the unique traditions of Liverpool FC and wanted to try to maintain them as much as he could, whereas Hicks was a hard-nosed assassin who saw all that culture and history nonsense as unwanted baggage which served only one point: to add value to the brand.

Which was why Hicks hardly ever spoke to the players and never met the fans. Gillett did meet with the fans though, and not only when he was ambushed at his hotel, on visits to the training ground or in city centre pubs.

Rick Parry had begun to realise that the Spirit Of Shankly was fast gathering members and credibility. He went along to several meetings in the Cross Keys pub in Liverpool city centre where he listened sympathetically to their frank and honest assessment of both him and the club.

At first SOS members were sceptical, guessing that he was attempting to claw back credibility after the disastrous sale to Hicks and Gillett and his Athens 'numbers game' quote.

The early meetings were fraught with anxiety because there were fans present who wanted to rip him apart, verbally, not literally – although I can't speak for all of them. Both sides soon realised that whatever had divided them in the past they were now united by one ambition. To see the back of Tom Hicks.

Spirit Of Shankly knew they needed allies in the boardroom and Parry realised he needed as many friends as he could muster outside it, especially with union membership climbing towards 10,000 and their spokesmen regularly articulating fan-base concerns in the national media. Eventually Parry decided it was in all of their interests to set up a meeting with Gillett, and both sides agreed. So on 13 September 2008, before the lunchtime kick-off against Manchester United, SOS members met Gillett and Parry at Anfield.

'It was all a bit cloak and dagger, to be honest,' recalls Paul Rice. 'There was four of us; Peter Furmedge, myself, Nicky Allt and John Mackin. Rick was there and this guy sat at the back dressed in classic Ivy League chinos and jacket. Gillett wore a suit with what I can only describe as monkey boots on his feet. I couldn't take my eyes off them. I was thinking, "Is this some kind of psychological ploy?"'

Naturally, Uncle George was very pally and it was all 'Hi, guys, how you doin'?' In a typical attempt to show they, not him, were the most important people in the room (but also a subtle way of sizing up his opponents and finding out useful information which could be used at a later date) he said, 'You guys know who I am so tell me who you are and what you all do.' They went around the table and metaphorically filled him in.

'I could tell by looking at him that he was taken aback,' said Rice. 'I think he was expecting us to say "hod-carrier, doorman, incapacity benefit recipient etc.," but instead he heard "chief executive, playwright, chief executive, etc." and you could see he was thinking, "Gee these guys might be able to string a sentence together, we could be in trouble here."'

Gillett upped his game. Out came the passionately regurgitated LFC crib-sheet, showcasing his knowledge of, and love for, their club. When they asked about his unworkable relationship with Hicks he admitted they didn't see eye to eye but they were looking at ways of working together (which was the same smokescreen Gordon Brown used to throw up when asked how he was getting on with Tony Blair).

Then Gillett cut to the quick by asking what their issues were with the ownership, and Rice listed the broken promises, the debt they'd thrown on the club, the lack of direction and leadership, the absence of a new stadium and the wanton undermining of the manager's position. 'I just gave it to him straight,' said Rice. 'I said, when you came into our club from nowhere you were welcomed warmly and you've basically gone on to shit on us from a great height, before adding that all four of us had better things to do that day than sit there telling him how appalling he was at his role of custodian of our great club. Like getting in the mood for our biggest home game of the season against the Mancs.'

John Mackin, co-author with Jegsy Dodd of the hugely entertaining book *Redmen*, also took his chance to lay it on the line: 'We've never needed to protest or demonstrate before,' he told Gillett, 'because in the past we all seemed to be pulling in the same direction – players, manager, staff and fans. But that's been ripped apart by you fellas.

'The old relationship used to be about everyone pulling in the same direction. Us behind the club and the club behind us. The club always there for us. We were never just turnstile fodder. We were never just there to be exploited. But that's changed and there's a feeling now that the club doesn't care who the fans are as long as they've got their money.'

They then brought up the £30 million interest being paid to keep the club afloat and the effect that was having on the strength of the squad.

A shocked and affronted Gillett hit back by launching into a speech about how the club was in 'a very, very healthy state' better than any other major club in Europe. 'We've spent more than anyone over the past few years except Chelsea. We've spent more than Man U. If your problem is with the quality of players then please, Sweet Jesus, don't blame me for that,' he said. When the SOS men loudly challenged him he asked them to keep the voices down because Rafa Benitez and his family were in the next office.

Now that Gillett had moved the conversation on to his favourite 'serial transactionist' he assured them that the real problem at the club was Benitez, before launching into an attack on him with Parry occasionally nodding in agreement. He talked about Benitez's obsession with doing things quickly: 'Deals take a long time. Alex Ferguson is prepared to wait until the last day of the transfer window but Rafa says "we have to act now". Well what do you think that does when we come knocking at a door. They start rubbing their hands together.'

They hit back by saying they didn't want a debate with him about the faults and merits of Benitez as an individual. What concerned them more was how he and Hicks had undermined the office of manager of Liverpool FC, regardless of who that manager was. Which was a cue for Gillett to tell them they didn't understand how difficult it was working with someone like Benitez.

It was at this point Paul Rice cut in to say: 'Look, George, can I be honest with you?'

'I would very much like you to be,' he replied.

'You've been relatively successful in business. If you were called in to study Liverpool FC, as a business, would you conclude that it's clearly dysfunctional and that it could not possibly move forward when it's split into two sides?'

Gillett's response was: 'Oh it's far worse than *two* sides.'

He wrapped up the meeting with the kind of diplomatic pleasantries you used to hear when Gorbachev met Reagan to try to end the Cold War: It's been very positive, we now both understand the other side's position, let's keep this dialogue going, here's my business card, you know how to contact me, do so at any time, my door is always open, etc.

But Gillett being Gillett, he had to top it with his own personal, empathetic touch by telling them, 'Let's fix this fricking club,' then, with reference to the well-publicised march the SOS had organised before that day's game: 'Now you guys go and do what you've got to do.'

He wanted them to walk away with the overriding impression that he was Uncle George, a good guy, who was on their side.

The impression they left with was of a patronising gnome in hiking boots.

CHAPTER TEN

'I was thinking, "Oh, come on, let's get these out, enough
is enough, the sooner these are out the better"'
— Steven Gerrard

The final straw for Steven Gerrard was watching Tom Hicks
by his Dallas fireside, clutching his Liverpool mug, pretending
to cheer on the Reds, while anarchy raged at Anfield.

Rafa Benitez was telling his captain of his increasing frustration, Rick Parry had been urged to resign, angry fans were
protesting, poison was seeping into every pore of the media,
people were persuading Gerrard to go public and demand
answers, and Hicks and Gillett were nowhere to be seen. Meanwhile, yet another trophyless season beckoned.

That positive meeting with the new American owners in
Manchester's Lowry Hotel, didn't feel like it was only fourteen
months ago. Gerrard thought back to how excited he'd been
to hear them say they were hell-bent on returning Liverpool
to their position as one of the most revered football clubs in
the world. Only to drag Liverpool to a place it had never been
before: a civil war battlefield.

The club's Huyton-born captain had long realised all those promises were empty, and like the vast majority of Liverpudlians he'd been conned by their charm offensive. Hicks had told his on-field leader he would always be there for him if he needed anything, but he never had a face-to-face conversation with him again. Or one over the phone for that matter. Not even a friendly 'how's everything going' bit of banter after being pulled aside at Anfield or Melwood.

Indeed the Sky News reporter, Alan Myers, whom he was now making his latest cosy film with, had more meetings with Hicks in the time he ran Liverpool than his team captain did. But as Gerrard watched that April 2008 interview in his Formby home, following as it did on the heels of the Klinsmann saga and the revelation that the Americans had shifted all their loans on to the club, even if they'd wanted to talk, they would have found their captain very reluctant to meet them.

He was telling friends he didn't even want to look at them. His frustrations, like those of the fans, made him wish they'd just pack up and go.

'I was thinking, "When is this going to end?" Will it carry on for one year, two years because the only people who are going to suffer are the team and the supporters,' said Gerrard.

He witnessed the internal warfare first-hand and feared a long and heavy fall-out with devastating repercussions. Journalists were telling him the extent of the briefings and counter-briefings, he could see the story moving from the back pages to the front and he was struggling to cope with the implications both for the club and for himself.

'I'd been at Liverpool since I was eight. I wasn't really interested in the media until I was fifteen or sixteen and started getting a big interest in Liverpool, but I'd never seen the club making national front-page headlines,' he said.

'When I was doing interviews a lot of people were saying, "Can I ask you about Hicks and Gillett and the break-down with Rafa," and I was thinking, "No, this isn't something to get involved in as a player. Concentrate on your own game and lifting the team."

'Because this wasn't an argument that was happening between them in an office, this was coming out in the public domain and you could see it was just going to get messier and messier.'

In that February 2007 meeting, Hicks and Gillett had promised Gerrard they were going to spend big, invest in the Academy and back the manager, because their main intention was getting it right on the pitch. The same sentiments they took into Anfield on the day of the takeover.

'I recorded the first press conference and watched it a few times and the key thing they were both saying is "we respect this club's heritage and history and the important thing is the team competing to win things,"' said Gerrard. 'But that wasn't the case. It certainly wasn't the case when they were dragging the club through the courts.

'That High Court hearing was a disgrace. The frustrating thing for me was knowing they were sticking out for more money and they were prepared to hang on to the club for a long time until they got out of it what they wanted. Because in that first meeting I thought they had our interests at heart.

'But I realised then how far they were prepared to drag this club down just to get some money. I can't find the right words to describe them. Let's just say they had some balls to do that.

I didn't think they would drag the club to those lengths for some money. It just shows how greedy they were.'

As Gerrard watched Tom Hicks's video in horror in his Formby front room, a few miles away in Blundellsands, Jamie Carragher was staring at his television in total despair. Like his fellow Scouse teammate, this was the moment when any respect he had for Hicks disappeared.

'That was when I thought it's got past a joke. To fly a TV crew over to your house, and dress your kids in Liverpool tops, and make them watch the game on your home cinema, coming out with stuff like, "Everton won't like that" I just thought, "Oh my God, what's going on?"

'Then he attacked Rick Parry, and whether you think he was doing a good job or a bad job you just don't do that. This is Liverpool. He's our chief executive and you're the owner. You don't start dishing the dirt on worldwide telly.

'When Hicks implied that we've never won the league under Rick Parry I thought, "It's not his fault," and if you're using that argument does that mean Parry won us the European Cup then? To attack him publicly was a betrayal of everything the club stood for. It was unforgiveable.'

Carragher, the boyhood Evertonian who broke into the Liverpool team in 1996 and came to typify the pride and character of the club for more than a decade and a half, eventually became emotionally exhausted with the civil war.

'It was like your mum and dad scrapping. You don't care what they're fighting about, you just want to scream at them to shut up,' he said.

'The manager and owners might not have liked each other but they should have concentrated on just letting us play football. I just wish they'd put their personal arguments aside for the sake of the team.

'I got sick of the rowing because it just wouldn't stop. No sooner would one fight die down, like the one between Rafa Benitez and Hicks, than another would blow up. Like Hicks and Gillett falling out. Everyone was trying to be too clever, playing politics with no regard for the damage they were doing to the club.

'I blame both Rafa and the owners for that. The manager would be coming out with things before a game like 'focus on coaching and training' and they would hit back through briefings or interviews. It was as though they were all playing their own games instead of worrying about Liverpool winning on a Saturday.

'Even when Rafa had a row with them you were put in a difficult position because the owners and the manager both wanted you on their side. But I just wanted to play football. Everything was going-off off the pitch, and I just wanted to say, "Can we forget about this and just play football."

'Sometimes Rafa would say something before a game and you'd think, "Don't say that, forget it, get on with the game."

'Before the Europa League semi-final against Atletico Madrid he comes out and says something about another club being interested in him, and the owners not supporting him and I'm thinking, "We've got a semi-final here, we can win a European trophy, what are you talking about that for? Just shut up and concentrate on winning the game."

'Don't get me wrong, it must have been hard for the manager dealing with the owners but there was too much politics being played. And we all suffered.'

One of the most obvious ways the players suffered was through a lack of investment in the team in the final eighteen months of the Americans' reign.

'The frustrating thing was the timing,' said Gerrard. 'We were so close. Two European Finals, finishing second, we weren't that far away from getting the League back. We were another two or three Torres, Reina and Mascherano signings away from competing with anyone, that was the big frustration.'

He felt the last three or four transfer windows held the club back because it stopped them competing with the best on the pitch, and consequently the squad didn't progress. Gerrard would never admit it in public because it would seem like an excuse, but friends say there were times when he thought that the lack of investment from Hicks and Gillett cost him medals. Certainly some of his teammates felt like that, including Jamie Carragher.

'I'm an ambitious footballer who wants to win medals and if they'd been better owners who'd put their money in like they promised then I might have won more than I did.

'I get very well paid but when you reach my age what really bothers you is how many medals you've got. You look at other players in other teams who are winning titles and it's natural rivalry, you want to be better than them.

'So when the transfer money dries up like it did with those two, because their plans went wrong, it gets you angry. It might sound selfish but I'm probably never going to win the League with Liverpool now because we're going to need to rebuild.

'I'd never come out and say they definitely cost me a League title medal because it was down to us players on the pitch, but if we hadn't had interest payments like we've had we could have been spending an extra £15–£20 million in the last few transfer windows which could have made the difference.

'Who knows? If the Dubai people had come in I might have won a Premier League title and I would probably have played in a new stadium. I'd have loved to have played in a new Anfield, and we may get one, but I'll never play in it. If they'd put that spade in within sixty days like they promised to, I'd be playing in it now.'

It wasn't just local legends like Gerrard and Carragher who felt badly let down by Hicks and Gillett's lack of financial backing; world-class foreign players like Fernando Torres and Javier Mascherano did too.

When Mascherano moved to Barcelona he gave an interview slamming the Americans, which appeared under the headline 'I Quit Kop For Two Reasons … Hicks And Gillett'.

In it he said he might still have been a Liverpool player had the pair left sooner, before giving this damning indictment on them: 'While Manchester City, Chelsea and Manchester United were spending big money, Liverpool couldn't because they had no money. The situation is clear to me. When you want to fight for big things like titles, you must have a big team to win. But, at Liverpool, that wasn't the case.'

Torres grew increasingly disillusioned during the 2009–10 season, when Liverpool were knocked out of the Champions League at the group stages and headed towards a seventh-place finish in the Premier League.

He had scored the goal that made Spain European Champions and was on his way to winning a World Cup. He had been shortlisted for the Ballon D'Or and was regarded as one of the top strikers in world football.

Here was a child prodigy, adored by fans of his boyhood club Atletico Madrid, whom he left as he approached his peak years because he wanted to win the highest honours in club football. So he joined Liverpool and won nothing.

When Liverpool began to fall out of the Champions League places he was made promises by the owners and the management that investment was on its way, and with it big-name players to share his burden. But none of it came. After Liverpool finished runners-up to Manchester United in 2009, they went into reverse. High-class colleagues like Xabi Alonso, Alvaro Arbeloa, Sami Hyypia, Yossi Benayoun and Javier Mascherano left and were replaced with inferior players.

To make matters worse, Atletico Madrid started winning trophies, while Liverpool looked further away from winning one than at any time for a decade.

Towards the end of the 2009–10 season, Torres spoke out in the press about his frustrations with Hicks and Gillett, telling them they had to spend to keep Liverpool competitive. But as they say in Texas, he was whistling Dixie.

When he flew to the World Cup in South Africa it was touch-and-go whether he would start the following season as Liverpool's number nine. The man who brought him to Anfield, Benitez, was on his way, and he was completely disillusioned with the running of the club, fearing that with no change of ownership imminent, the one thing he had yet to own, a winners' medal with a club side, was as distant a dream as ever.

His agents set about listening to offers, but few came. A combination of factors were to blame: with three years left on his contract Liverpool would be asking a colossal fee but his injury problems and the poor World Cup made potential suitors think twice about breaking the bank. Barcelona, the only Spanish side he contemplated moving to, signed his Spain striking partner David Villa, and Chelsea, the one English side he privately pined to join, threw in a derisory £30 million offer, without following it up.

As much as Hicks and Gillett may have loved to trouser such a debt-shrinking sum, Torres was deemed as not only pivotal to Liverpool's ability to compete on the pitch, but their chances of being sold. A global superstar who shifts replica shirts by the container-load, and has a hefty sell-on fee, is a handy card to pull out during negotiations.

So managing director Christian Purslow got to work on Torres, promising him that big things were around the corner, pleading with him to stay for at least another season, offering him more money and a clause in his contract enabling him to leave the following summer for £50 million. He agreed to give it a go.

'I am really happy to stay with all my teammates,' Torres said at the time. 'My commitment and loyalty to the club and to the fans is the same as it was on the day when I signed.'

As my mum used to say, 'Try telling that to your gob, then.' With another poor transfer window, a shocking start to the season and a new manager so out of his depth at Anfield he looked like he'd caught the bends, Torres's face and body spent the next six months screaming 'get me out of here'.

When Roman Abramovich eventually threw him a lifeline he grabbed it without a second's hesitation, handing in a written transfer request three days before the end of the January 2011 transfer window.

His timing was almost as shocking as his words on arriving

at Chelsea: 'The target for every player is to play for one of the top clubs in the world and I can do it now, so I'm very happy,' he said, neatly forgetting the history of the club he'd left and the fact that during his time at Liverpool, UEFA had ranked them number one in Europe, which equates to being the best in the world.

Despite the £50 million he earned Liverpool, his exit was classless and insulting, and in the eyes of most fans he went from being a beloved legend to persona non grata. Just another self-serving, love-feigning imposter. A plastic idol heading to a stadium of plastic flags.

Such criticism was valid, especially as Torres had spoken so passionately about his love for Liverpool, its people and its culture. How he wanted his kids to grow up with Scouse accents and how he could never think of joining another Premier League side because Liverpool were his English club.

However, it would be naive and unfair to underplay the toll the Anfield Civil War had taken on this highly driven footballer's ambitions. People around him cited the 'broken promises' made to him during the summer of 2010 at the fag end of the Hicks and Gillett reign, and when Torres faced his first Chelsea press conference he firmly fingered our friends from across the pond.

'It wasn't just last summer really,' he said. 'It's the last two years maybe, especially with the old owners. They wanted to sell the club too many times and during that time the team was being weakened.

'I once said I didn't think I would play for another club because at that moment Liverpool were giving me what they promised, but not now.

'I was feeling a big deception about everything that was happening with the sale of the club. There were too many things to think about, too many promises, too many false hopes.

'I accept that my performances were not the best, but if the promises they made had been true Liverpool would be fighting with Man United and Chelsea now.'

Four months after the civil war ended the casualties were still being counted.

Steven Gerrard had total empathy with the foreign superstars, as did Jamie Carragher: 'You can't blame top foreign players looking at their mates who are winning at other clubs and thinking "My career's going nowhere at Liverpool,"' said Carragher.

'Torres left Atletico to come here for medals and that club went past us. The reality is the top players get offers from top clubs and you can't blame then for being unsettled, especially when they're not from this country, let alone this city. They want to win things.

'Me and Stevie didn't necessarily care more about Liverpool than them, we just had more of an understanding what was going on because we're from here.'

Many onlookers found it baffling that foreign players, who had been brought up with deeper passions for clubs in their own countries, should feel moved to risk their careers by speaking out, while Scousers like Carragher and Gerrard, who were far more affected by the civil war, stayed silent.

Spanish goalkeeper Pepe Reina told the pair he was amazed they hadn't come out and demanded the owners sort out the mess. He told them they were too respectful towards the people above them at the club, and too readily adopted a 'whatever will be will be' attitude. The Spain international believed that at other big clubs around the world like Real Madrid, Barcelona, Bayern Munich and the two Milan sides, local legends who had been there since they were kids would have been issuing threats and demands, knowing they were secure because of their iconic status.

Neither Gerrard nor Carragher disagree with Reina. In fact, they readily admit that the dilemma tortured them at the time and still plays on their consciences today.

'I totally understand why some of the fans were frustrated that we didn't speak out,' says Gerrard.

'When I'm down at England I hear stories about what big players have said at big clubs, but when me and Jamie speak we're worried about taking a lot of criticism like "Who does he think he is? Does he think he's bigger than the club?"

'So it's a horrible situation because you want to come out and use your status to help but on the other hand you're terrified of it backfiring and creating more of a mess. That's the frustrating thing.'

There were times when Gerrard was on the verge of going public, demanding answers and pleading with owners and manager to sort out their differences. But so murky had the waters become, and so politicised the atmosphere, he could never be certain who was in the wrong or the right. Moreover, he didn't believe it was a player's role to openly criticise the management and he feared the consequences.

'"Should I say something, would it make any difference, and who are we to criticise our bosses?" They were the questions I kept asking myself. It wasn't my thing but there were times it was on the tip of my tongue.'

He had another dilemma. If he was to speak his mind, who did he speak it to, and how did he speak it?

'Their honeymoon period was all good and they were around so there were people to talk to, but when the public spat hit the press there was no one here. I had fans and friends telling me to speak to them and ask when it's all going to end, but there was no one here. So what do you do? Do you go through the press to get to them? It's not right. There wasn't an office here when you could speak to them because they'd gone. It was a mess.'

There was a further concern haunting Gerrard based on self-knowledge. He sensed if he became as major a player in this saga as he could have, and if he'd done some of the things people were asking him to do, such as make phone calls to America, he'd have become too deeply involved and wouldn't have been able to concentrate on his job.

When people like Rafa Benitez tried to speak to him and draw him into the civil war, he didn't want to know because he felt if he got too heavily involved in the in-fighting he would take it on to the pitch. Plus there were people at the club telling him that to cause a public spat by letting the world know the extent of the problems at Anfield would not have been The Liverpool Way.

'Never mind that what was going on wasn't The Liverpool Way, it wasn't my way. I'm not one for doing big exclusives, making big noises and getting pats on the back from people saying "We're made up you said that." For me it's about when that whistle goes and you show the fans how much you want to be successful. That's my job.'

The fact that some fans accused him and Gerrard of cowardice still rankles with Carragher but, like his friend, he's not convinced that publicly registering his anger would have been the right thing to do: 'Maybe me and Stevie should have done more about it. Maybe we should have come out when we had the power, and said something. I don't know.

'It's different for me and Stevie. We're from here. We love the club and never like saying anything negative about it. Even if you're upset with things, as we were about the owners, you don't want to be seen to be criticising in public.

'It's what we believe in. So whatever happens, whatever is thrown at you, you feel you have to take it. It's like if someone in your family does something wrong you'll still stand behind them even if you want to slag them off.

'But as a foreigner you can understand the frustration. Getting promises about top players coming in then seeing top players leaving and not being replaced, I can see how they got frustrated. They must have been thinking they'd walked into a loony bin.

'But don't believe that they were all thinking like that. The really top ones were but some of the others weren't that bothered. Without wanting to criticise my own fellow professionals too much, footballers are different. Some of them would only have been unhappy with the Americans if the money wasn't going into their bank account. As long as they were getting paid they didn't worry.

'To be fair, if I was abroad I wouldn't be too bothered who the owners were as long as I was playing every week, getting my money and we were winning. I think the problem gets worse when the team isn't winning. When it's winning no one cares who the owners are.

'But my attitude is whatever's thrown at you you take and get on with it. In the 2008–9 season when we fell from second to seventh I wasn't looking at the owners, I was looking more at us, the players, the staff, the manager and thinking, "Hang on, what can we do?"

'We'll never know if it was a good or a bad thing that me and Stevie didn't speak out but no one could ever question our commitment to the club and the fans.'

The pair's major cause of worry was how the fans were suffering. They both come from big football families, have a wide circle of friends, and through being at the club since they were boys are close to hundreds of passionate Liverpool supporters. They could see how badly they were hurting.

Gerrard found it extremely depressing to see the fans marching and having sit-ins because it just wasn't what he was used to at Anfield. He'd seen it at other clubs but he never thought it would happen at his own.

'The lowest point was doing warm-downs after games. You see the Kop is half full and you get home and see it on the news. I was thinking, "Oh, come on, let's get these out, enough is enough, the sooner these are out the better." I'm thinking the way the fans are thinking but from a different perspective.'

It was during the post-game sit-ins after the last two home matches of Hicks and Gillett's reign, organised by the Spirit Of Shankly, that Gerrard and Carragher ditched any protocol and openly sided with the fans. The first followed a 2–2 draw with Sunderland in September 2010, the second after a turgid 2–1 defeat by Premier League newcomers Blackpool the following month.

As thousands of Kopites sang about lying bastards and Yanks

Out, the two Scousers applauded as they went past during their warm-down.

'We clapped them and we were always going to because we were on their side,' said Carragher. 'And to be fair to fans, no matter how frustrated they were, or how low they got, they were always on our side. They hardly ever vented their anger during games.

'But I was thinking when I read about us applauding them in the papers, "I hope no one thinks we were trying to get out of that performance against Blackpool."

'I hated it when people used to make excuses for us after a bad game by blaming the owners. I hated that because it wasn't about them, it was our responsibility. None of us were thinking about the ownership issue during the game.

'I don't think it helped but you can't tell me the ownership problem takes away from our individual performances. We've had great performances while they were there, great wins, we even finished second in the league. So we could never use them as an excuse on the day.'

Gerrard would never say the team was suffering because that would appear to be an easy cop-out for bad results, but he told people it didn't help when the players were talking about it on the way to games and the papers around the training ground were full of it.

He had to give team talks in the dressing room where he told players to forget all the stuff going on in the media, and to not let it affect their mind-set. All you can do, he told them, is go out there and get three points for the club.

The truth was the players knew a civil war was raging around them, battles were being fought in the boardroom, in the chief executive's and manager's offices, on the terraces, but also that it could never be used as an excuse for dismal form on the pitch. That said, they knew it didn't help, and it definitely got to them.

'In the end I stopped reading newspapers and just switched off because everything was so negative,' said Jamie Carragher. 'I wasn't reading about football, I was reading about backbiting and bitching and plots and people slagging each other off. The game wasn't getting played on the pitch but off it. Political games. It became a bad soap opera, didn't it?

'You're not just thinking about your game, you're thinking, "Whose side should I be on, who said what and did you hear this?" And I probably get too involved in that side of things because I speak to people all the time about football and Liverpool.

'Sometimes I wished I could just do my training and go home and think about nothing else but my game, but it became impossible. I was taking it all home with me.'

Towards the end Gerrard just wanted to see the back of Hicks and Gillett and never hear their names again. He often thought back to how positive he'd felt after that initial meeting with the new owners and, as he did, the anger would rise over all those promises which went unfulfilled. Promises like the new 70,000-seater stadium which he was told he would one day lead Liverpool into, and which he was asked to endorse.

'When I saw the design for the new stadium it looked unbelievable. I was thinking, "Wow, they're some plans them, imagine that stadium being up in two or three years."'

Although Jamie Carragher was also impressed by the plans, looking back he feels he and Gerrard were being slightly used by the Americans to win Scouse approval.

'We were the ones who were always dragged out to endorse things like new stadium plans, and I sensed they thought if me and Stevie say it's OK the fans will buy it. It was just another part of being pulled in different directions.'

But the stadium is the one area where Carragher feels a slight sympathy towards them: 'The stadium didn't remain unbuilt on purpose because they had nothing to gain by not building it. The stadium was the reason they came here in the first place because that's how they hoped to make their money. And I don't knock them for that.

'We all knew that was what they were after. They weren't here because they loved Liverpool, the great fans, our history, the players or Rafa. It was the stadium, pure and simple. It gave them a fantastic chance to make tons of cash and increase the value of the club.

'They're wealthy people who had worked and made money since leaving school, and realistically they were never going to come to Anfield and give us £150 million of their money to risk on the transfer market. That money was for their kids.

'I just think they made a stupid press comment about the spade being in the ground in sixty days. They were Parry's plans which they ripped up. A year later we see a new stadium which looked brilliant but then the credit crunch kicked in and it screwed them. They were never going to build the stadium out of their own money. No one does that. Look at Arsenal.'

How would he describe his relationship with the owners? 'I didn't have any relationship with them. I met Foster Gillett when he had an office at Melwood and he'd chat to us at lunch and ask questions about football. He was a very nice lad, and like most people at the club, I always tried to make him welcome. But with the owners, apart from that first meeting and the time Gillett pulled me over to his mates and asked me to "do my Scouse", I never really saw them. They just used to come to the game then get off.

'If I had to choose I'd say I preferred Gillett to Hicks simply because I hated the way Hicks was always talking on Sky, and I just wanted him to button it.'

Gerrard, too, preferred Gillett, because at least he would speak to him, ask how the team was doing and give words of encouragement.

Both players look back at Hicks and Gillett's reign less with outright anger than a deep sense of regret about what might have been for the club and for them.

'I think some of the fans were a bit naive,' said Carragher. 'Maybe they were so desperate to see change that they believed everything they were told. But these were ruthless businessmen who saw LFC as a golden opportunity to make money. It wasn't charity.

'Unless you're a Sheikh Mansour or a Roman Abramovich, when money really doesn't matter, you're not going to throw it around to keep people happy.

'The problem with them was putting the debt on the club. They tried to run it like just another business but football is different.

'At the start we couldn't complain about what we spent in the transfer market. We were buying players for around £20 million when we'd only ever paid £15 million at the most. But where that money was coming from is the question. It turned out it was the banks' money not theirs.

'We hoped they'd do it a different way and the team would

be successful and we'd have a new stadium. But the fact that they didn't put the funds in and tried to take it out the other end really wound me up.

'I was pleased they walked away with nothing because they had their chances to sell the club and make their profit but chose not to. Once the recession kicked in and the money dried up they were fighting for their lives. At that point they didn't care about Liverpool they just cared about themselves.'

They are sentiments you could never accuse Jamie Carragher or Steven Gerrard of. The fact that both players were paranoid about letting fans down through not taking a public stand tells you all you need to know. Few fans expected that stand to be taken. The vast majority saw it as their role to lead on the pitch and bring some hope and happiness among the gloom and despair. Plus they knew that at least one of those two was as disillusioned with the manager as he was with the owners. So it was wise, The Liverpool Way even, to not act like those above them, maintain some dignity, and concentrate on doing your job.

There were many shades of grey in this civil war, many uncertainties and untruths, but one shines out like a beacon. Carragher and Gerrard are two of the finest players ever to wear the red shirt, and they are as much victims of Hicks's and Gillett's empty promises as the fans are.

These two, the only genuine stars to come through Liverpool's youth system since the 1990s, were the main reasons (along with Benitez's tactical acumen) that Liverpudlians travelled to Istanbul and had the greatest night of their lives.

Back then, in May 2005, Gerrard was about to turn twenty-five, Carragher had just turned twenty-seven. They were heading into their golden years which, after such a Champions League victory, should have meant a cabinet full of medals, including a Premier League title winner's. But the club never built on that phenomenal triumph and when it believed it had, by selling to Hicks and Gillett, it was a cruel delusion.

Gerrard and Carragher stayed loyal to the club, but who of those running the club stayed loyal to the promises they gave to keep them there?

They don't like saying that Hicks and Gillett, and by implication those who naively sold Liverpool, cost them the Premier League, in case it sounds like they're making excuses. So let me say it for them: thanks to the combined failings of the last two sets of owners and directors, Steven Gerrard and Jamie Carragher were robbed of their birthright as Liverpool legends.

CHAPTER ELEVEN

'Blow me, fuck face. Go to hell. I'm sick of you'
— Tom Hicks Jr.

January 9 2010 was a typical Saturday morning in the Horner household in Loughton, Essex. Steve, a 29-year-old freelance quantity surveyor, woke up at half past eight, walked into the kitchen of his two-bedroom apartment, made a cup of tea, went into the lounge and switched on his computer.

With his girlfriend out at work and his six-year-old daughter staying at her grandma's, it was time for a spot of self-indulgence (this is not going where you think). He clicked on to the *Liverpool Echo* website for the latest news about the team whose spell he fell under when John Barnes was torturing full-backs back in the 1980s, and was drawn to the headline on Dominic King's Blood Red column, 'Rafa Benitez should not have to manage Liverpool's debts'.

He clicked again, took a slug of tea, and read a very interesting piece about Birmingham City bidding £9 million for Ryan Babel, which Liverpool had rejected because they felt he was worth closer to £12 million, despite the vast majority of

Liverpool supporters thinking Brummie hands should have been snapped off at the wrist.

As King pointed out, the reason Rafa Benitez chose not to sell him at that price was because he knew he wouldn't have been given a penny of it to spend, as it would all have gone towards interest payments on the £240 million debt. The manager's only chance of getting a transfer kitty that January, he argued, was to buy a Lottery ticket and cross his fingers.

For the third window running Benitez was told to forget about quality signings and sniff around for loans or free transfers. In the end he brought in Maxi Rodriguez for next to nothing, despite raising £6.4 million by offloading flops Andriy Voronin and Andrea Dossena. The message to fans being: forget about trophies, all we want to do is pay down the debts.

King warned that were Liverpool to miss out on qualifying for the Champions League that season (which they did) and some of the star players were sold to make up the shortfall in revenue (one was), they would struggle to keep up with the best teams in England (they have) and could end up falling off the European map (we'll see).

He ended his excellent and, for a local paper, brave article with this statement: 'What is not right is a club with Liverpool's history and pedigree being forced to rummage around for bargains with nothing other than loose change.'

Steve Horner had nodded throughout and, although a mild-mannered man, felt his anger levels rising. He got up, walked around his flat, and thought about getting on with his day but he couldn't. It had got to him. The Spirit Of Shankly member had been going to Anfield since 1990 but hadn't set foot in the

ground or bought any club products since 2008, in protest at
the Hicks and Gillett ownership.

He would vent his anger sporadically on the Liverpool Way
website forums and had occasionally sent emails to members
of the Hicks and Gillett clans, striking up a dialogue with Tom
Hicks's son Mack. There was nothing abusive or aggressive in
the missives, because that wasn't his style. He just sent them
critical observations about their business model and asked con-
structive questions about the future. This had been the last one
he'd sent them on 22 December 2009:

> Gents,
>
> When are you going to let Liverpool fans know what is going on at
> the club?
>
> Our club is in crisis both on and off the field with the team strug-
> gling, the manager's future up in the air, and talk of £60m repayments
> not met last summer coupled with £310m worth of debt loaded onto
> the club as a result of your leveraged buy-out.
>
> It is time to talk to us fans or sell up for the GOOD OF THE CLUB.
>
> If you love Liverpool FC as we do then be straight with us. You will
> gain more respect that way.
>
> Regards,
>
> Steve

King's column had stirred something in him and he knew what
he had to do. So at 9.12 a.m. he sat down at his screen, copied
and pasted what he believed to be the pertinent points of the
article, with a link to the *Echo* website, added no comment of
his own, and sent it to Tom Hicks, George Gillett and Tom
Hicks Jr.

He wasn't expecting a response as none of them had ever replied to him in the past, but it felt good to get it off his chest. He went back into the kitchen, stared at the snow outside, and made himself some toast and porridge. At 9.30 a.m. he went back to his computer and noticed he had mail. From Tom Hicks Jr. Which surprised him, especially with it being 3.30 a.m. in America. When he opened the email surprise turned to shock. There was a single-word reply: 'Idiot.'

After eight minutes spent staring at the screen trying to digest the implication of this response to a fan from a member of Liverpool FC's board of directors, and trying to work out whether it was a hoax, or if he'd sent it to another Tom Ollis Hicks Jr., he decided to email back.

Thanks for your prompt response Tom. Your command of the English language is nearly as good as your knowledge of English football and Liverpool FC. Why not address some of the points raised in the piece written by Dominic King in the Liverpool Echo or has it touched a nerve?

And then he sat hunched, like an angler on a riverbank, and waited. Four minutes later, he hooked a whopper:

'Blow me, fuck face. Go to hell. I'm sick of you.'

The shit had hit the fan (kind of literally) and the blow came at him like a Yosser Hughes headbutt. 'I was just left absolutely stunned, but when it sank in I was really saddened that a Liverpool director could respond to a supporter in such a manner,' said Horner.

He was now certain it was from Hicks Jr., as the email was copied in to the club's finance director Philip Nash and commercial director Ian Ayre. He had clearly caught him off-guard at a bad time, probably, with it being 3.40 a.m. over there, just before going to bed in a 'tired and emotional state' (as bank managers' wives say after necking a bottle of Gordon's gin and burning hubby's Ford Mondeo for leaving a deposit in his secretary's drawers).

Horner paced around, thinking what to do next. Did he really have dynamite here? Could he prove it was Hicks? What should he do with it? He needed to speak with someone, but was home alone, so he decided to share the email exchange with fellow fans by posting on the Liverpool Way forum.

'I have just received the following response from Tom Hicks Junior when I emailed him the link to Dominic King's piece in the *Liverpool Echo* this morning. What a charming individual he is. I think it touched a nerve,' Steve wrote in a commendably understated style.

The story now assumed an unstoppable momentum. He phoned Paul Rice at the Spirit Of Shankly who alerted his media contacts. He emailed sympathetic journalists like Chris Bascombe, who assured him the Hicks address was genuine and that the *News of the World* would be running the story the next day.

'I sensed blood and felt that this could be a small but significant breakthrough in our attempts to oust Hicks and Gillett,' said Horner.

'I was dying to put a nail in their coffin because I hated them with a passion for the damage that they were causing to my football club. They had eroded away my passion for football and for Liverpool FC and I was desperate for them to sell up and never darken our door again.'

Shortly before nine p.m. Texas time, with the Sunday newspapers out on the streets and, more importantly, the worldwide web screaming headlines such as 'Blow me **** face. Go to Hell. I'm sick of you' (*News of the World*) and 'Hicks jnr in email war with furious Reds fans' (*Mail on Sunday*), Tom Jr. crawled back to his computer and hit the grovel key:

> Stephen,
>
> I apologize for losing my temper and using bad language with you.
> It was a kneejerk reaction.
> Tommy.

Freuds, the expensive PR agency charged with the impossible task of improving Hicks's and Gillett's image, was now on the case. And they needed to go into overdrive on the Monday after the Sunday papers carried the line that Liverpool FC were declining to comment on the matter.

During that Sunday, *The Times*' football editor, Tony Evans, had tried to contact the club's managing director Christian Purslow for a statement, only to be told he wouldn't be saying anything because he was 'having a Me Day'. Evans was so infuriated he wanted to run the 'Me Day' response in the paper but was talked out of it.

The Spirit Of Shankly condemned what they called a 'conspiracy of silence' and released a statement demanding the immediate resignation of Hicks Jr.

'It is a great surprise and an even greater disappointment that Liverpool FC have thus far failed to make any comment on what we feel is a very serious matter,' said SOS spokesman James McKenna.

'Is this what the club has come to, that a board member can speak in such derogatory terms to a supporter but can go without censure or any public criticism? The conspiracy of silence which has followed this unsavoury incident is totally unbecoming of a club which has always prided itself on its relationship with the fans.

'Are we to presume that the Liverpool hierarchy condones the comments made by Tom Hicks Jr. or is it simply a case that the deeply flawed regime of Hicks and Gillett has left the entire club in a state of paralysis? Surely the very least the Liverpool supporters deserve is an open and honest explanation from the club, an indication on their feelings about the objectionable behaviour of such a senior member of the board and a commitment that such an incident will not happen again.'

Within hours the club responded by removing Hicks Jr. from the board and replacing him with Casey Coffman, the executive VP of Hicks Holdings, who had recently revealed to an interviewer that her favourite book was A *Confederacy of Dunces*. Meaning she was perfectly qualified to fly into the Anfield loony bin.

That wasn't the end of it for Poor (non) Scouser Tommy, though, who was forced into a second grovel, this time to the entire Liverpool fan-base.

'I have great respect for Liverpool Football Club, especially the club's supporters,' he said in a statement which had clearly been written for him by one of the various PR firms working for his father.

'I apologise for my mistake and I am very sorry for my harmful words. I do not want my actions to take away from the club's future; therefore I am resigning from the board. To the fans and to the club, please accept my sincerest apologies.'

Unsurprisingly, the Spirit Of Shankly snubbed his act of contrition, calling instead on his father and his co-owner to resign: 'Tom Hicks and George Gillett bought the club and talked of respecting the legacy and tradition, as well as family values by passing the club on to their children. If these are the kind of values they see fit for Liverpool Football Club, and this is how they respect our legacies and traditions, it underlines the need to remove them from the club.'

The impact of Blow Me Fuckface-gate (as it should have been christened) cannot be underestimated. To most outsiders, and some Liverpool fans, all Hicks Jr. had done was give an honest (if utterly naive and suicidal) reaction to receiving grief from a faceless enemy. Even Jamie Carragher, who over the years, like all footballers, has had to bite his tongue when fans have got on his case, saw the funny side. 'I laughed my head off when I heard about it. I know it upset the fan but we've probably all come in after a row with our missus at three in the morning, read someone slagging you off on an email and thought of doing that.'

But it gave the Spirit Of Shankly and other protesting fans hope, during a lull in hostilities, that if they could force a Hicks to resign from the board over his thuggish behaviour, then wider change could be effected. It reminded the more gullible Liverpool fans who saw the likes of the SOS as reckless militants, and still gave the Americans the benefit of the doubt, exactly what the club's owners thought of them. And it made members of the wider footballing community, some of whom were beginning to pigeonhole protesting Kopites as whingeing

Scousers who had been fooled by Benitez into demonising his paymasters, rethink their opinion.

Certain London-based commentators, who resented Liverpool fans for believing they were part of a unique and special tribe, were sceptical. They claimed there must have been more to the email exchange than was being offered up. This Spirit Of Shankly man was obviously a bolshie crypto-communist who had been bombarding this poor stressed-out American with a blizzard of vile abuse and the guy snapped. But the email exchange (which was never contested by the owners or the club) disproved such a theory. Horner had simply exposed Hicks Jr. as the arrogant, moronic charlatan he was.

Tony Evans sees it as the defining phrase of their tenure: 'It summed up to perfection their attitude to Liverpool fans. They completely saw us as commodities. If someone drops off so what, someone else will come in and take their place. They didn't realise that football is about more than that. OK, the lad was probably being a bit of a pest but there you had the moment that told you what it was all about.'

Hours after Tom Jr.'s resignation was announced, his father responded to another supporter who had emailed him with concerns about Benitez's lack of spending power: 'Our debt is very manageable (see Man U) and we never use player sales for debt service. Our interest on £200m is about £16m. The new stadium will be the game changer. Christian Purslow is working very hard on it. January is a poor-quality market. The summer window will be big.'

It wasn't. But that wasn't the point. After Blow Me Fuckface-gate the fans stopped listening. That one outburst had stripped away any pretence of decency or any doubts about their attitude to the fans. No Tom Hicks–Alan Myers cosy fireside chat espousing his family's love of the city and its people, no slick PR statement, no folksy email exchange with a fan could disguise their utter derision and contempt for Liverpool and everyone connected with it.

It cut through the pretence and said it like it was. We are the Masters of The Universe, you are the plankton which feeds our pool of wealth and elevates us even further from your scummy existence.

Like many other Liverpool fans, by early 2010, with no sign of the Americans leaving and the team looking increasingly likely to fall out of the Champions League places with frightening consequences, Horner was suffering from a genuine depression. The emails and the change they forced on the Hicks family gave him a huge lift.

'I was getting seriously depressed about the situation because I really love the club, I hated what was being done to it and I couldn't see a way out,' said Steve. 'To think one harmless email from me had resulted in one of the Americans being thrown off the board really picked me up. More than that it whetted my appetite to do more to get the rest of them out.'

However, there was a downside to Steve's new-found fame. He was hit with a barrage of emails, phone calls, messages and interview requests from the world's media and struggled to cope with the intrusion.

That was when a fellow SOS member and Liverpool Way poster Mick Carroll got in touch and advised him on what to expect and how to handle it. Mick had achieved notoriety four months earlier, under his forum pseudonym Dougie Do'ins, by confronting George Gillett at the Academy, taping an interview with him on his mobile phone and posting the transcript on the Liverpool Way site. To say Gillett emerged from it as a slippery buffoon would be a severe understatement.

It was the morning of the 6–1 home rout of Hull at the end of September 2009 when the boy from Wisconsin was showing his latest non-buyer, Saudi prince Faisal al-Fahad bin Abdullah bin Saud, and his entourage, around his Merseyside empire. The Spirit Of Shankly had got word that the party were at Melwood and fifteen members drove there in the hope of putting some questions to him and letting him know that cowboys, their debts and their evasions, weren't welcome here.

When Gillett and his party emerged from the training ground the protestors unleashed some verbal volleys. 'Gillett's face was a picture which I'll never, ever forget,' said Mick Carroll. 'It was one of total shock. He just never saw it coming and you could see he was embarrassed.'

The party sped off to the Academy with the SOS in pursuit, but when they arrived at Kirkby the fans were barred from entering. So they stood outside staring in, waiting to catch a glimpse of the enemy. When Gillett appeared on a balcony Carroll shouted: 'George would you mind answering a few questions about the club's finances?' and to his great surprise he said: 'I'll speak to you but I'm not speaking to any of your friends.' He recognised a few of the faces, like Jay McKenna's, from past confrontations and he didn't fancy going head to head with them again.

This was Gillett doing his Man of The People act, no doubt attempting to put flesh on the statements he'd just fed to his Arab guests about having an open and honest rapport with his punters. He asked Carroll his name and two minutes later he was at the door, shaking his hand and inviting him inside. Obviously the first thing that caught Mick's eye was the owner's alternative footwear.

'He had these massive boots on,' said Carroll. 'I think he had them on to give himself a bit of height or something but he shook my hand and then stood on my foot. I'm not sure whether it was deliberate or not.'

Gillett ushered him upstairs into an office and with the pleasantries out of the way, Carroll demanded to know where all the money that should be going to the manager for his transfer budget had disappeared to. Gillett came back with, 'Let's try and have you take your attitude out of these questions' before blitzing his interrogator with a string of facts and figures most of which had no bearing on reality.

'When we bought the club it was with our own money. Cash. A year and a half later, when the credit crisis hit we each put our portion of the club up as collateral for a loan to go into the club and refinance the business. Today, the club has the lowest to each dollar of profit of any of the major clubs in this sport.

'We have all the debt documents. The club is in an extraordinarily good financial condition. Far better than United, Chelsea or Arsenal.

'The club had £40–80 million debt when we bought it, but no earnings. We have invested massively. We have put more money in than anyone, than Man City with the craziness they have got.

'The vast majority came from Tom and me and our personal cash, not the club, not from borrowings.

'The question is how is the debt relative to the earnings. If you have a mortgage on your house and you don't have a job, that mortgage is in jeopardy. If you have a mortgage on your house and a very good job, that mortgage is very sound. The debt on this club is very sound.'

Carroll was recording him on his mobile phone, which Gillett hadn't spotted. Until it rang out and he fumbled to switch it off.

'Hey! That's not switched on, is it?' asked Gillett.

'No, it's a mobile phone. I'm just rejecting a call,' replied a red-faced Carroll.

The then 41-year-old fan didn't feel it was going well. For years he had dreamt of getting one of the owners in the room and grilling them (sometimes literally). Now he had Gillett alone, but felt he was being blinded by science. He told him he didn't recognise his figures and that the fans and the media saw the funding of the club in a completely different light.

'That's bullshit. The media don't understand how to write about cash flow and profit and loss. Good idea to come and say where the club is at. Not being drip-fed anything by me. I tried to support our manager and let him have freedom of rule to spend the money in his way, as wisely as he can, to do the proper scouting and get us the best young men he can. That's what we try to do. I don't get into strategy or individual players.

'I've tried to keep to The Liverpool Way, being silent in the background and providing funds for the manager. The status of the club, the general financial condition, the debt versus earnings is the only thing that matters.

'Our budgets are taken over the last six years of the club, we're not planning on getting to Champions League finals or anything like that. The budgets are done conservatively. It is based upon a relatively limited run in the Champions League. The debt wouldn't go up without Champions League football. We have enough cash flow to pay the minimum interest we have, which is not very high, to give Rafa the capital he needs.

'If I told you that Arsenal by law cannot spend as much as we do, United cannot spend any more than we can, would you say we are underspending?'

Carroll pushed him on the previous summer's lack of transfer activity, claiming all the money that was spent had been recouped in sales. Gillett replied:

'The £30 million went straight back in from Alonso. We didn't do what Man Utd did. They took all of their money from the player sale and owed so much money they had to use it to pay down the debt.

'We have invested in keeping with the history of the club more money than our competitors, which means it should be getting better. Now if it's not getting better, it's not Gillett and Hicks, it's the manager, it's the scouting. So make sure you balance out your analysis.

'It is the case that the money went back in. Rafa had the money from Xabi plus another £22–23 million this close season in addition to the money that came from selling to buy players. There is no leakage in the system – whatever came in plus whatever we had given him as part of our budgets he had available.

'We have spent net between £20 and 25 million. I had probably the best writer in the country call me this last week asking why people are trying to demean the true level of spending. The £20 million-plus is not a cap, it's an estimate. When you put a budget together on your house and you decide you're going to spend a little more here and a little less there, it's not a cap, it's a goal, a programme for spending.

'A budget is what it is, and it's the same in a business. We spent more than the £20 million cap in our budget, plus all the money from sales, so there was plenty of money, so any complaints you have you should take a look at the ins and outs. Hicks and I did not take any money out to pay down debt, there was no money taken out. It's all been spent on players.'

Carroll attempted to cut through this lengthy spiel by asking if he had invested any of his own money in the club, and he replied by saying he refused to go there. He then told him Liverpool was falling behind the other big clubs, which Gillett utterly refuted.

'What are you talking about? We have more cash flow than they do. You want a bigger stadium and if we could figure how to do it I would have done it yesterday. Not going to use our own capital because that is not the way a smart investment occurs for this club.

'Look at Roman Abramovich; he is massively wealthy. He didn't put his own money in. He used loans to borrow the money from Russian banks, and that's why he's in so much trouble.

'We have put £128 million in to buy players on top of what's come in in the last eighteen months. The media write about it, they criticise us relative to United and Arsenal, but we're putting more money in than they are. Let's focus on one set of challenges. When I was in Spain trying to understand the economics of those clubs I realised that they spend crazily every five years and get bailed out. It's now in its third cycle and it's not going to happen here to have the government step in. That's a model that's difficult to compete with on a short-term basis. That money is all borrowed from the government. We will give Rafa enough that through his genius we hope to be competitive.'

The figures, statistics and historical rewrites were coming Carroll's way at such a speed he couldn't digest them, so he switched to a subject he knew would embarrass Gillett. The stadium and his vow to have a shovel in the ground in sixty days.

At this point Gillett lost it slightly, coming out with words like 'horseshit' and denying he ever used the sixty-day phrase, claiming it was Hicks who said it. Carroll, having seen him say it on a video recording of the initial press conference, told Gillett it was him.

'It was Hicks who said that sixty days. Bullshit. That was not me. It's wrong. I have never talked about that,' he replied, only for Carroll to reiterate it was. His stubborn refusal to cede ground on the issue carried on for a while but Gillett was so convincing Carroll began to question his own sanity, telling him if he was wrong, he apologised, despite being able to see him say it in his mind's eye.

Which allowed Gillett to go on the attack: 'I think that what happened was that Hicks was convinced we were going to start to move dirt on the foundations within a sixty-day period. In the period of time, the world credit market collapsed and he had big egg on his face, not living up to what we said. I don't talk about absolute dates when we're talking about credit markets.

'When a bank issues you a commitment on a mortgage there are lots of commitments. One of those is a *force majeure*, which means that if the world falls apart, that commitment doesn't mean anything. That could have been claimed to have happened to us.

'Is that what this whole controversy is about, about Tom Hicks saying sixty days? Do you think I don't want to build a new stadium? Nothing is going to happen, good or bad, that we don't take credit or blame for. I want to build a new stadium as soon as the commercial markets allow. I can't speak for Hicks, but you can tell I would love to build a new stadium.'

He then asked, 'What's so symbolic about the stadium?' which completely threw Carroll.

'I just thought, "You mustn't have had any intention of building a stadium if you've just asked that question," because that point would have been paramount when they were dealing with banks trying to get finance to back up the building of the new stadium. I think he was that used to talking rubbish about the situation that he believed his own bullshit.'

Carroll was, by then, feeling confused and uncomfortable and wanted to get out. Before doing so he warned Gillett that he may have fans queuing up to get into Anfield right now but if the team was to go through a couple of seasons of mediocrity the good-time day-trippers would soon disappear.

Inevitably Gillett put on his best understanding face and tried to reassure him that he was panicking in vain and has misjudged the owners. 'You shouldn't be worried. You may not like me and may not trust me, but what I have said is fact. I have never taken a cent from this club. I get no salary, no compensation. The money taken out is for the benefit of the club, not the detriment. The fact was that Hicks promised a stadium in sixty days. The cash flow, the money reinvested, etc., which came from the media were wrong. A dumping on me of vitriol, suspicion, calling me a liar on half a dozen different counts. The one thing I plead guilty to is that I have a partner promised a spade in the ground within sixty days and then credit markets collapsed. There's no way I can deny that. But the rest of the things he and his group have got very angry with because of things reported that were inaccurate. He was charging me with taking money out of the club, but I take nothing out of the club.'

He then implied it wasn't he or Hicks who were threatening the club's future but groups like the Spirit Of Shankly, before issuing a plea for everyone at Anfield to live together in peace, love and harmony:

'You're not on the inside. Why can't we figure out a way for you guys to understand we are better off working together? When you guys go and protest and we have a commercial interest in, they say why would we invest in that club?'

Carroll thanked him for his time, they shook hands, and Gillett had a warm smile that said, 'Gee, sucker, thanks for the opportunity to do a little PR job in front of the Arabs.' The American probably thought that would pretty much be that, but then Dougie Do'ins went home, transcribed the conversation from his phone, posted it on the forum and all of his bullshit and horseshit made its way into the national media.

Fans can accept football illiteracy from their owners because they know the vast majority are only in it for kudos or profit. They can also excuse a lack of cash, if, like David Moores or Everton's Bill Kenwright, they're in it mostly for love. They can even live with arrogance, aloofness and a poor knowledge of the club. But they cannot accept having the truth distorted or hidden from them.

The vast majority of what Gillett had said to Carroll fell into that category. Here were five statements which didn't stand up to scrutiny:

'The debt on this club is very sound.' It was £44.8million when he took over. By then it had reached £245 million and rising.

'It was Hicks who said that [about the stadium]. Sixty days? Bullshit. That was not me. It's wrong. I have never talked about that.' As tens of thousands of clicks on YouTube then showed, it was Gillett. Check it out.

'We have put £128 million in to buy players on top of what's come in in the last 18 months.' Rafa Benitez's net spend during that period had been £20 million.

'The club is in an extraordinarily good financial position.' So how come the Royal Bank of Scotland had told him and Hicks to find new investment, sell up or they would repossess the club?

'[The club is doing] far better than Manchester United, Chelsea and Arsenal.' The Glazers may have burdened United with huge debts but the club was still an enormous money-making concern, with a vast global fan base and 75,000 fans at every home game. Chelsea had a pocket as deep as a Siberian gas field and Arsenal was the best-run club in Britain. In the previous financial year they had generated profits of £38 million and what debt they had revolved around a state-of-the-art, 60,000-capacity stadium, which ensured a golden future.

Meanwhile, Liverpool was crippled with interest payments

of £35 million-plus and nowhere near starting on a new stadium three years after the Americans arrived. Plus they were run by two men who couldn't stand the sight of each other and whose sole intentions were selling up at a profit.

Gillett's deceit just added insult to the many injuries. Like Steve Horner, Mick Carroll had, through determination, initiative and luck, exposed the contempt felt by the American board members to the fans. Both were morale-boosting victories for Spirit Of Shankly at a time when their critics were asking if they had become just another self-indulgent talking shop. Following the early meetings with senior Anfield figures and a whirlwind of media coverage things had quietened down.

There had been leafleting at matches and fund-raising events to help free Michael Shields – the Liverpool fan wrongly imprisoned for attacking a Bulgarian waiter after the 2005 Champions League Final, who was pardoned and released from prison in September 2009. The union's provision of cheap travel to away games was proving very successful, they were about to unleash a brilliant 'Debts. Lies. Cowboys. Not Welcome Here' poster campaign on billboards across Merseyside and because of SOS intelligence, Hicks and Gillett knew they couldn't come to Anfield without unleashing chaos.

But radical members wanted to adopt a more aggressive approach by taking the fight directly to the Americans, and Spirit Of Shankly organisers knew that smarter, more lateral, thinking was called for. Blow me Fuckface and the Academy ambush, or rather how those two incidents became huge news stories, made the fans realise they had another, highly potent weapon in their armoury: the internet. Steve Horner got together with Mick Carroll, another SOS member, Alan Kayll, the Liverpool Way forum organiser Dave Usher, forum posters Simon Green, Andy Perrin, Dan Thomas, Richard White and Jon Salmon to form Kop Faithful. Their numbers would later be boosted by a group from the Red and White Kop website called Save LFC.

The idea of Kop Faithful was to build up a following of like-minded fans who wanted to take direct action through organised internet campaigns. They were the Provos to the Spirit Of Shankly's Sinn Fein. A splinter group, which ended up with 15,000 recruits and could engage in the kind of swift, concerted cyber attacks the constitutionally bound union could not be seen to be condoning.

The SOS had its SAS and The Noise was about to get louder.

CHAPTER TWELVE

'What have I got to apologise for? Everyone told us
they were good for their money'

– David Moores

Mick Carroll and Alan Kayll had cased the house three days
after Blow Me Fuckface-gate broke, and could see no problems.

It nestled in a secluded spot on a country road leading up
to Southport. Opposite were fields, to the sides and rear were
scrub and woodland, and behind the electronic gates lay a green-
lined path up to the front door of the large family home.

They would undoubtedly be caught on CCTV but then what
offence were they committing? Was it wrong to throw 10,000
mock £10 notes carrying a cartoon of a man being handed
bags of loot as two shady figures whisper 'Come on, Dave, the
club will be in good hands with me and Tom' into that man's
garden?

Was it a criminal offence, or merely an expression of one's
democratic right to protest, to throw an 8ft x 4ft banner over
his gates with the slogan 'Hope The Extra £8million Was Worth
It Dave'?

The two independent-minded Spirit Of Shankly members

didn't believe it was. So at 10.30 a.m. on a bitterly cold January Sunday morning, Mick parked his Citroën Picasso in a nearby sports field, Alan grabbed the flag from the back seat, and the two heavily dressed forty-somethings advanced on David Moores' house to do a deed they'd been wanting to do for more than two years: shame the man who sold their club.

No sooner had they crossed the road than a thought hit them. Maybe they should give him a chance to defend himself. Maybe, before showering his manicured garden in bent notes and covering up the initialled motifs on his gates with their flag, they should ring the intercom and ask him to explain his actions and his intentions?

As long shots go it was up there with a Xabi Alonso halfway-line chip, into the wind with Petr Cech in goal, but then so was Mick's interview request to George Gillett and that had hit the back of the net. Besides, Moores must have been aware of the growing anger towards Hicks and Gillett over their refusal to let go of their prized asset, and therefore the growing anger aimed at him.

For almost three years he had refused to break his silence. Shying away from the microphone was nothing new to the hermit-like Moores, who had even refused to do interviews the morning after Istanbul, his ultimate moment as Liverpool chairman. But he could feel the enmity all around on Merseyside and he was crippled inside over his monumental error. He'd even stopped visiting Anfield, the focal point of his life, since resigning from the board around the same time as Rick Parry in June 2009. With skin thinner than an ultra-smooth, featherlite condom, he was buckling under the weight of criticism and guilt. A deeply unhappy man, undoubtedly.

Mick pressed the intercom buzzer. After a short silence, a well-spoken mature woman's voice asked who it was. They said they were Liverpool fans who wanted to have a word with David. The woman, David's wife Marge, told them politely that that would not be possible because her husband had been instructed by his solicitor to say nothing on the subject.

As Carroll and Kayll did their best to persuade her, it became clear she was worried they were undercover journalists trying to trap her husband into breaking his silence. They told her they were nothing of the sort, just a pair of lifelong fans, now in their forties, trying every avenue possible to save the club that they and her husband loved from falling into the abyss.

As she stared at the CCTV pictures, three options presented themselves to her. She could be looking at a pair of lying reporters, a pair of *Crimewatch* suspects, or genuine fans with innocent intentions. She took an instinctive gamble and told them to wait. If they were who they said they were, and they did only want to talk about the future, they may actually help her husband break free from the dark thoughts that must have been tormenting his peace of mind.

Minutes later, David Moores' deep Scouse voice was heard over the intercom, asking them what they wanted. Alan replied: 'We're here because the club is on its knees and we think it's time you came out and said something. You helped put us into this mess, David, you've got to try to get us out of it.'

As he interrogated them through the intercom, convinced he was being set up and any words he said would end up twisted in tomorrow's papers, Mick persuaded him to come outside, speak to them face to face and discover for himself that they were just a pair of genuine fans.

So there they were on this bleak January morning, two fans talking through the railings to a broken man, as though visiting an old lag in Walton. Both Carroll and Kayll were unnerved at how fragile and weak Moores appeared and went easy on him. As they stared at a man who looked like he hadn't found much sleep since his last visit to Anfield, both felt relieved they hadn't forced him to confront the flag and the notes. Christ knows how ill he'd be looking now if they hadn't rung his intercom.

The conversation was amicable. They put their point across, telling him they weren't interested in going back over old ground and assigning blame for what had happened three years before. They were only thinking about the future and what they could do to keep the heat on the Americans. Moores was told that if he were to call for them to sell up in a reasoned and passionate way, it could hasten their removal.

They hammered home the point that he had a part to play in salvaging something from this mess and if he could do that, he might salvage his reputation. They sensed his reluctance, his fear that if he spoke out – especially during a season when they were challenging for honours – and it backfired, or his motives were misinterpreted, he would be accused of creating even more damage.

Mick and Alan told him that was impossible, because things couldn't get any worse than they already were, and he owed it to every Liverpudlian to say something. Moores pointed out that he had emailed the Americans when he stood down from the board, telling them he was disgusted with the way they were running the club and he wouldn't be attending any more games while they were in charge. They didn't even afford him the courtesy of a reply.

Something that disturbed Alan Kayll, who had been scathing about the ease with which Moores had sold the family silver, was how he became offended when they told him a good first step with the fans would be an apology. 'What have I got to apologise for?' he asked. 'Everyone told us they were good for their money, even the bankers Rothschild's.'

His refusal to acknowledge personal error almost bordered on the arrogant, but what Moores did take on board was his need to speak out against Hicks and Gillett, and he told the pair he would give it serious thought. They left their contact details, told him he had nothing to lose and much to gain, and he said he'd be in touch. They shook hands through the railings, headed back home and posted details of the meeting on the Liverpool Way website.

Alan emailed another SOS member, Kevin Sampson, who had been friendly with Moores for many years, and asked him to vouch for the pair. A fortnight later a meeting was arranged in the Catholic Cathedral's cafe with Rick Parry and Sampson flanking Moores. This time the mood was more relaxed. Moores had read about the Academy ambush of George Gillett and asked Mick Carroll if he should be frisking him for a wire. His wife had also read out some of the comments Alan Kayll had posted about him on the Liverpool Way forum, forcing Moores to jokingly ask if he was packing a baseball bat.

Once again they hammered home the message that he couldn't just sit there doing nothing because he had a responsibility to help the fans he had sold short. They asked him why he made the calamitous mistake of selling to Hicks and Gillett, when all the available information showed that at least one of them was the opposite of a fine custodian of sports clubs. The one who had had his face plastered all over *Time* magazine above the headline 'Leverage Buyout King Tom Hicks'.

Moores wasn't evasive and there was no scripted defence running though his head. He kept repeating the fact that the prestigious firm Rothschild had said they were good for their money. After a while spent dwelling on the past, Carroll and Kayll told him that whoever was or wasn't to blame for Liverpool being in a hole, had become irrelevant. It was now about how they were going to get out of it. You have to make a statement, they told Moores, or the club you say you love so much will be finished.

Moores conceded the fact, but when they asked him to do it immediately he was reticent. Mr Paranoid feared if the season went badly wrong after he'd spoken, or if prospective buyers pulled out amid a media storm, fingers would be pointed at him.

All agreed that the best timing would be at the end of May when the season was over. Without any format being discussed they shook hands and went their separate ways, knowing at least one miracle had taken place in the house of God – Alan Kayll had bought a round of five coffees, two of them for Moores and Parry.

Down in London, another Liverpudlian had been chipping away at Moores to break his silence. Since the previous summer *The Times*' Tony Evans had been writing letters urging him to do a piece in the newspaper aimed at putting pressure on Hicks and Gillett to sell.

Evans, who had written the excellent LFC book *Far Foreign Land*, heard the intensity of the criticism Moores was receiving and despaired. Not for the Littlewoods heir, whom he felt had 'ballsed up big style' in selling the club to the Americans, but over the destructive in-fighting that was tearing Liverpool fans apart. He thought that for all of Moores' faults he could be a key unifying figure.

'I knew that he was devastated,' said Evans. 'People talk about the extra £8 million he got for not selling to DIC but I reckon he'd burn that, and more, just to turn back the clock.'

The Times' man's plan was to get him in a room and do a *Reservoir Dogs*-style interrogation on him in the hope he would become so emotional he'd say anything Evans wanted him to. And what he wanted him to say above all else was that he may have made a huge mistake but it wasn't him who was killing the club now. It was the Royal Bank of Scotland.

His ideal scenario was to have the entire back page of *The Times* saying Hicks and Gillett may be shysters but they're shysters who are being propped up by a state-owned bank that has been bailed out by tax-payers. Nail that, he believed, and it could really force the already disgraced RBS to put the pressure on the Americans to sell.

On three occasions Moores agreed to meet Evans before pulling out because he couldn't go through with it. With Liverpool's season over, Evans made one last attempt to persuade Moores to do the decent thing.

Three days later, *The Times*' sports desk took a phone call saying Moores didn't want to do an interview but he had spent all night writing a long letter which they were free to publish. Typically, Moores didn't have email. So, in time-honoured transfer style, he faxed it through.

On first sight Evans was disappointed because Moores wasn't saying what he'd wanted him to say. But then he read it properly, and reread it, and realised it wasn't so much what Moores was saying, but how he was saying it, that was poignant. The power of the letter came from the fact this was Moores speaking, for the first time, from the heart, and in his own words.

On 26 May 2010, five years and a day since Istanbul, *The Times* ran his entire letter under the headline 'For the sake of the supporters, let Liverpool go'.

Dear Tony,

Thanks for getting in touch again. I'm writing to you not out of any mission to clear my name – if I felt I had anything to apologise for I would have done so, without hesitation, a long, long time ago. I'm sending this to you, in good faith, because my family, particularly the younger members, are continually being wounded by the combination of hearsay, mistruth and malicious gossip regarding my decision to sell the club, and the process that led the sale.

I'm writing because it's 5 years this week since the miracle of Istanbul – my greatest moment as a fan and as Chairman of Liverpool Football Club – but which now feels light years away from happening again. But above all I'm writing to you because I care deeply about the club, the team and the fans. I hope against hope that Messrs Gillett and Hicks will see this letter, or some portion of it, and do the right thing. In holding on and holding out, they risk damaging a sporting institution of global renown and if they have any conscience or nobility they will stand aside and allow new owners to take over the club for its future benefit and that of its lifeblood – the club's fans.

One of the principles that unites us as Liverpudlians, gives us pride and informs our sense of identity is the philosophy of doing things The Liverpool Way. On the pitch this evolved from Shankly's fearless attacking football into a simple but wonderful game of pass and move, founded on hard work and a team spirit that relied upon everybody fighting for each other. Off the pitch things were not so different. We would put our faith in the manager and support him to the fullest extent we were able. Since the day I accepted the honour of becoming Chairman of Liverpool FC to the day I stood aside, that has been my guiding principle; back the manager, invest in his vision and ensure that the heartbeat of the club – the methods and ethics that we hold so dear – are preserved and continue in The Liverpool Way.

When I asked Rick Parry to join the club as Chief Executive, I knew that he too cherished these ideals. While we were both very eager for success and both dearly longed to help guide the club back towards the good times, we equally knew that there was a correct way, a Liverpool way of doing things. And one thing we would never countenance was any notion of borrowing against the club to create a phony wealth for some 'jam today' spending splurge. I can say with certainty that our housekeeping was immaculate. I have always acted with the very best interests of the club at heart, and if I've made mistakes – which I know I have, and not solely with regard to Gillett and Hicks – then they have been honest mistakes.

To give a proper context to the situation we find ourselves in now, it's important to trace things back to their roots. I became the majority shareholder of LFC in 1991, and underwrote a new share issue in 1994. Pre Euro 96, football was incredibly unfashionable. There was nobody else on the scene in Liverpool who was even remotely interested in taking on the financial challenge of LFC. I became involved for one reason – for the love of the club.

But in the wake of Euro 96 with the influx of more and more overseas superstars on superstar wages, I was aware the game was changing beyond all recognition and deeply worried, too, about my ability to continue underwriting the financial side.

I was from the ever-decreasing pool of old-school club owners, the locally based, locally wealthy supporter like Jack Walker who stuck his money in out of his passion for the club. If we'd have done it as an 'investment' we'd have come unstuck pretty quickly. Back then, football was a mug's game when it came to the finances. You did it because you loved your [sic] club – although, unlike the Chairmen of other clubs, I would never entertain the idea of a stand or a stadium being named after myself. That wouldn't be Liverpool, and it wouldn't be me.

If loyalty is a weakness then I'm loyal to a fault. I stuck to my guns in terms of backing the people I trusted, and it began to work. Under Gerard Houllier we began seeing the results of a long-term strategy. The Academy, the new training facilities at Melwood, investment in the squad all required serious money – much more money than the club could ever generate in those pre-Champions League, pre silly-money years. It's easy to overlook the fact that we only qualified for the Champions League for the first time in 2001, and only really started making money in Europe thereafter. But 2001 was a year we'll all remember with great affection – the year we finally began our concerted fight back. Rick and myself felt satisfied that the time, the patience and the investment was finally amounting to the targets we aspired to: winning the League again, and re-establishing Liverpool FC as a force in Europe.

I'd pinpoint 2002-2003 as pivotal in what led to my ultimate decision to stand aside if the club was ever going to truly progress

– and if we could find the right calibre of investment, and curator. At the end of a terrific 2001-2002 where we made a bold and realistic scrap of the Premier League title chase and came agonisingly close in the Champions League, I backed Gerard in a significant summer of signings. The £20 million we spent was a huge outlay in those pre-Abramovich times, and it was done in the knowledge that we couldn't repeat the spend again without significant progress – a proper go at the Champions' League and, chief among our goals, the return of the League Title to Anfield. Very regrettably, 2002-03 failed to deliver our aspirations, and the players we invested in were unable to make a difference.

Rick was always vocal about planning for success, and after much soul-searching from everybody close to the club we bowed to the inevitable. We began to accept that the only way we could continue to compete was by building a new stadium. Anybody who cares to dredge the archive will find myself on record as finding the decision difficult to come to terms with; but looking back now, the thing I was finding most difficult, was the transformation of the game I loved. Football clubs were beginning to be seen as a source of profit rather than a source of pride; they were as much financial institutions as they were sporting legacies. The Abramovich era was upon us, and I knew that I could never compete.

The search for suitable custodians began in earnest. I don't really care whether the supporters like me or approve of me – but it's important that they believe me. I would never lie, never – and I have nothing to hide. We looked long and hard for the right person or institution, we followed up every lead. We WANTED that fantasy investor to come forward – the infinitely wealthy, Liverpool-loving individual or family with the wherewithal to transform our dreams into reality. And so sincere was our commitment to finding that person or company, that we invested huge sums and massive amounts of time investigating potential investors, only to conclude that they were not the right people for Liverpool. It would have been easier, I assure you, just to take the money, cross our fingers tight and hope things worked out – but we dug deep into every file and asked all the tough questions, knowing the answers might scupper any deal.

To give just one example, we responded to overtures from Thailand – the figures discussed were so enormous we were obliged to take a closer look. We had just persuaded Rafa to join the club as manager and were eager to back him in the transfer market. No matter how dizzying their wealth though, we would never simply rush into a relationship with an unsuitable partner, and so it transpired with Thailand. After looking closely at the deal we withdraw from the proposition, and did so for all the honourable reasons you'd expect from our club. So it was ironic that Manchester City was subsequently sold to the same entity, without so much as a murmur of disapproval from their fan base. When it suits them, football fans can turn a blind eye to the things they'd rather not have to acknowledge. We did acknowledge it though – we confronted the reality that the Thai offer was unethical, made our decision to withdraw and carried on the search. Rick's remark about selling the family silver has been used repeatedly against ourselves and the board – but it was said in all seriousness, with all sincerity. Several years down the line, I do sometimes wonder if we took the process too seriously. Do the majority of fans just want owners, whoever they are, who'll buy all the best players, come what may? Speaking for myself, I could never square that outlook and that legacy with our own unique football club.

Around that time, by the way, I experienced my first real back-lash from the fans. It started with a few letters in The Echo and quickly grew into a campaign aimed at forcing me to sell. There's an irony there somewhere that, in holding on and giving prospective new owners the third degree I was somehow seen as deliberately holding the club back! It was [a] loud minority giving me stick, but this growing ill-feeling was certainly a factor I took into account. Our search for funding took us to the US where we spent time with the hugely impressive Robert Kraft.

Both Rick and myself were disappointed that the Kraft family decided not to take their interest any further – Robert is a good man, and would have been a fitting custodian for LFC. Around the same time we met George Gillett for the first time, liked him very much as a man and were struck by his sheer passion for the club he owned, the Montreal Canadiens. There was a cultural similarity between the Canadiens and LFC, in that Montreal is perhaps the most un-Canadian of Canada's major cities; the fans see themselves as separate (and perhaps superior) to the rest of the country. They are devoted to their team, which gives them a sense of pride and identity. Importantly, too, all the fans we spoke to on the street and around the stadium had nothing but affection and praise for their owner, George Gillett. Sadly George was unable to follow up his very real interest with the necessary funding to take our club forward.

We have been accused of failing to capitalise on the Istanbul Effect – in fact our talks with Dubai International Capital stemmed directly from winning the Champions League in 2005, with Sameer Al Ansari from DIC introducing himself to Rick Parry in Istanbul and making it known that he was an ardent Liverpool supporter. Rick wasted no time in following up this lead, and having laid

*out our needs (significant investment for players; a new stadium)
we spent the next year working out a deal with DIC. On 1st
December 2006 we informed DIC that they were our preferred
option – and that the deal would have to be completed by 31st
December 2006, for 2 reasons.*

*Firstly, so that Rafa could take advantage of the January transfer
window, and secondly the timeline of non-negotiable targets we
had to hit if we were to start the new stadium on time. Several
things happened (or didn't happen) that gave cause for concern.
Our being made aware that DIC had devised a 7-year exit strategy
was one such issue, along with a suggestion they intended to raise
£300 million in working capital (i.e. debt), secured against the
club. But by far [the] biggest reality check came when we got
down to the practicalities of planning a schedule of works on the
new stadium. Under strict terms we had negotiated with the various agencies, local and European, with whom we had to deal
over grants, planning permissions etc, we were on course to complete the stadium in time for the 2009/10 season, but we had to
keep resolutely to the timetable. Therefore (also in December 2006),
the club put it to DIC that it was essential we placed an immediate order for the steel required for the new ground's infrastruc-
ture. The steel was going cost in the region of £12 million. Deadlines
passed before and after Christmas. New Year 2007 came and still
no steel, and quite frankly (and, I think, justifiably) we began to
have misgivings.*

*At this juncture – January 2007 – George Gillett returned with
a new proposal. We asked to hear more, and George introduced
his partnership with the Hicks family. On 30th January 2007 (the
day we played West Ham away) we put the Gillett/Hicks proposal to the board, and they voted in favour. I was conscious of*

the fact I'd agreed a deal with DIC, and telephoned Sameer Al Ansari to tell him that the board preferred Gillett and Hicks's offer, and I wanted 48 hours to think things through. DIC representatives confronted me prior to the game and put it to me that I had to sign off on their offer immediately or the deal would be withdrawn. I told them I wouldn't be held to ransom – and they withdrew the offer. With hindsight, we may have had a lucky escape there as Dubai is not the buoyant market it was in 2007.

We moved ahead with Gillett and Hicks with all due speed (even now I cannot accept that we were hasty) – and here is an element of the process I accept we could have handled better. We had looked into George Gillett's affairs in detail, and he came up to scratch. To a great extent, we took Tom Hicks on trust, on George's say-so. There was still the very real business of obtaining approval of the shareholders, however. I was the 51% majority stakeholder, but I was obliged to – and I wanted to – obtain a mandate from Liverpool's shareholders great and small. Gillett and Hicks produced a very substantial offer document containing all the key assurances re debt, the stadium, investment in the squad and respect for Liverpool FC's unique culture, traditions and legacy. It was impressive stuff – and it did the trick. For the motion to be carried we needed around 90% in favour. Over 1700 shareholders voted and the result was 100% in favour of accepting Gillett & Hicks's offer.

So many times I have had people ask me, and write to me, and quiz the people who are close to me: 'Wouldn't a simple Google search have told you all you needed to know about Tom Hicks?'

I could be flippant and tell you I don't know what Google is (I have never used a computer in my life). I could point out that internet searches are as likely to mislead as to inform. But the truth is that we went way beyond Google in our check-ups. We retained Price Waterhouse Coopers to advise us on the fabric of the deal, and they received assurances from Rothschild's, one of the most respected and respectable names in global finance, who vouched for both Tom Hicks and George Gillett. Indeed, Rothschild's – who were representing Gillett and Hicks – telephoned a non-executive director of LFC, Keith Clayton, to assure him that both were good for the money. Could we have done more? Probably – though under those circumstances, in that time-frame, probably not. We did our due diligence on Messrs Gillett and Hicks and if we're guilty of anything it is that, after four years searching, we may have been too keen, too ready to hear the good news that George and Tom had passed their tests.

The Google question, along with any suggestion that the shareholders and I preferred the Gillett/Hicks bid because it promised to net us more money, is a source of anger to me. Internet culture is inexact and gossip-driven ... to suggest anyone at our football club would run a financial health-check via a search engine is just silly. Don't forget that everyone was delighted with their takeover at the time. Significant shareholders like Granada and Steve Morgan were insistent the board of LFC should accept the G&H offer, and left me in no doubt about my legal duty to accept the offer. George and Tom were carried shoulder high through the city centre on the afternoon of the Barcelona game in March 2007 – it wasn't just me who was taken in. And as for the extra money I netted from the G&H deal – you really don't know me if you think that was a factor. Ultimately, the deal we signed up to was laid [out] in unambiguous terms in the share offer document. That is a matter of fact. But at the end of the day you can carry out any number of checks with infinite degrees of scrutiny and certainty, but I doubt there's any procedure available that will legislate for a guy you've come to trust looking you in the eye, telling you one thing and doing the exact opposite.

As I've already said, I feel no duty to justify myself and in writing to you now there is much I've withheld out of decency, more than duty. There's also the very real possibility that, in speaking out, I might derail the process that many believe I can positively effect [sic]. But it has been hard for me, sitting mute on the sidelines as the club I love suffers one blow after another. Since resigning from the board I have not set foot inside Anfield – and it hurts. I hugely regret selling the club to George Gillett and Tom Hicks. I believe that, at best, they have bitten off much more than they can chew. Giving them that benefit of the doubt – that they started off with grand ideals that they were never realistically going to achieve – I call upon them now to stand back, accept their limitations as joint owners of Liverpool Football Club, acknowledge their role in the club's current demise, and stand aside, with dignity, to allow someone else to take up the challenge. Don't punish the club's supporters any more – God knows they've taken enough. Take an offer, be realistic over the price, make it possible. Let the club go. It is a sign of strength, not weakness, to concede for the greater good.

Yours faithfully,
David Moores

Friends of his say it was an emotional but cathartic process for Moores which allowed him to say things that he couldn't say before. Many fans refused to read it and plenty of those who did struggled to get all the way through it. Richie Pedder, the chairman of Liverpool's supporters club, gave the press a comment which probably summed up the view of the vast majority: 'Hindsight is a wonderful thing, but Moores and Parry should have done their homework, and they didn't.'

The *Guardian* ran an opinion poll on its website asking if Liverpool fans now felt sympathy for Moores: 18 per cent said Yes; 82 per cent said No. Comments underneath ranged from 'It's time we gave him a break and moved on' and 'You can't doubt his love for the club' to 'This bleeding heart letter is beyond Krusty The Klown' and 'You were a clueless owner. I just hope you enjoyed your £88 million.'

To most Reds it didn't change much. They were pleased he had finally broken his silence and begged the Americans to leave, and the greater insight into the reluctance of DIC to commit themselves earned him some sympathy. But the big, stupid mistake still stared them in the face. Moores had allowed Gillett to vouch for his business partner and they took his word. Moores looked into their eyes and asked them to promise they wouldn't put the debt on the club and he fell for their act.

So he may not have been greedy, but he was greener than a plastic Paddy with a leprechaun's hat and a Guinness shillelagh in Flanagans' Apple pub on St Patrick's Day.

The timing may have left Moores feeling better, in so far as no one could say he had wrecked the season, but that had been wrecked months before and Liverpudlians were heading for an all-time low. Rafa Benitez was on the brink of leaving, Jose Mourinho was making noises about finally landing Steven Gerrard, and Fernando Torres and Javier Mascherano headed off to a World Cup refusing to guarantee they would be around next season.

As Liverpool had staggered over the Premier League finishing line in seventh place, missing out on Champions League
football and its money, many fans said they couldn't blame
either for heading to Spain. Liverpool had just paid £40 million in interest loaded on by American owners who were in
deep trouble back home with Hicks filing for bankruptcy pro-
tection and trying to sell his baseball team, the Texas Rangers.
So maybe it wasn't the best of moments for the man who helped
put them in that dark place to paint himself as a victim.

His sympathy-seeking line about how hard it had been sitting on the sidelines as the club he loved suffered one blow
after another, did not go down well among the real victims
who felt distraught and battered by the state of Liverpool. Victims who didn't have an £88 million cheque to soften the blow.
And the least he could have done in a 3,000-word attempt at
self-justification was use the one word Liverpudlians wanted
to hear above all: Sorry. He didn't.

Tony Evans though believed his sorrow and pain shone
throughout the letter with his personal devastation plain for
all to see. 'I feel for him in many ways. The truth is Moores
was no better or worse than most other chairmen or owners
but at a time when he needed to be surrounded by dynamic
people with intelligence and vision he wasn't,' said Evans.

'The people around him told him the club had to be sold if
it was going to move forward and he believed it. And it was
crap. He listened so he's got to take responsibility for it, but
he's not the only one. Had there been a chief executive with a
bit of gumption none of this would have happened. That's not
to excuse Moores but it's true. The sale was just a symptom of
a bigger malaise at the club.'

When David Moores stepped down from Liverpool's board he barred himself from going to the place he loved more than any other on earth, staying at home to nurse a broken heart. In that respect he was similar to Bill Shankly, and like the great man, he knew there was no one to blame but himself. That broken heart eventually killed Shankly, and as much as I've had my run-ins and vented my fury at Moores, I don't want history to repeat itself. Cut him to the core and he is a genuine Liverpool man. I hope one day he feels relaxed enough to return to Anfield. If he does it would be a potent symbol that the civil war is an historical footnote, hope has replaced despair and the good times are back.

For all his faults and mistakes, Moores deserves to enjoy them as much as any other Liverpudlian.

CHAPTER THIRTEEN

'This is business and in business I am Fernando Torres'

– Christian Purslow

When Rafa Benitez was growing up in 1970s Madrid he would while away his spare time brooding over a military board game called Stratego. So often did he engage in this test of martial skills and battlefield leadership, and so obsessed did he become at improving his performance, by the time he reached adulthood he was convinced there was no better Stratego player in the world. An opinion he shared, unprompted, with baffled journalists at a press conference en route to winning the 2005 Champions League.

The point he was making was that he may not have had the best team in Europe – he didn't even have the best team in the Liverpool postcode of L4 that season – but he had the best strategies. A boast that was proved to be correct. How else do you explain winning a European Cup with djivin' Djimi Traore, Igor Biscan, Milan Baros and the star of more *Casualty* episodes than Charlie Fairhead, Harry Kewell?

However, in the summer of 2009 Benitez's Stratego skills

would be put to the test on several occasions, and through all of them he would be outmanoeuvred and left licking increasingly gaping wounds. After missing out on the Premier League by four points (or was it two deflections by Man United's Federico Macheda), Benitez knew expectations of delivering the title the following season would be colossal. But still he felt relaxed about the task.

His analysis was that Chelsea were on the wane because Roman Abramovich had turned off the rouble tap, United would lose Cristiano Ronaldo and become too reliant on ageing players like Ryan Giggs and Paul Scholes, and Arsenal were, as they always were, a work in progress. He was telling people that if he could keep what he had and bring in a couple of attacking players to turn the draws into wins, Liverpool were set fair for their best title-challenge in twenty years. All he would need, he said, was a perfect summer in the transfer market. Sadly, it ended up as far away from perfection as the results of the Bride of Wildenstein's plastic surgery work.

On the last game of the season Xabi Alonso, who had felt undermined by Benitez's attempts the previous summer to sell him and bring in Gareth Barry, told him he was leaving. His agent followed that up by telling him he was off to Real Madrid.

Javier Mascherano was pushing for a move too, and Benitez sensed one of them would get away. Alonso had only two years left on his contract, Madrid were once again awash with cash, so he calculated if he got £35 million from them he would take it, hold on to Mascherano, bring in Barry and have a tidy profit to add to the £15 million transfer kitty he'd been promised by the owners.

In his head the Barry move would be a doddle. He was

convinced after all the spadework he'd put in the previous summer that Barry's heart was set on Anfield and Aston Villa were resigned to losing him, so he had plenty of scope to play hard-ball. When he lodged a £7 million bid they told him it was an insult, claiming he knew the asking price was £12 million. When he came back in again with an extra million he was informed (with much pleasure) that Manchester City had bid the full £12 million and Barry was holding talks with them. Actually City didn't so much talk to him as lay an annual salary figure below his startled eyes and hand him a pen.

Benitez was stunned. He had told Alonso's agent he could move to Madrid if they came up with the right fee, so he was now potentially missing a key midfield player plus his replacement. His entire summer transfer strategy was in chaos.

Having lost an English international to the up-and-coming, money-no-object, Abu Dhabi-run Manchester City, Benitez told the board that if they lost another one to them, the perception would be that Liverpool were no longer a top four team with clout and may as well wrap up their Champions League spot with a light-blue bow and send it down the M62 to Eastlands.

When both clubs made a move for Glen Johnson, Benitez was determined not to lose out again. The result was he paid £17.5 million, and wages of £100,000 a week, for a full-back who struggled as a defender. Meanwhile, Real Madrid snapped up Alvaro Arbeloa for a piddling £3.5 million.

The perfect summer was shaping up to be a poor one until chief scout Eduardo suggested the ideal replacement for Xabi Alonso, and it became bleaker than a fortnight spent in an Anglesey caravan, with the rain continually dancing off the roof and the entire family struck down by swine flu. Alberto

Aquilani was not only injured (and would stay so for the first two months of the season) but he was also totally unsuited to the rigours of the Premier League, and at £18 million became arguably Benitez's worst piece of business.

Actually Aquilani wasn't his worst piece of business, Eduardo was; the scout he brought in from Spain in 2006 who failed to unearth any unknown gems from his homeland, and whose knowledge of Italian football can be summed up with the words Andrea Dossena. Or Alberto Aquilani.

There then followed a defining moment which would cast doubt not only on Liverpool's ability to challenge for next season's title, but possibly for years to come. Benitez, through his contacts in Madrid, believed Real were prepared to pay up to £35 million for Alonso, because they had earmarked him as a vital cog in their new Galactico set-up. When the price reached £30 million and Benitez refused to budge he was told that the club was accepting it because the money was needed to meet the crippling interest payments.

There was now no pretence. The Royal Bank of Scotland was effectively in charge at Anfield and looking for its money back. It felt like the club was in a form of unofficial administration, its professional negotiators being told how far they could go by bankers.

Former player John Aldridge, who has supported the Reds since he was a kid growing up in Garston in the 1960s, views this moment as the lowest in Hicks's and Gillett's reign: 'That was when the shit really hit the fan. I knew when players were going out and the money wasn't getting spent that the game was up, because something similar happened to me when I was managing Tranmere.

'Suddenly the owners were robbing Peter to pay Paul. When Real Madrid buy a player off you they give you the cheque in full. So that summer £30 million came in for Alonso and £3.5 million for Arbeloa. That's the best part of £35 million going straight from Real Madrid to the bank. Yet when they bought Aquilani it was on the never-never, meaning the money from player sales was servicing the debt.'

If being outflanked by the banks was bad enough for Benitez, things were about to get markedly worse. With fringe players, and a legend in Sami Hyypia, being sold, he believed he had more or less balanced the books, with still enough left to bring in a striker (especially as the money he received back from selling Robbie Keane had not been invested) and a centre-half. His targets were Fiorentina's Stevan Jovetic and West Ham's Matthew Upson.

As a bid was prepared for Jovetic, Benitez was told he didn't have the money. The rules had changed without his knowledge. The cost of all the new contracts awarded to Steven Gerrard, Fernando Torres, Dirk Kuyt and Daniel Agger now formed part of his budget, as did the payments which were still being made for players signed in previous windows. The bottom line was all he had left in his kitty was £1.5 million – the price of a Sotirios Kyrgiakos.

The king of Stratego had been outmanoeuvred to a monumentally embarrassing and barely credible degree. When asked a year later why Liverpool slipped from second in the Premier League to seventh, Benitez would reply, 'Christian Purslow'. The troubled Spaniard had found his new nemesis.

Purslow appeared to meet every criteria as a replacement for Rick Parry – the yin to Parry's yang. Here was an extremely successful businessman (his MidOcean Partners private equity firm had made him millions through buying and selling companies like Center Parks), a lifelong Red and season-ticket holder who spoke fluent Spanish and had already been involved with the club as an adviser to Steve Morgan's buyout team back in 2004. The 46-year-old was a Cambridge and Harvard Business School graduate, was passionate and energetic and had a brain the size of Jan Molby's arse. He was also friendly with Royal Bank of Scotland chief executive Stephen Hester.

By the summer of 2009 RBS was running out of patience with Hicks and Gillett. Although they were still making a tidy profit out of the interest repayments they wanted their money back, preferably with the Americans gone, as the loathing the nation felt for these bailed-out bankers had shifted up a few notches on Merseyside. PR-wise, Hicks and Gillett stank.

Hester more or less told the Americans they had to take Purslow on and allow him to sell the club or bring in new equity to pay down the loan. So although Hicks and Gillett didn't make Purslow their new managing director, they were forced to rubber-stamp his appointment.

His remit was to sort out the ownership problem in whatever way he could. With a global credit crunch, owners who loathed the sight of each other and were suspicious of Purslow, and half the Middle East refusing to deal with them, that was never going to be easy.

From early days Purslow was telling people that Hicks and Gillett were the worst type of leverage buyout merchants imaginable, because they refused to put their own money in. Virtually all of it was borrowed. He also believed their £800 million valuation of the club was so ridiculously high that no one would come in for it. Which was what he felt Hicks in particular wanted. He believed the Texan's plan was to keep refinancing the loan until, at some magical future point, a mug would give them £800 million, they could pay off the banks and pocket £300 million each.

Purslow's appointment in June 2009 was warmly welcomed even among people who would go on to be his most savage critics. At least with his enemy Parry out of the way, went the thinking, Benitez would stop all the politicking and concentrate on that final push to a nineteenth League title.

At first things went well. Purslow was far more communicative than Parry had been with Benitez, and was instrumental in giving him his new contract, but the honeymoon didn't even survive the summer. When Benitez was told he had spent all of his transfer kitty, had to keep schtum and get on with it, the battle-lines were drawn. The dynamics of the Anfield civil war were shifting yet again. Purslow had merely replaced Parry as the man who was killing Rafa.

Months after Benitez left Liverpool, during a press conference before his Inter Milan side played Tottenham, he was asked to explain why Liverpool ended up falling out of the Champions League places in 2010, and he gave an answer which made Eric Cantona's seagulls and trawlers speech seem perfectly sane:

'We have a saying in Spanish, which is "white liquid in a bottle has to be milk". What does this mean? It means that after eighty-six points and finishing second in the League, what changed?

'The Americans, they chose a new managing director and everything changed. The managing director is involved in all the decisions: new lawyer, new chief of press, new manager, nine new players, new medical staff, and new fitness coaches – they changed everything. They changed the managing director who was talking with some players, and they changed everything that we were doing in the past.

'So, if you want to ask again what was going on, it's simple: they changed something and, at the end, they changed everything. So, white liquid in a bottle: milk. You will know who is to blame.'

Reporters looked even more baffled than they had been at his Stratego press conference five years earlier, and one asked him if he could explain the milk analogy. He replied: 'White liquid in a bottle. If I see John the milkman in the Wirral, where I was living, with this bottle, I'd say, "It's milk, sure." John the milkman's priceless response to the bizarre outburst was, 'Rafa was a very good customer. Just three bottles of semi-skimmed. They didn't have to be placed on his step zonally or anything.'

Journalists who fronted Purslow about the changing of the transfer rules that summer were told there had been no change, just a long overdue ordering of affairs. He had simply introduced something called a Players' Account, which incorporated agents' fees and improved contracts. But the club's former CEO was telling any journalist who would listen that this was something new. Even Rick Parry believed Rafa had been shafted.

An ally of Purslow's at the club said there were two reasons why his relationship with Benitez began to unravel: 'For the first time Rafa was being held to account financially over the players' budget and for the first time someone was chipping away at his omnipotence.

'One of the criticisms of Christian was that he had only been brought in to drum up finance, not make wider decisions, but that's nonsense. He was the managing director, or the CEO, and therefore he ran the club, especially with Hicks and Gillett hardly ever there. He made a mistake when he joined by saying he had been brought in to sell the club because he was actually brought in to run it. That was slightly naive and it came back to haunt him.'

There were other moments of naivety too. Notably his meeting with the Spirit Of Shankly when they taped the conversation and asked for his approval of the minutes so they could release it to their members. Purslow had been far more frank about the owners than he intended, and asked if they could agree an edited version of the minutes. The SOS refused and printed them anyway. He instantly cut off all dealings with them and began referring to them as Sons Of Strikers.

Peter Hooton went to the meeting with an open mind, especially after Ian Ayre had told the group that it would be in their interests to give Purslow a chance. 'His whole demeanour was patronising from the start. His persona was all about "I don't need to be doing this job. I'm only here for the benefit of Liverpool." It seemed like he was thinking "I'll try to get down to their level."

'He started swearing about the Yanks. I was thinking, "This is an act and I don't believe a word you're saying."

'Every question we asked he'd say "fantastic question". I was thinking, "Stop being condescending." I got the impression he looked around the room and thought these are a bunch of fairly militant lads who haven't got great jobs.'

Fellow SOS committee member Paul Rice said: 'When he

was given that Liverpool job he was like the kid who got the keys to the sweet shop. He completely undermined the office of the manager, far more than Rick Parry did. He interfered in transfer policy, took part in the plot to unseat Benitez then landed us with a new manager.

'If he'd have kept to the financial side, the role he was brought in for, there wouldn't have been a problem but he overstepped the mark and started playing Football Manager with Liverpool FC.'

An Anfield source who advised Purslow how to handle the SOS meeting said he warned him there would be no such thing as 'off the record' and he should choose his words carefully. But he proceeded to tell the fans what he thought: he hated Hicks and Gillett and it was his aim to get them out.

'If you get it wrong first time with Scousers you're knackered,' said the source. 'Christian didn't get it wrong he actually said what he felt, that he agreed with the fans that the Yanks were bastards and he wanted them out. His crime was to ask if he could change the minutes, but was that really such a crime when he is on the board of directors, and the club's MD, and can't be seen to be slagging his bosses off to the fans?'

Whatever the rights or wrongs, from then on the newly christened Sons Of Strikers viewed Purslow as the enemy. Or Cecil as he became known due to his middle name – there is still a Cecil Purslow twitter page out there with his head superimposed, *Blackadder*-style, on the body of a World War One general.

'They undoubtedly hated him because he was posh,' said the Anfield source close to Purslow, 'but that whole Cecil thing summed up how much he was misunderstood. The implication was here was Cecil, a Little Lord Fauntleroy figure born with a canteen of silver cutlery in his mouth. The truth was he was named after his uncle Cecil, an electrician who worked on the docks and who died of cancer, aged twenty-three, the same year Christian was born.'

The perception of many hard-core fans was that Purslow was a Hicks and Gillett stooge who would keep on propping them up in return for living his childhood dream by sitting in the dressing room alongside Steven Gerrard and Jamie Carragher, even though events would prove the first part of that observation to be patently wrong. Tony Evans wrote that people at Anfield had nicknamed him 'Forrest Gump' due to his uncanny ability to put himself at the centre of every major event. You could see where he was coming from. At one point the players took bets with each other over who he would put his arm around first, after a game. Purslow had briefed ITV's touchline reporter about a Steven Gerrard injury after his half-time visit to the dressing room, and Sky bagged an interview with him after a draw with Lyon put Liverpool out of the Champions League.

'He came in to raise £100 million and he couldn't do it,' said Evans. 'He thought he was cleverer than anyone else in football and he'd be able to run rings round them but it turned out he didn't have a clue.

'I found it unbelievable that a man who was brought in to raise capital could end up firing and hiring managers, selling and buying players. He thought he knew it all.

'He thought he could pick players better than Rafa, he could manage better than Rafa. I told him it was wrong for a managing director to go into the dressing room and he answered, "No, it's my job to pick the players up." I said, "No it's not, it's the manager's job." Here was a man in the wrong place at the wrong time making big decisions.

'The best I can say for him is when it came to the vote which sold the club to NESV he voted in the right direction.'

One journalist who changed his mind about Purslow after taking an instant dislike to him was *The Times*' Tony Barrett: 'I once stormed out of a briefing he was giving because I thought he was contradicting himself with every sentence. To be fair to him he could have thought, "That's an insult, sod you," but he rang and told me I had to trust him. He said the Yanks didn't know this but he was operating behind enemy lines. And to be fair, in the end, he was proved right. He delivered on that promise. If only he'd kept out of the football side of things that he was totally unqualified to dabble in, Purslow could have been a hero.'

The criticism hurt Purslow, especially when a banner appeared at the front of the Kop bearing his face next to Hicks, Gillett and Martin Broughton, under the words: 'Four riders of the apocalypse'.

'That was outrageous and so, so wrong, as was proved at the end when the Americans tried to sack him from the board,' said his Anfield ally. 'He probably was a bit star-struck at first, which was why he got close to the players, but he felt after the Parry years they might be glad of some encouragement from above.

'What clearly wound people up is that he's an enormously intelligent, multilingual, multimillionaire, Cambridge scholar and Harvard graduate who has been hugely successful in business and was trying to save his football club, not for money but for love.'

There is no doubt that many people at Anfield believed the

managing director thought too highly of himself. At its heart Liverpool is still a modest, self-deprecating club. So anyone saying to a Scouse member of staff who queried one of his decisions, as Purslow did, 'This is a world you don't understand. This is business and in business I am Fernando Torres,' is going to struggle on the popularity front.

The 2009–10 season started badly, with two defeats by Spurs and Aston Villa in the first three games, and never recovered. With five league losses before the clocks went back, Kopites knew in October that the push-on from second to first was never going to happen. In fact the way they were playing and the way their luck was panning out (you only have to think of that superb match-winner by the Sunderland beach ball) it was clear they faced a major battle for Champions League qualification. And so it proved. They were only in the top four places for one week out of the final twenty and ended up limping in in seventh, their worst finish for eleven years.

For once there was no Champions League progress to mask Benitez's domestic failure as his side never looked like making it out of a relatively straightforward group containing Debrecen, Lyon and Fiorentina. The lack of depth in the squad was the most worrying aspect of the decline. Aquilani got close to fitness by the end of October but it was clear he was too lightweight for English football and when Torres was injured all goal threat disappeared because the only back-up strikers available were young David N'Gog, porn-star lookalike Andriy Voronin, and the perennially under-achieving Ryan Babel. It was as though without Xabi Alonso, the purring Ferrari of the previous season had lost its engine and become a spluttering old Lada.

The media smelt blood and intensified the attacks on Benitez, pulling apart his transfer dealings and questioning his mental health. When he offered a 'guarantee' of a top four finish, obituaries were being written and filed away for the following May.

Rafa didn't look great. He was white and gaunt through too much worry and too little sleep, he picked up infections and coughs and kept coming out in cold sweats. When friends told him how awful he looked, he'd invent stories about his daughters waking him up. The truth was Liverpool's decline was eating him up and as a result he would stay up all night devising ways of outflanking his growing army of enemies. He was playing Stratego again, but with far more at stake.

The pressure affected his wife Montse too. She loved living in their Caldy home on Wirral, and had no desire to move back to Spain, or anywhere else for that matter. She would break down in tears at parties when asked about her future. She would sit in the directors' box at games rubbing rosary beads between her fingers, praying throughout the final half-hour of a game for victory. All so the pressure would be eased on her husband.

Apart from hard-core fans who still idolised him for the European glory he had brought to the club, and who saw him as the most potent anti-Hicks and Gillett symbol, Benitez was now dangerously short of allies.

As the Americans fought to stop their empires crumbling back home they were more and more distant from the club, meaning Hicks was never there to offer his hypocritical support. Members of the League Managers Association hated Benitez for not crawling up Alex Ferguson's backside with them and former players openly questioned his managerial ability (my favourite being Graeme Souness, whose thirty-six wins in eighty-three at Newcastle set him on course for the JobCentre and the Toon on course for the Championship). The national press was slaughtering him and an increasing number of fans decided they could no longer stay loyal. Worst of all, he had alienated key sections of his playing squad.

Footballers can change loyalties from team-sheet to team-sheet and many switched allegiances for or against Benitez on a regular basis, but throughout his final season the dressing room was nearly always split between those who had no time at all for him, and those who did. This breakdown in respect boiled down to the fact that he was having too many fights on too many fronts. He was too distracted with what was happening off the pitch. He became too obsessed with the politics of the club, which was understandable when virtually every match day he would be wheeled out before different prospective owners, the vast majority of whom were simply there on non-serious ego-trips. He took his eye off the ball, forgot what he did so brilliantly, and the players could smell it.

Meanwhile, he and Purslow were at war, briefing and leaking against each other and cooperating as little as possible. Whenever Benitez tried to take the fight to him by demanding clear-the-air meetings, he would be told, 'We've got investors coming in and we can't afford to be seen to be fighting. RBS needs stability.' So he would bite his tongue and help sell the cunning masterplan for world domination to another group of sheikhs.

The problem was most of the sheikhs, American, and Far

East groups were fake, and those who weren't baulked at the unrealistic asking price. The only genuinely serious offer to materialise came in April 2010 from New York-based private equity firm the Rhone Group. They offered £118 million for 40 per cent of the club, meaning they would take control and Hicks and Gillett would become sleeping partners with 30 per cent equity each. Rhone also pledged to put an extra £25 million on top of the annual budget for transfers that summer. Purslow had brought his £100 million to the table, and sold it to the owners on the grounds that when Rhone paid down the debt and financed the new stadium, the club's stock – and thus their 30 per cent stake – would soar, meaning they would finally make the profit they so coveted.

Within hours of the offer being made, Hicks's favourite TV reporter Alan Myers was on Sky Sports News saying the owners would be turning it down. It was to be a fatal mistake. An incandescent Royal Bank of Scotland decided the days of bluff and counter-bluff were over and they were calling in their loan. They had always worried about the backlash from allowing a national sporting institution like Liverpool to go to the wall (although not that much that they stopped bleeding the institution dry with interest payments) and now feared that was where the Americans were taking it.

So they told Hicks and Gillett that they'd had enough. They agreed to give them one last six-month extension of the loan (with severe financial penalties imposed) in return for them appointing an independent chairman to sell the club and reconstitute the board so it was made up of Hicks, Gillett, Purslow and Ayre, with the chairman having the casting vote. It meant if the new chairman sided with Purslow and Ayre on a sale of the club, the Americans, despite being the owners, were effectively passive shareholders.

Former Citibank big cheese Michael Klein, a friend of Tom Hicks's, suggested British Airways chairman Martin Broughton, and RBS approved it. Hicks believed he had pulled off another coup by keeping the banks from his door in return for approving some stuffy, old school London toff he would be able to manipulate with ease. So buoyed was Hicks by the situation he predicted he would sell the club for £800 million, making 'three or four times our money'.

The 64-year-old Texan was losing his touch and showing his age. Beneath the gentlemanly manners, public school charm and floppy hair, Broughton was a hard-nosed operator. Inside the silk glove, the former CBI president packed a steel knuckleduster. He was well up for earning a £500,000 cheque for selling Liverpool, and having such a prestigious addition to his CV, but he was never going to be anyone's patsy. The stark reality was that when Hicks signed up to the new board arrangements, he signed away all of his power.

The day after the twenty-first Hillsborough anniversary, Broughton was officially appointed as the new independent chairman, with Barclays Capital replacing Rothschild and Merrill Lynch (Hicks and Gillett's previous choice of bankers) to conduct the search for new investment. RBS shot down fans' criticism of the refinancing by saying it was the only way forward for the club, as it gave them stability while trying to find a new buyer. The alternative would have been a summer firesale of key assets such as Fernando Torres and Steven Gerrard, because their previous arrangement with Hicks and Gillett meant they had to reduce the club's £237 million debt by £100 million before July.

Naturally, there were some choice comedy quotes from Waldorf and Statler, as they let it be known they wouldn't be setting foot in Anfield again. In a joint statement (a joke in itself) they said:

> *Owning Liverpool Football Club over these past three years has been a rewarding and exciting experience for us and our families,* [making them the only families in the world who actually enjoy being escorted by police outriders away from Anfield in blacked-out cars as a raging mob tries to get at them.]
>
> *Having grown the Club this far we have now decided together to look to sell the Club to owners committed to take the Club through its next level of growth and development. We are delighted that Martin Broughton has agreed to take the position of Chairman, working alongside the club's excellent senior management team. Martin is a distinguished business leader of excellent judgment and with a great reputation. He is a genuine football supporter and will seek to oversee the sales process in the best interests of the Club and its supporters.*

Within six months they would be asking a Dallas court to jail Broughton on the grounds that he had stolen the club from them.

Initially there was suspicion about Broughton at Anfield, even among fellow board members Purslow and Ayre. With his Sir Humphrey Bufton-Tufton persona he seemed about as at home around the fields of Anfield Road as an Eskimo would at the equator; he was a committed Chelsea fan and he'd been recommended by one of Hicks's business buddies. But they knew, once he grasped the truth of the Liverpool horror show, that if he had any decency about him, he would feel compelled to do the right thing, if only for the sake of his own reputation.

And what a horror show it was as the season staggered towards its death. The fourth Champions League spot had been lost, Fernando Torres had done his knee in after setting up a Europa League semi-final showdown with his old club Atletico Madrid, and stories about Benitez's agent holding talks with Juventus were all over the back pages.

Fans looking for a chink of light to brighten these darkest of days could only find it in the season's final game, as Chelsea won 2–0 at Anfield to stop Manchester United taking their nineteenth title. It said it all. Liverpudlians were quite happy to surrender to the detested Cockney Rent Boys, and take their nineteenth defeat in a season they hoped would bring them their nineteenth title, so long as it denied United.

'You're ancient history … you're ancient history,' taunted the triumphant Chelsea fans, with Kopites lacking either the will or the evidence to disagree.

The end-of-season lap of honour was surely the most excruciating any set of Liverpool players had had to endure. It was difficult to work out who was the more embarrassed, the players or the fans who'd stayed behind. It had been a devastatingly disappointing season, with anyone emotionally tied to the club left feeling battered and drained. All you wanted to do was forget about the whole horrible mess for a few months, but the chances of that happening were zero. The future of the club's ownership, star players and manager would dominate the summer. Starting with the manager.

Benitez's body language as he acknowledged the Kop chanting his name during the lap of honour, was similar to Xabi Alonso's a year before. He knew and we knew this was goodbye. In fact he'd suspected as early as January when he was told he couldn't spend the money he was bringing in for selling Andriy Voronin and Andrea Dossena, that his time was up.

The distance his new chairman was keeping from him only confirmed those suspicions. Broughton didn't introduce himself by phone or email when he was appointed, and made a tentative agreement through a third party to meet Benitez after his first home game in charge, but headed straight back to London.

Liverpool's senior management were now convinced that Benitez's outspoken nature could lose them prospective buyers if he was still at Anfield during any delicate future sale. Within days of taking over, the new chairman realised his first job would be easing out his manager as cheaply and cleanly as possible.

It was made easier by the fact that Benitez had no allies left on the board, and by his own erratic behaviour. Three meetings were eventually set up between him, Purslow and Broughton, and three times Benitez cancelled at the last minute. Rafa claimed they were scheduled at ridiculous times, almost inviting him to cancel, Purslow claimed vindication for all he'd told Broughton.

The third cancellation, on the day after Atletico Madrid knocked Liverpool out of the Europa League semi-final, genuinely shocked Broughton. He could not understand how an employee had reached a position in a company where he could be allowed to treat board members in such a way. When he eventually ordered Benitez to a meeting in London there was only one intention on his mind and the fact that Rafa had alerted his employment lawyers meant he knew what it was.

There was more than one meeting and there was more than one version of events.

At the first one Benitez insisted Purslow leave the room before reading out a long list of notes containing every instance in which he believed the managing director had undermined him.

At a second meeting he told Broughton he could turn things around in the summer, even if big names left, so long as they could assure him he would be allowed to reinvest all of the money. No such assurances were given. It was a cat-and-mouse operation, with hints being dropped about how attractive that Juventus job was, and Broughton diplomatically trying to make Rafa agree that both knew why they were having these talks, so let's stop dancing around legal handbags and get to the point. We're splitting up.

In the end Benitez told Broughton and Purslow he was taking his family on a half-term break to Sardinia but he'd like to carry on talks when he got back. No sooner had he hit his sun lounger than he realised the unworkable situation was wreaking too much damage on the club, and instructed his agent to negotiate a pay-off.

On 3 June his exit was officially announced with Benitez putting out a statement which read:

It is very sad for me to announce that I will no longer be manager of Liverpool FC. I would like to thank all of the staff and players for their efforts.

I'll always keep in my heart the good times I've had here, the strong and loyal support of the fans in the tough times and the love from Liverpool. I have no words to thank you enough for all these years and I am very proud to say that I was your manager. Thank you so much once more and always remember: You'll never walk alone.

He made the right decision for himself, his family, the club and the many supporters who had stayed loyal to him but who were now happy to see him put out of his misery. His position had become untenable. Had he refused to go Benitez would have become increasingly paranoid and frustrated, and he never would have survived the medium-term. A clean break was best for all.

His last email exchange with the Americans had come in the April when he emailed Hicks (cc-ing Gillett out of courtesy) enquiring about his summer budget. Hicks told him he couldn't give him a figure because they were looking for new investors and he wouldn't be able to tell him until new money came in. Gillett's was characteristically quirky. A one-liner to the effect of: 'As always we are fully supportive of every Liverpool employee and will continue to be so.'

When his departure was announced, neither got in touch with the only Liverpool manager they'd ever had to thank him for his efforts and wish him well. It says a lot about them. As it does about Rick Parry, who sent his old enemy a text saying, 'Thanks for all you did at Liverpool. Good luck for the future.'

Rafa texted back: 'I fear for our club.' Parry replied: 'I fear you're right.'

Rafa's parting memory of Purslow was being hastily pursued out of the final meeting by him, being looked in the eyes and told: 'I would be so upset if you thought this were personal.' Benitez laughed at that one, and realised that his constant battle to be rid of Parry was a classic case of being careful what you wish for.

When he returned from holiday people were turning up at his Wirral home in tears, hugging him, Montse and the girls, thanking them and leaving gifts. When his pay-off was sorted he gave £96,000 to the Hillsborough Family Support Group, and hefty donations to other charities such as the Rhys Jones Memorial Fund and a Hoylake care home.

Benitez would eventually hear his name mentioned by Hicks four months later when the club was sold and the Texan did his last Sky News propaganda film. The real people to blame for Liverpool's fall from grace, said the Texan, were Benitez and the fans who became internet terrorists.

'Rafa lost the club. We didn't finish at the top – that's not the fault of the owners, we spent good money. Rafa has to take accountability for his own results.'

Since that Athens press conference in 2007 Hicks had never stopped detesting Benitez, even when he was pretending they were happy bedfellows. He hated him because he could never sack him due to the love fans felt for the Spaniard, and the loathing they felt for him. These were business currencies he had never before had to deal in, and it blew his very large cranium.

That was another reason, set alongside those many glorious

European nights that restored Liverpool to its place as one of the most feared and respected teams in world football, for declaring that Rafael Benitez was a true Liverpudlian legend.

And always will be.

CHAPTER FOURTEEN

'You do know that you crashed the entire Blackstone/
GSO system don't you?'
— *Wall Street Journal* reporter David Enrich

As sobering news bulletins go, this one came straight from the
Head of Reformed Alcoholics at the Salvation Army's top drying-
out clinic.

'Italian treble winners Inter Milan have just announced Rafa
Benitez as their next manager,' said the Sky News anchorette on
Wednesday, 9 June. 'Meanwhile Harry Redknapp has distanced
himself from stories linking him to the vacant Liverpool job.'

Now here was a reality check. The newly crowned European
Champions were saying, 'We'd like to take your manager off
you, if you don't want him, Liverpool', while the London media's
favourite Cockney uncle who had won one major trophy in a
twenty-seven-year managerial career (the FA Cup, against
mighty Cardiff City) was saying, 'What? Me go to Anfield? Leave
it out, my son.'

Not that Liverpool had a reality many felt like checking. The
preferred fantasy manager option, Jose Mourinho, had gone to
Real Madrid and the preferred fantasy but at least attainable

option, Guus Hiddinck, swiftly let it be known he wasn't interested. In fact the only man to openly tout for the job at this stage was Sven Goran Eriksson, who was so keen he broke a career-long silence on his tribal loyalty to say he had been a Liverpool fan all his life. Sadly, few people in Liverpool knew anyone who'd ever been a Sven fan.

The Liverpool board (seeing itself as being back in old-fashioned Liverpool Way mode) made the expected diplomatic noises about taking its time to ensure it found the right man to take the club to the next level etc, etc. But in truth they had more or less decided that man was Roy Hodgson, and it wasn't the next level they were after. More a decibel level in the manager's office that was low enough to allow them to get on with the real job in hand: selling the club. Hodgson was safe, Establishment, League Managers' Association aristocracy who would toe the party line and play the white man. He was also relatively cheap, would take a short contract and not demand to bring in a huge backroom staff. Plus Danny Murphy had told the players who matter that Roy had done a terrific job at Fulham, and was a gentleman to deal with, so he was a shoo-in. That wasn't how Kenny Dalglish and many fans saw it though and with hindsight they were spot on.

It was fitting that the lie about harmony breaking out all over Anfield once Benitez had left should be exposed so risibly and so quickly. Kenny Dalglish, the man Christian Purslow and Martin Broughton asked to help sift through the managerial shortlist (but really to give a selection panel containing non-football men some credibility) took one look at it and decided the most suitable candidate was not on that list. The candidate's name? Kenneth Mathieson Dalglish.

Even worse, he told a journalist of his feelings and thus the news that Liverpool had appointed a headhunter who effectively said, 'None of these are worth hunting, so hunt me,' wrote itself into the public domain. Dalglish was immediately slapped down by the board, being told to his face, 'We can't let you do this, Kenny, because we don't want you to put in jeopardy your iconic status as the club's number one legend,' and, 'We envisage an Academy/ambassadorial role for you which will far outlast any manager.'

But the briefings behind his back were more frank. How long had he been out of the game? Where was the evidence he could handle the pressure these days if he couldn't handle it twenty years ago? We're not sure what he's supposed to be doing to earn his club salary now, so what confidence could we have in him earning it by doing twelve-hour days, seven-day weeks as manager?

Seven months later, as Liverpool lurched from one miserable defeat to another, and the fans were chanting 'Hodgson For England' followed by Dalglish's name, the club would be forced to send an embarrassing distress call to a cruise ship in the Persian Gulf begging the Prodigal Son to return and save their season.

Liverpudlians let out a collective scream of relief and joy that January Saturday morning, on the eve of the FA Cup third round tie at Old Trafford. Not just because Roy Hodgson had gone but because it meant that the only major player left from the Hicks and Gillett era was Ian Ayre. Who was one of us. With Kenny back, it felt as though your dad, who had run away to sea many years before, allowing your mum to let a string of undesirables into her bed, had returned to tell every outsider to sling their hook.

But back in June there had been no mass campaign to reinstate Dalglish following Benitez's exit. There was no huge appetite among fans to see the 59-year-old legend step back into the dugout for the long haul. Most wanted a young but experienced European coach like Didier Deschamps to come to Anfield and establish himself as the next Jose Mourinho. However, when it came to choosing between a safe Roy Hodgson and a king called Kenny, the majority instinctively sided with the monarch. It partly explains why, with Dalglish employed at the club and hovering around in the background, Hodgson was doomed from the outset.

As often happens to club legends, they are useful to those who will never attain a fraction of their status. Cynics suggested that Purslow was happy to keep Dalglish close by to protect him from growing anger that a City figure who had been brought in to raise £100 million investment was now sacking and appointing managers.

To be fair to Purslow, he hadn't been the only Anfield Civil War general to involve King Kenny in the hostilities. When Rafa Benitez brought Dalglish back to the club it wasn't just to help develop the young talent. It was in the hope he would persuade some of the ranting ex-players to get off his back, and that he might become a big hitter in Premier League and FA circles, taking on the many vested interests which had coasted past Liverpool. Neither happened.

It also has to be pointed out that there are few men in the football or business worlds cannier than Dalglish, who knew exactly what he was letting himself in for by taking a job in the Hicks and Gillett snake-pit. Besides, there was an endgame being played out at Liverpool in the summer of 2010 that was much bigger than any individual, including Kenny. In fact, for a few weeks it appeared the game could end with a glorious conclusion, thanks to a second King Kenny.

On the night of 25 June, Tony Evans was sitting in his *Times* office with his feet on his desk, watching Spain play Chile in the World Cup, when a highly respected contact rang and said they needed to meet. Evans pointed out how decent this game was shaping up to be, and was told it really would be in his interest to meet, as Liverpool were on the brink of being bought by Chinese investors.

It was a representative of Hong Kong-based investment banker Kenny Huang, who was fronting a wealthy Far East consortium, telling Evans the takeover was becoming unstoppable. Huang had bought out Gillett's debt and his group were in a position to call in his shares, he said. Evans was told that Huang had very serious big hitters behind him and had been in dialogue with RBS for weeks, but progress was slow, so he was asked to sit on the story until a deal was imminent.

By August Huang's people were becoming restless with Liverpool's unwillingness to dance to their tune, and went public with their own story. Cue a week of utter midsummer madness in the papers. 'You'll Never Wok Alone' and 'Chinese Takeaway' were to be expected splashes in the tabloids, but it was in the traditional quality papers where Huang-mania really took hold.

On 5 August *The Times* led its front page with a picture of the Kop in full flow and a headline 'China set to buy Liverpool', claiming the mystery backer behind Huang was China Investment Corporation (CIC), who were prepared to pump millions into the club to make it the number one team in Asia.

Other broadsheets then went out of their way to rubbish the story, mainly on the grounds that no one at CIC was admitting a link with Huang.

Broughton, in particular, was far from impressed with the hysteria surrounding Liverpool being under direct rule from Beijing, when he had yet to see an offer. Meanwhile, journalists couldn't track Huang down or establish if the Chinese government was on board.

All the time the vultures were circling. Yahya Kirdi's exotic name kept appearing, billed as some wealthy Syrian businessman, but all anyone could establish about him was a chain of Canadian pizza stores, and a tenuous link with George Gillett. The Rhone Group were still in the picture apparently, as were the al-Kharafi family from Kuwait, and Keith Harris kept ringing up every couple of weeks to say he had a big player on board who was about to declare his hand. He never did. The reality was, for all the talk and promises, hype and self-publicity; by the start of the new football season, Broughton had no firm offers on the table to buy the club.

Those close to the Huang deal said he was about to be given preferred bidder status, but that Broughton had wanted to put a rider into the agreement stipulating that if another party came in with a better bid he could withdraw that status. That's when he walked away and waited in the wings, calculating no one else would come in with the money, and as it neared the October sale deadline, Hicks would flog his shares to his group, who would then get Liverpool off RBS for a song.

The club's take on Huang was that despite being suspicious of his publicity machine they took him seriously. Until he was asked to show them the money, at which point he demanded a month's exclusivity to check out the books and put his financing in place. This was the month in which RBS were piling penalties on Hicks and Gillett, and thus the club was technically falling deeper and deeper into debt. They couldn't afford to jump into bed with one unknown quantity, no matter how sexy his PR machine.

Tony Evans, who was close to the Huang bid throughout, said: 'They tried to be too clever. They were convinced that Broughton had no one lined up and they thought if they left it to the last minute and went to RBS they could go, "Look, here's Gillett's shares, give us the rest cheap." They were too complacent and Huang screwed it up.

'To be honest I was sick of them at the end because I thought this has rumbled on long enough. I told them, "If you really want this club you're still getting it cheap at £300 million, so put your money down on the table."

'They said to me: "No, we'd rather put that money into players and the stadium," and I told them, "But if you don't get the club you're not going to put that money anywhere."

'I have no doubt the Huang bid was a genuine attempt to take over the club, and that CIC were backing them, because there were too many serious people involved for it not to be. But too many people involved were trying to be too clever for their own good.'

What was interesting was how little opposition there was among Liverpudlians to the prospect of their club being run by the Chinese government, which had a very dubious human rights record. Before the arrival of Hicks and Gillett serious questions were asked by fans about whether they should be entertaining an offer from the much-maligned Thaksin

Shinawatra. After three and a half years of the Americans, Kopites would have flown 'Fuck Tibet' banners and turned a blind eye to dead babies in gutters, if it meant losing the cowboys.

Since the meeting with Moores and Parry in January, Kop Faithful had been building up a healthy internet following, honing their techniques and focusing their campaign solely on the Royal Bank of Scotland. It was their continued funding which allowed Hicks and Gillett to survive and it would be their refusal to refinance which could kill the Americans. It was RBS, therefore, who bore the brunt of the first wave of Kop Faithful cyber-terrorism.

An RBS senior executive, Rebecca Oliphant, had replied sympathetically to a Steve Horner email, leaving her email address (obviously) and her phone number (ill-advisedly). Within hours her inbox was bombarded by hundreds of mails from Liverpool fans urging RBS not to refinance Hicks and Gillett, and when Mick Carroll phoned her in Edinburgh for her response, she went ballistic. 'I'm so glad we were 200 miles away because I fear if we'd been in the same room she'd have ripped my head off,' said Mick. 'For the first and only time in my life I realised what that phrase meant about hell having no fury like a woman scorned.'

Far from scaring off Kop Faithful, the eruption of Mount Oliphant was an inspirational turning point as it made them realise how effective their campaign could become if they really applied themselves. If that was the response of just one RBS executive to a small-scale email drop, imagine the effect a much bigger assault would have on every key executive in the company.

The process was simple. An email would be put together by one of Kop Faithful's handful of writers, it would be posted on the website with a list of recipients and instructions to copy, paste, send and distribute among friends, fans, other websites and Facebook accounts. A young generation of techno-savvy fans were surmounting all obstacles placed in front of them by anti-spamming agencies. Members were encouraged to use different email accounts to beat filters, advised on which key words to exclude and ordered not to write anything abusive.

So the bombardments were stepped up and the executive base continually upgraded, meaning every Monday morning every senior employee of RBS would turn up for work, switch on their computer only to be faced with several thousand anti-Hicks and Gillett emails clogging up their inbox. Then, as the October refinancing deadline approached and Tom Hicks began looking elsewhere for backers, the game changed. Whenever a bank, hedge fund or equity house was linked to Hicks, the addresses of all key personnel would be unearthed, an email would be posted and they would all be made aware of who they were dealing with.

The day the Kop Faithful came into its own was Saturday, 18 September 2010, on the eve of the 3–2 Old Trafford defeat. After the *News of the World* had gone to press Alan Kayll was told by Chris Bascombe that the paper was running a story saying Hicks was on the verge of securing a two-year agreement with a company called Blackstone/GSO, to pay off RBS and refinance.

The Texan had called a three-hour board meeting in London earlier that week where he delivered the news of his plans to deal with Blackstone, telling Martin Broughton he had no intention of selling the club at the RBS debt level, and that the board had no authority to prevent him repaying that debt and keeping the club with whatever funds he could muster.

It was the nightmare scenario. Hicks bypassing the sales process by giving ownership of Liverpool to a US equity firm, with the only proviso being they made RBS, and with it Broughton, disappear. Minutes from this meeting also show Hicks famously refer to the protesting Liverpool fans as 'Noise we have been dealing with.'

By Sunday afternoon 14,000 emails had hit the inboxes of Blackstone/GSO executives and those of allied companies, telling them the following:

> If your company agrees a £280 million refinancing deal with Tom Hicks to retain his share in Liverpool Football Club, then the only return that you will see on your investment is bad publicity and a severe backlash from Liverpool supporters worldwide.
>
> As you are aware, Hicks is trying to refinance his debt to the Royal Bank of Scotland before October 6th so that he can continue his disastrous ownership of Liverpool Football Club.
>
> There is no point in us listing the countless and well-documented offences of the grossly destructive reign of Tom Hicks and George Gillett. The media is full of articles about them. And that is the point. No longer do we rely on the occasional heroic journalist to expose corruption within institutions we hold dear. This is a new age, an era of organized resistance at the click of a mouse.
>
> You are facing an energized, well-informed mass of Liverpool fans from around the world. We are tapped into a constant stream of information on the ownership situation. Every day, dozens of web forums buzz with the latest news. Protest marches, newspaper ads, boycotts

and billboards are organized. Every move Hicks makes is scrutinized. And every associate of his is warned.

Refinancing is our nightmare scenario. Anybody who helps Tom Hicks refinance will become our primary target.

We have a decent track record of taking on and beating those who attempt to blacken the name of Liverpool Football Club. As an example, the boycott of the Sun Newspaper following their disgraceful coverage of the Hillsborough Disaster in 1989 is said to have cost News International an estimated £10 million a year.

If the Blackstone Group/GSO Capital Partners join forces with Tom Hicks in raping and pillaging Liverpool Football Club, then you will be making a very powerful enemy.

You have been warned.

Throughout the Monday, as Alan Kayll drove around in his taxi, he received texts telling him that Blackstone were rumoured to have pulled out. He wanted proof before calling off the campaign, so armed with the phone number of Michael Whitman, the senior Blackstone/GSO executive who had addressed the Liverpool board the previous Wednesday, he rang for clarification.

At 4.50 p.m. he left a message on Whitman's answerphone explaining who he was and asking him to call back by ten a.m. the following day. 'If you don't call me by then I'm going to put your name and phone number on every single Liverpool FC website,' Kayll warned him. The next day he decided to check with Whitman's PA that her boss had got the message. Within minutes of ringing her, the 'Senior managing director of the Blackstone Group and Head of the European Business of GSO Capital Partners', Michael Whitman, rang Alan in his cab.

'There are reports in the press that your company has pulled out of refinancing Tom Hicks, but there's no statement from your company. Can you confirm to me that you are not going to refinance Hicks?' asked Kayll.

'The reports are accurate, Alan,' replied Whitman.

Kayll told Whitman he hoped he understood why he'd been inundated with emails, before explaining that Liverpool is more than just a football club to many people. It's their lives and their community, he told the American, and it's being destroyed by Tom Hicks.

Whitman replied: 'We have taken the passion and commitment of Liverpool supporters into this and I wish you well with your campaign.'

Alan was still struggling to get his head around a major Wall Street player admitting that the Kop Faithful had impacted on one of his company's investment decisions, when David Enrich, a reporter on the *Wall Street Journal*, rang from New York to ask about the story. 'You do know that you crashed the entire Blackstone/GSO system, don't you?'

As Enrich was interviewing Kayll, another story was breaking in the Big Apple. A Scouse-born New Yorker, Paul Wilson, had spotted Hicks and Tom Jr., sitting on a bench in the same Manhattan street which housed the headquarters of Deutsche Bank AG and J.P. Morgan Chase & Co. Wilson, a 35-year-old financial consultant, guessed the pair might be rattling their begging bowls at either bank so whipped out his BlackBerry, photographed them and sent the images to his wife, Erin, before following Hicks into the lobby of the building that housed Deutsche.

Confident he had nabbed Hicks at work he told Erin to post

the photos on Twitter with a brief explanation, and soon they were picked up by Kop Faithful. Key addresses of J.P. Morgan and Deutsche executives were pasted on to the same email Blackstone had received, with the same orders, and within an hour one J.P. Morgan banker was telling the *Wall Street Journal*: 'It's totally viral right now.'

On Thursday Enrich rang Alan Kayll to say, 'You're going to be famous tomorrow … you're on the front page of the *Wall Street Journal*.' Which he was, in a long article, under the headline 'A Texas Tycoon Learns a Lesson: Don't Mess With Liverpudlians'.

These were a few of the highlights:

> In the old days, English soccer hooligans settled scores with knives and broken bottles.
>
> As Texas billionaire Tom Hicks is learning this week, the weapons of choice these days: camera phones, twitter and spam e-mails, can be almost as scary.
>
> Mr. Hicks, co-owner of England's hallowed Liverpool FC, is on the run from a mob of angry fans who blame him for the team's tailspin. Liverpool faithful are waging a fierce campaign to evict the American owner. Their strategy: Scare away banks and other financiers who might throw Mr. Hicks a lifeline, starving Mr. Hicks of needed cash and forcing him to sell. To do that, they are using the tools of the digital age to track Mr. Hicks' efforts to drum up money, then bombard would-be lenders with thousands of irate emails, phone calls and tweets.
>
> Lately, financial institutions have borne the brunt of Liverpool's rage. Fans have been flooding RBS with let-

ters and phone calls urging the bank to seize the club and give Mr. Hicks the boot. Top executives' inboxes sometimes have been hit with several hundred emails per day.

A few weeks ago, some fans started a Facebook page encouraging people to boycott RBS. Mr. Kayll, the cab driver, drew up lists of financial institutions Mr. Hicks is believed to have approached, posting them on a website he helps run that urges fans to help oust Mr. Hicks.

The campaign hit Stephen Schwarzman, the billionaire co-founder of Blackstone Partners, whose GSO Capital Partners hedge fund considered participating in a deal to help Mr. Hicks refinance the RBS loan. By Monday, GSO had backed out of the talks.

There was scepticism in some quarters over whether Kop Faithful's email campaign against Blackstone/GSO had actually killed the deal. Some observers say Blackstone was never going to proceed anyway, and that the scheming Texan was overplaying the significance of his talks to con the board into believing he was still very much in control of his destiny. We'll never know the exact truth, but there is no doubting the fact that the email storm warning did have an impact on influential American decision-makers in those key days when Hicks sought the refinance.

If the decision was in the balance, and any negative thoughts about Liverpool FC were harboured, Kop Faithful (especially after the *Wall Street Journal* front page) gave Hicks a mountain to climb. Even Hicks himself blamed the 'cyber-terrorists' for leaving him with nowhere to run. They may not have eventually trapped their prey but they bricked up a lot of his escape routes.

A senior Liverpool executive believes you cannot underestimate the influence the Spirit Of Shankly and their offspring Kop Faithful had on driving Hicks and Gillett out of Anfield.

'If it wasn't for the intensity of the fan opposition towards them I'm in no doubt they would have become worse than the Glazers and put more and more debt on the club. Thanks to SOS, their protests, constant vigilance and media profile they were very wary of how far they could go,' he said.

'As for the email campaign as major people were about to come to the table, that was really effective. I know that worked because we had the banks and financial institutions ringing us up and asking what the hell was going on. Hicks and Gillett knew that too, but there was nothing they could do about it.'

Kop Faithful knew the Blackstone victory would mean nothing if RBS decided to give Hicks his refinancing, so they re-trained their sights on Edinburgh.

As a new blitz of emails was sent out demanding they call in the loan, Alan Kayll rang Roger Lowry, their head of public affairs, and left a message saying he could stop all the mails coming RBS's way if he'd pick up his phone and have a chat. Alan was sat in his cab outside Liverpool John Lennon Airport, one late September morning, waiting for a fare, when Lowry called back. 'Just to let you know, Alan,' he said, 'we don't have a problem with your emails. We are reading them and so are all the senior executives.'

It threw Kayll because that wasn't the kind of message he had been expecting. He sensed he was now dealing with people who understood. He began to hope that maybe they were looking at Liverpool's situation like normal, caring individuals, instead of faceless bankers chasing their next bonus pot. As the possibility of achieving real justice washed over him, Kayll poured his heart out to Lowry.

'I just sat there and gave this stranger the most passionate plea I've ever given anyone in my life,' he said. 'Please, please, please pull in this loan now. You have to understand that it's destroying a great football club and it's destroying a great community. You've got to do it for us, please.'

There was a short silence, and then Lowry replied: 'We can't say anything to you because there's a confidentiality agreement but believe me we're listening to you.'

Kayll went straight on to the forums demanding a change of tactic. Forget the standard emails to RBS, because they're listening. In future everyone should write a personal one, telling the bankers exactly how it feels being a Liverpool fan right now and how much you fear for the future if RBS refinance Hicks and Gillett. Just give it to them straight from your heart, he said. And in their thousands, they did.

This is the part of the Hicks and Gillett saga that should fill Liverpudlians with genuine pride. It started as a gathering of 350 fans in the backroom of the Sandon pub and spawned a grass-roots union, mass protest, media campaigns and internet warfare. It led to meetings with representatives of some of the richest and most powerful men on earth and eventually made the Gordon Geckos of Wall Street quiver in their Prada shoes. Those fans refused to just sit back and take what Hicks and Gillett were throwing at them. They exposed these two for what they really were and made them pariahs in their own moneyed community.

There was something quite noble about that, especially when you consider how low the average football fan is viewed by the rich and the powerful. They could have done nothing, as many fans did, in which case Liverpool might now be in administration or being run into the ground by an American hedge fund. But they stood up, stayed united and fought the American imposters on every front possible, and made rich men realise that real power doesn't lie in how many friends you have in the White House, how many companies are listed in your investment portfolio or how well you can schmooze big, corporate cheeses over dinner.

It lies in that old trade union maxim of strength through numbers, and more importantly the intensity of the passion that glues those numbers together. No group of sports fans has ever left so many rich men feeling so powerless, confused and unsure about their decisions as Liverpool's did during those forty-four months.

They did not ultimately evict the Americans from Anfield, the Royal Bank of Scotland did, by taking them to court. But those fans made it increasingly difficult for the bank to not follow that course of action.

In decades to come, when social and football historians look back, it may well prove to have been the Twelfth Man's finest hour.

CHAPTER FIFTEEN

'They are guilty of unconscionable conduct which conclusively demonstrates just how incorrigible they are'

– Mr Justice Floyd

Towards the end of July something called football broke out again at Anfield as a strange oasis of calm was sighted amid the madness.

For a short while, on-field progression took precedence over the off-field frenzy, with fans allowing themselves a rare feel-good moment, optimism even, for the coming season. In hindsight, strange doesn't start to cover it. New manager Roy Hodgson was saying all the right things a Liverpool leader should, coming across with a calmness, humility and old-school decency which reassured the Rafa-haters who'd become exhausted by the Spaniard's brinkmanship.

Fernando Torres (after much persuasion) and Steven Gerrard (after no persuasion) let it be known they were staying. Joe Cole snubbed offers to move to Arsenal, Spurs and Manchester United, instead choosing Liverpool. Or, in words that gave Liverpudlians more of a lift than Cole will ever know, 'The biggest club in the country.'

Few had expected Cole to flee London for Anfield, and it brought smiles back to troubled faces, especially as the nation had recently been screaming for him to start every World Cup game, and he was leaving a Double-winning Chelsea side whose fans were last heard telling Kopites 'You're ancient history.'

But, quicker than you could say Milan Jovanovic, that summer oasis turned out to be a heartless mirage. The rest of Hodgson's buys would have failed to inspire the Wigan unfaithful (although, to be fair, he was working on a relative shoestring and had no Champions League to offer); and when the season began it was clear why Chelsea had allowed Joe Cole to leave on a free, and why Hodgson had never won a trophy outside Scandinavia.

The football was dour and unambitious, the team lacked spark and cohesion, and by October they were down among the relegation sides. An epoch-defining low-point was imminent and duly arrived on 3 October when Blackpool won 2–1 at Anfield. The result only tells a fraction of the story.

It was the second home game running that a Spirit Of Shankly-organised mass march on the ground and a sit-in afterwards was called-for. For thirty minutes half of the Kop stayed behind to demand the removal of Hicks and Gillett and as embarrassed players went through their warm-down exercises, some like Steven Gerrard and Jamie Carragher applauded in a show of unity while the majority didn't. Their lack of empathy with the protesting fans was in keeping with the 30,000-plus empty Anfield seats on all three stands but the Kop. Here was a club dying a death by many cuts. Not least, apathy.

It was hard to blame any fan for feeling defeated by the struggle. Hicks and Gillett had taken so much away from them, and appeared to have the ability to survive every attempt at removal, that many supporters had long ago lost the will to oppose. However, hope could be gleaned from across the Atlantic, where Texas Rangers fans, who had been dragged to an almost identical pit of despair by Hicks, found the courts coming to their rescue.

In early 2009 the Hicks Sports Group, the holding company for Hicks's empire, had defaulted on repayments for $525 million loans (it is no coincidence that Liverpool never had a net transfer spend in any future window under Hicks).

According to sources who saw original documents relating to the loans, Hicks defaulted on a $350 million bank term loan, $100 million second-lien loan and a $75 million revolving credit facility.

Days before the banks announced that Hicks had defaulted, he hired Merrill Lynch to explore the sale of a minority stake, of up to 49 per cent, in the Rangers. That failed and Hicks was forced to place the Rangers into administrative bankruptcy, known as Chapter 11, to fend off creditors while he attempted to sell the club in a deal that would have allowed him to stay on as a shareholder.

But other parties took legal action to halt any potential 'sweetheart deal' and baseball's governing body, Major League Baseball, had to become the team's administrator, loaning the Rangers $40 million so they could carry on paying salaries and bills.

In August 2010, a court ruled that the team had to be sold by auction, and Hicks was removed from the process. The new owners were a group headed by Chuck Greenberg and base-ball legend Nolan Ryan, who, with Hicks gone, had led them in fairytale style to that year's World Series final.

The Hicks default with the Texas Rangers is still regarded as the most dramatic manifestation of the recent economic crisis on the American professional sports world. Ironically, Gillett was in similar dire straits, having to sell the Montreal Cana-diens in 2009 for $550 million, just to stay afloat.

Before the sale of the Rangers, Hick Sports Group owed an estimated forty lenders $600 million in loans, unpaid interest and fees. As a result he sold his luxury chalet in Aspen for $18.5 million (claiming that his family preferred to go on holiday elsewhere) and tried to sell the Dallas Stars ice hockey team. How was a man estimated to have been a billionaire in 2009 in so much trouble? What was his true worth? Was it all on paper? And if so, when the American markets went into melt-down, did Hicks's wealth prove not to be worth the paper it was written on?

Hicks had spun the same fiction to all of his sports fan-bases in that his days of making fortunes through leverage buyouts were behind him. Now he was in semi-retirement mode, and his sports clubs were his reward for a lifetime's graft, his chance to smell the roses and put something back, but most of all they were for his family. Here, he told every fan of every club, was the proof he was in it for the long-haul. These were multi-generational, family investments.

But in an interview with American magazine *Sports Business Journal* in early 2010, Hicks admitted his sporting purchases were never going to be 'dynastic' assets. In other words, Liver-pool, the Texas Rangers and the Dallas Stars had nothing to do with love, care and long-term growth. They were Weetabix, pure and simple.

Reading the comments from American sports fans underneath that article (and cutting out the odd douchebag) you could almost have been on the Liverpool forums.

'Tom Hicks most certainly doesn't give two shits about what any one of us thinks. But I think the outrage stems from the fact that, as sports fans, we desire, whether it's a realistic desire or not, for the owners of the teams we support to actually care about the success of the teams, not just their own bottom line. It just sucks to see that Hicks' involvement with the Rangers and Stars is such a passionless investment.' – zobzerto

'What Hicks, that big douchebag, fails to understand is that sports teams aren't just some investment vehicle for letting fat white guys turn a profit. They are public trusts – the public puts its trust in you to do the right thing! That means having the means to field a competitive team without borrowing out your ass, then defaulting.' – G. David

'All this time he sold his team ownership to us as a family deal that he wanted to pass on for generations. He tried to make us believe he cared about winning but as we all suspected he was a money hungry ass-hat. I can't wait for the day he is out of our lives.' – Scotts Merkin

Asses of the world unite. You have nothing to lose but your hats.

The more Liverpool's phantom buyers came and went – like nosy pensioners sneaking around Barratt showhouses checking out the colour schemes – and the longer the silence about the club's future dragged on, fears grew that, come the October refinancing deadline, Martin Broughton and Christian Purslow would be powerless to evict Hicks and Gillett.

Broughton had said, on the day he became chairman, that the fans would only hear from him when there were serious offers to consider, but this was drifting so close to the deadline the common perception was he had nothing to say. Hatred towards the Americans was becoming so intense, most fans were now letting it be known they would prefer to be taken over by RBS, risking administration and a nine-point deduction, rather than suffer their ownership any longer.

That awful choice looked like proving unnecessary less than a fortnight from deadline, as Sir Humphrey Bufton-Tufton appeared to pull a pair of credible rabbits out of his top hat. His overriding fear, though, was whether he had the power to sell Liverpool FC against the owners' wishes. Which was why he spent the summer taking advice from top London solicitors Slaughter and May and working hand-in-glove with the Royal Bank of Scotland, so he was ready to do battle with Hicks and Gillett if, as expected, they tried to block any sale which left them without a profit.

On Sunday 3 October Broughton emailed both Hicks and Gillett to tell them he had two buyers lined up: Singapore businessman Peter Lim, and the Boston Red Sox owners NESV. As the NESV offer would expire on 5 October he convened a board meeting for 3.30 p.m. Tuesday, in London, to consider the offers.

On the same day in Liverpool, Hollywood producer Mike Jefferies directed a viral video called 'Dear Mr Hicks,' starring John Aldridge, actors Ricky Tomlinson and Sue Johnston, playwright Jimmy McGovern, comedians John Bishop and Neil Fitzmaurice and other fans and celebrities, appealing to the Texan to sell up and go. Jefferies posted it on YouTube, and as well as provoking much bile from rival fans and reassuring old Brookside viewers that half of its cast were still alive, it attracted three-quarters of a million worldwide hits. But the men it was aimed at weren't heeding its message. Far from it.

On the Monday, unbeknown to Broughton, Hicks and Gillett, realising they were powerless to outvote the three British directors, agreed by phone to reconstitute the board, replacing Ian Ayre and Christian Purslow with Hicks's youngest son Mack and Lori Kay McCutcheon, the financial controller of Hicks Holdings. As Broughton, Purslow and Ayre, plus bankers and legal teams from all sides, gathered in the first-floor boardroom of Slaughter and May, mid-afternoon on Tuesday, 5 October, awaiting the transatlantic conference call board meeting, nerves were strained.

A senior Liverpool source described the tension thus: 'We'd taken a lot of legal advice and the view was we had the right to sell the club. The Americans also had the right to stop the sale, but if they did, it would probably turn out to be a hollow victory as it could be eventually overturned in court.'

The problem for Broughton, Purslow and Ayre was they knew Hicks and Gillett would try to frustrate the sale, but didn't know how. Thirty minutes before the meeting was scheduled to start, Broughton received a message which told him. The board had been changed, a listing of the new members filed with Companies House, and therefore any meeting held this afternoon would be invalid.

The first anybody outside the room heard of the drama came in an email sent from one of the Liverpool board members to the press team, who were waiting in nearby offices to announce news of the sale. The email read: 'Everything is on hold. World

War Three is starting. Await instructions.' This was the final, dusty Main Street, High Noon, shoot-out scene in the Anfield Civil War.

After the British board members digested Hicks and Gillett's tactic, there followed intense discussions with the legal teams, with RBS advisers assuring Broughton the Americans were in clear breach of their agreement. So the Liverpool chairman decided to ignore what he believed to be an illegal stalling action, told the room he was about to start the meeting, and made the calls to Hicks and Gillett.

'I'd like to officially declare this board meeting open,' said Broughton before being brusquely interrupted by a deep Texan voice which reminded the assembly that Purslow and Ayre were no longer on the board, so he was proposing they postpone the meeting for another month. When he asked, 'All those in favour,' a small Wisconsin voice was heard to squeak: 'Aye.'

Broughton went on the attack, reminding the pair he was chairman of the company and they had no legal grounds to change its constitution without his consent. He informed them he was refusing to go along with the removal of Ayre and Purslow, but was calling an adjournment for further legal advice, after which the meeting to sell the club would go ahead regardless of whether they chose to attend or not. The American lines had gone dead before he finished.

After another hour of legal advice Broughton decided to go ahead with the sale.

The Americans were phoned to take part, but neither answered. So a sub-committee was formed, consisting of Broughton, Purslow and Ayre, which unanimously voted to sell the club to one of the two credible bids.

By mid-evening the most amazing press statement ever to appear on a British football club's website was posted, effectively announcing that a coup had been staged by a British group of directors, declaring independence from the American owners:

> *The board of directors has received two excellent financial offers to buy the club that would repay all its long-term debt. A board meeting was called today to review these bids and approve a sale. Prior to the meeting, the owners, Tom Hicks and George Gillett, sought to remove managing director Christian Purslow and commercial director Ian Ayre from the board, seeking to replace them with Mack Hicks and Lori Kay McCutcheon.*
>
> *This matter is now subject to legal review and a further announcement will be made in due course. Meanwhile Martin Broughton, Christian Purslow and Ian Ayre continue to explore every possible route to achieving a sale of the club at the earliest opportunity.*

The owners were thus being told back home in America, via their own television channel, that their club was about to be sold, and there was nothing they could do about it. The workers (albeit the very well-paid ones) had literally taken control of the club. Viva la Revolution, gringos.

The three-man board then went back to the Slaughter and May boardroom and began to assess the two offers. By two a.m. they decided to go with a £300 million bid from New England Sports Ventures (NESV), a seventeen-member consortium which is the parent company of the Boston Red Sox, rejecting the higher offer of £320 million from Peter Lim on the grounds that NESV appeared to have a superior track record in club development. Insiders claim another factor in their favour was that NESV were offering to pay off more of the Hicks and Gillett financial 'PIK' penalties imposed throughout the summer by RBS than Lim was.

Shortly after seven a.m. on Wednesday, a new statement was put up on the LFC website announcing the sale to NESV. Broughton had also pre-empted Hicks and Gillett's next tactic by saying he intended to go to the High Court to confirm the legitimacy of the board which had just sold the club.

A Liverpool employee who was close to the action throughout the day said: 'It was probably the most dramatic twenty-four hours in the club's history. You had a transatlantic boardroom war going on over the phone, with Martin Broughton magnificently standing up to Hicks's bullying 3,000 miles away, and four different legal teams [LFC's, RBS's, Hicks's and Gillett's] listening in. There was no confidentiality because Hicks's and Gilletts' legal teams were in the same room, so small knots of people had to huddle outside the boardroom passing on information and making decisions.

'Then you had the club's own communications structure ignoring the owners' wishes and communicating against them. It meant the Americans were reduced to briefing external media to get out a message which contradicted their own publicity machine.

'It was like something you'd see happening in a Third World Country when there's a military coup. They had had their own power taken away from them after being boxed into a corner by a very clever guy who had the balls to stand up to them, because he'd made sure when he took the job he had the power to do this, and he knew what he was doing was right.'

That was in effect what Liverpool's sale came down to. Broughton's decision to be no one's patsy. A decision he ensured he had in writing, and one he was determined to see through the longer he worked with the Americans and saw the horrendous damage they were inflicting on a great British sporting institution.

Broughton then seized the initiative by going public about Hicks and Gillett. In a series of interviews he said he pitied them for choosing to walk away from Liverpool 'humiliated' and claimed the pair had 'flagrantly abused' undertakings they had given him and the RBS not to oppose a reasonable sale.

Furthermore, they had abused the club's constitution and its articles of association, by seeking to sack the managing director, Christian Purslow, and commercial director, Ian Ayre, and replace them with Hicks's son and his assistant, to give Hicks a majority on the board.

Liverpool's articles of association stated that only Broughton, as the chairman, had the right to appoint or remove directors. The key clause was paragraph 81a of the thirty-page document, which stated: 'Each director appointed to the office of chairman of the board of directors of the company may appoint any person as a director of the company and may remove any director (other than George N Gillett Jnr and/or Thomas O Hicks). Any appointment or removal shall be made in writing and signed by the then current chairman.'

Crucially for Broughton, the RBS backed him all the way. Indeed it was the bank's decision to take the Americans to court and bring an end to this damaging, drawn-out mess. Broughton said he was 'confident' a High Court judge would rule in the board's favour the following week, before adding worryingly for Liverpudlians, 'You can never be 100 per cent confident when you go to court.'

Hicks's spokesman in New York nonchalantly claimed that his client had given no such undertakings to Broughton, stating that, as owner, he had the right to sack and appoint directors: 'The board has been legally reconstituted and the new board does not approve of this proposed transaction,' he said.

With the club five working days away from possible administration, and the Americans' almost superhuman ability to defy death, no Liverpudlian was feeling the least bit confident. In fact everyone was waiting for the next awful twist, the next blow to the teeth from those Liver Bird-encrusted cowboy boots.

Mick Carroll awoke at 5.30 a.m. on Wednesday, 13 October, in a north London B&B on a flea-bitten bed that rocked through the sound of his mate Ben Crone's snores, and the early morning trains pulling into nearby Euston station. He flicked on the dingy TV to see the first of the trapped Chilean miners being released from his dark, hellish existence and took that as a good omen for his day ahead in the High Court.

At six a.m. the pair set off in (roughly) the direction of the Royal Courts of Justice, using the London Underground map as a satnav. An hour and a quarter later, after non-helpful directions from a Cockney ('You're fackin' miles away, fellas') and helpful ones from an exiled Scouser ('Here ya go, lads, I'll walk ya there') which they took as another omen, they were standing in The Strand, outside the imposing grey stone archway and black railings of the High Court. They were the first people there, so started their own queue, convinced they'd just bagged rights to the view of a Liverpool victory that would rank up with any of the five European Cup wins.

Over the next two hours more Liverpool fans turned up, mainly London-based ones who had been there the day before to hear the legal battle commence, along with the media and the occasional well-wisher. A woman in her early twenties, on her way to work, stopped to offer support: 'It's not right what's been going on, they need to go. Good luck, lads'. A City gent, in his seventies, dressed in a suit and long overcoat, made his way across the pavement to them: 'Bloody bastards they are, the pair of them. Hope it all works out OK for you chaps. Bloody good luck.'

At this point Mick and Ben were stunned and humbled. If London workers old and young, rich and not rich, male and female, sense the burning injustice inside their souls, surely Mr Justice Floyd would reflect that, and deliver them victory this morning.

The previous day had seen QCs do legal battle over Liverpool's future in the same wood-panelled courtroom Mick and Ben were hoping to gain a seat in for that day's verdict. Hicks's and Gillett's barrister, Paul Girolami, QC, insisted his clients were not 'trying to throw a spanner in the works' of Liverpool's sale to New England Sports Ventures. Rather they were trying to save the club for better owners who valued it higher.

They believed the 'English directors' had blatantly ganged up on them, calling themselves the 'home team', and excluding the Americans from the decision-making.

'The English directors have gone forward with the NESV bid

without properly considering alternatives when those alternatives at least appear to give better prospects,' said Girolami.

Thus their complaint, m'lud, was not that they would lose out personally from the sale, you understand, but with this rush to do business at such a low price, the club would. It was the fans they were thinking about all along, you see. Honest.

Liverpool's QC, Lord Grabiner, won the argument about the Americans being in breach of their contract with RBS, through reconstituting the board without Broughton's approval. He also demolished their claim that the club had not been properly marketed. He said the board had spoken to 130 parties by the previous Tuesday, a necessary deadline set because it was ten days before the club could be forced into administration. Lim's and NESV's were the only two offers on the table and although Lim was 'credible', the board decided NESV's bid was marginally better.

'It was a thorough and well-thought-through process,' Grabiner said, rejecting the accusation from Hicks and Gillett (still unexplained) that the 'English directors' did not want the best bid for Liverpool.

Lord Grabiner derided their decision to snub the crucial board meeting by reconstituting the board: 'Someone who is invited to a meeting and says, "I don't want to come to your meeting because I've done something else which makes that meeting irrelevant," said Grabiner 'is ridiculous and unarguable.'

RBS's barrister, Richard Snowden, accused the Americans of 'breathtaking arrogance', as they sought to derail a potential sale of the club: 'It is quite astonishing for two businessmen who are owners of their company to say, "We don't care that we owe the bank £200 million by Friday. They can wait."'

As the High Court drama unfolded Steven Gerrard was a stones-throw away, following it through his mobile phone. He was on England duty in London during an international break and was holding a business meeting in the Savoy Hotel. A meeting he kept being distracted from as texts from friends kept him up to date on how events were unfolding in court. When progress was frustrated he sent a couple of texts back saying he was only a quarter of a mile away and was tempted to head down to court to give the legal team a hand.

Jamie Carragher was also being blitzed with texts asking him what was going on, to which he replied, 'I'm back at home watching it on the telly, same as you.' Like every Liverpool fan, the frustration was killing him.

'I'd be thinking "We're nearly there", and then Hicks would come out with something and you'd think, "No, we're not are we?" I was chuffed that it was all coming to an end but kept thinking, "Why is Liverpool in this situation?" Seeing LFC in court was just another stain on our history.'

At nine a.m. on the Wednesday, Mick and Ben could see a security guard making his way towards the big wooden doors of the court, just inside the stone archway, and primed themselves for a New Year's Sale dash. After a visit to the X-ray machine and body scanner they rushed along a corridor, up stairs and down a smaller corridor until they found Court 18.

Fifteen minutes later, a woman usher in a black gown called the press forward, followed by the first block of public witnesses, showing Mick and Ben to the middle of a bench at the back of the court. They couldn't believe their luck as they were directly in line with the judge's chair and in the row behind the Liverpool delegation of Christian Purslow, Ian Ayre, Martin

Broughton and their legal team. It felt like they'd been given free tickets for a European Cup Final only to discover they'd surfaced right behind the directors' box.

Purslow turned round, shook their hands, thanked them for making the effort and asked if the Spirit Of Shankly coach had arrived. They told him it was on its way. Ben nudged Mick and asked if he'd spotted the name on the courtroom clock face. He hadn't. When he looked he could make out, beautifully written in a curve just above the bottom set of numerals, the words 'Gillett & Co.'

It freaked him. He began to feel sick and scared by the enemy's name staring back at him as the pendulum swung. 'Lose this case,' he said to Ben, 'and we may as well go home and bull-doze Anfield to the ground.' Ben too felt the fear kicking in. It was the fear that all courtrooms stir, even in the stomachs of the non-participants, but also the fear that someone's freedom is about to be taken away by one stern old man's words.

At 9.50 a.m. the worried usher called a colleague over and pointed up at the gallery: 'How did you lot manage to get up there?' she yelled. There was an uncomfortable silence until a Scouse voice rasped back: 'We, er, told the security guard we were from the RBS and he let us in.'

'Well you'll all have to come down from there immediately,' she told them.

'Why?' asked the defiant Scouser.

'Because nobody is allowed up there, it's a health and safety risk.'

'Can we appeal?' was the reply which sent the packed court-room into fits of laughter.

At ten on the dot Mr Justice Floyd entered, bowed, sat down

and began talking to the legal teams for the best part of an hour. There was a tap on the window behind Mick, who turned to see that the corridor had filled up. The SOS coach had arrived. He lip-read a fan's words 'What's happening?' but not having a clue what was going on, just shrugged back.

As Mick turned to face the judge, Christian Purslow swivelled around in his seat, gave a thumbs up and said: 'One nil to us.'

Mick looked over at Broughton, but saw not a blink or a twitch. Cool as ice. He turned round to the corridor window and gave a thumbs up. The judge started to talk again, to which Purslow turned and said: 'Two nil to us.' Mick relayed the score to the corridor.

By 10.40 a.m. Purslow had turned, winked and raised his thumb a further three times and a Press Association journalist nudged Mick and told him, 'You've won this hands down, mate', before shaking his hand and leaving court to file his story.

By eleven a.m. court costs were being argued, with that, too, going against Hicks and Gillett, whose barrister looked like he'd been pummelled around all four corners of the court with a mace. Purslow turned to Mick and Ben for the final time, with fist clenched and a beaming smile, and announced: 'Seven nil.'

The humiliation for the Americans could not have been more complete, with Mr Justice Floyd coming down categorically on the side of RBS, Broughton and the directors. He said he could find 'no basis' that what Hicks and Gillett did 'was justified'.

'The true position is that in order to ensure additional loans, they had released absolute control of the sale that they are now seeking to regain,' he said.

'When it became clear that it was proceeding on a basis unpalatable to them, they sought to renege on an agreement.

'I do not see that the evidence even begins to establish a case of repudiation,' he said. 'They ceased of their own volition to take any part. I fail to see how any of which occurred could be the substance of complaint by the owners.

'I see no justification for interfering further in the running of the company. That's a matter for the newly reconstituted board.'

The damning verdict on Hicks and Gillett left them with no right to appeal, facing a legal bill of £500,000, and being told Broughton could continue with a sale which would see them make a loss. As slaps in the face go, this must have felt like coming from Grace Jones on steroids.

Back in court, Mick Carroll pulled out some photocopied posters. He'd superimposed Broughton's head on a famous photo of Al Capone holding up a post-prohibition Chicago newspaper bearing the headline 'We Win.' As it was passed along the Liverpool bench Broughton snapped out of his deep focus and gave a huge guffaw. The court emptied out onto steps which basked in autumnal sun, to be met by the world's media. There were handshakes, hugging, back-slapping plus the belting-out of a really bad, tuneless version of 'You'll Never Walk Alone'.

Ben and Mick had microphones waved at them for quotes, but pushed through the scrum towards the George pub, across The Strand, to celebrate this famous victory. The last alcoholic drink to pass Mick's lips had been on 5 March 2008. As he stared at the pint of Guinness Ben pushed in front of him, he knew there was no turning it down. The victory he had just witnessed eclipsed anything he'd seen on football pitches across

Europe, and that pint was beckoning him in: 'It's had my name written on it since the day David Moores fucked up his "homework,"' he told his mate. Then proceeded to get bladdered.

More Liverpool fans headed into the pub, and well-wishers popped in to congratulate the fans on their victory. A party of pensioners poured off a coach and filed past towards the food tables. A finely dressed lady in her eighties spotted the red shirts and stopped: 'How did we get on, lads?' she asked. 'We won,' they told her, and she almost burst into a jig of joy.

Obviously, the jigging, singing and cork-popping turned out to be a tad premature. This being Hicks and Gillett there was always going to be another sick trick to be played. Their death-grip was never going to be released, not while there was still time to take the club with them down the chute to hell.

Shortly before eight p.m. that night, as Liverpool directors were about to sign over the club to NESV, a restraining order from a Texan court, banning the sale, landed in the offices of Slaughter and May. It was risible, casting RBS as bully-boys who had forced the directors to sell against their will, and attempting, through some powerless little judge in Dallas, to overturn the will of the British High Court.

'The Director Defendants were acting merely as pawns of RBS, wholly abdicating the fiduciary responsibilities that they owed in the sale,' read the legal suit.

'RBS has been complicit in this scheme with the Director Defendants. RBS has informed investors that it will approve of a deal only if there is no economic return to equity for Messrs Hicks and Gillett.' This is, they said, 'a grand conspiracy'.

It was a pathetic, cack-handed rehashing of the argument they had just so soundly lost before the highest court in Britain.

Hicks's lawyers bizarrely claimed that the Texan jurisdiction was valid because it was based on damage done to an American Corporation. Broughton and RBS could have ignored it and proceeded, but decided to use the two days before the refinancing deadline to kill the order, and in doing so, the Americans. So back to the High Court they went, this time to face an almost apoplectic Mr Justice Floyd.

During more than two hours of evidence, he heard that Hicks and Gillett's Texas injunction was 'oppressive, offensive and grotesque' and that they had misled the Dallas judge by not disclosing that they had had a similar action rejected in the UK court the previous day.

David Chivers, QC, for NESV, said: 'The owners, from beyond the grave, are seeking to exercise with their dead hand a continuing grip on this company. This is simply not acceptable.'

Mr Justice Floyd labelled them guilty of 'unconscionable conduct', said their behaviour 'conclusively demonstrates just how incorrigible they are', and ordered them to withdraw their injunction by four p.m. the next day or face contempt of court charges. Meanwhile, over in Dallas, the judge was hearing a demand from Hicks and Gillett that Martin Broughton should be jailed.

It had clearly descended into farce and the Americans had chosen to go out with minimum dignity and maximum contempt. Right to the end they gambled recklessly, caring nothing about the effect their actions were having on the football club they had claimed to be custodians of.

At one p.m. on Friday, 15 October, the Dallas court lifted the restraining order, and Hicks and Gillett were forced to drop their £1 billion damages claim. With four hours remaining

Liverpool was free to be sold, thus clearing their debt to RBS, and being allowed to continue functioning as a Premier League football club.

Fittingly, I heard about it from the man who, with some justification, is called King of the Kop. I was sitting at my desk, just about to send my Saturday football column, when a text came through from Steve 'Mono' Monaghan. It said, 'Happy Xmas War is Over.'

In another south-Liverpool house, a couple of miles away from mine, John Aldridge felt a wave of relief wash over him: 'I just felt so utterly elated. My first thought was "At least we're not going to become another Leeds United." That could have happened. We were losing £110,000 a day through interest on our debt. Once that was gone we knew we had stability and therefore a chance. We could start again. In the end, Hicks and Gillett were drowning men and they were pulling the club under with them. That afternoon it felt like we'd been given a lifebelt to get us to the shore.'

The three-year-and-eight-month ownership from hell had ended. The seven-headed hydra had finally been stabbed through the brain, unable to rise and spew its poison for another day. But as the corpse lay there twitching, the final drops of ugly pus seeped from its septic wounds. Hicks threatened to pursue 'every legal avenue possible', vowing to mire Liverpool in litigation for years to come, and, of course, he called in his loyal Sky Sports News crew to deliver his uncensored message to the world.

There he sat in his Dallas mansion, the plans of the New Anfield stadium framed behind his head (probably the most costly drawing hanging in his house, and let's not forget he owns a Matisse), looking tired, hurt and broken. As he choked back the crocodile tears, he blamed Rafa Benitez for losing the club, the internet terrorists for driving away investors, the players for not playing as well as they could, the British media for using 'inaccurate numbers' and an organised conspiracy between RBS and Broughton, which, he said, had left him feeling shocked and devastated because 'this was a valuable asset that was swindled away from me in an epic swindle'.

Not since *The Thick Of It*'s Malcolm Tucker turned to junior immigration minister Ben Swain after he'd been grilled on *Newsnight* and told him: 'I've never seen anyone look so fucking ugly with just one head. Who did your media training? Myra Hindley? You were like a sweaty octopus trying to unhook a bra,' has a TV interview made me laugh so long and so loud.

The phone started to throb. It was the *Daily Mirror* Features desk. I guessed that the way the day was panning out they wanted me to do an I'm Feeling Yankee Doodle Dandy now we've been Beverly Hills Kopped by new owners, piece. Twice in the past six months I'd refused to do a 'praise the Lord' type article to celebrate the demise of Hicks and Gillett on the grounds that I didn't believe they were history until I saw stakes sticking out of their hearts. The stakes had been served.

'You finally happy now it's all over then?' I was asked, but clearly the happy tones weren't coming through in my voice.

'Typical bloody Scouser. You've spent three years whining about how these horrible Yanks are screwing you into the ground and when you get rid of them you're still not happy.'

How do you begin to clarify just how much the past forty-four months, encapsulated in the final traumatic fortnight, had left you mentally scarred and physically exhausted? How do you explain, as you look at a league table that sees your team in the relegation zone, that you're more angry and embarrassed than euphoric? How can you measure in words your shame and disgust at watching the club you've loved all of your life dragged through courts in two continents as it flirted with extinction?

How do you get across how the backbiting and bitching, the spinning and the briefing (by all sides) made you fall out of love with football because you realised it was all a horrible lie?

How do you express your gratitude for the one positive to emerge from the mess: the radicalising of the fans. The noise that started in the back room of the Sandon, as the Sons Of Shankly, which grew into the 50,000-strong organisation Share Liverpool-SOS, determined one day to buy the club they emotionally own.

How do you point out just how much these cowboys stole from you? How they actually managed, on certain days, to make you hate going to Anfield? How, instead of talking about teams and tactics you spoke of bank loans and PIK rates. Instead of holding flags and singing songs in support of your players, you devoted all your efforts to getting rid of the owners.

How do you portray a civil war in which brother fell on brother over the right to protest and fans turned on fellow fans for doing too much or too little? A war which made us stop laughing during after-games drinks in the Albert, the Salisbury, the Sandon and the Park, and just argue, argue, argue.

How do you explain to outsiders that there is a little part of every Liverpudlian which those Americans will keep for ever?

How can you even begin to portray the cynicism you have

towards the fine promises of the new American owners, when you still cringe at your naive acceptance of the last ones?

You bang out 300 words for the front of the paper that employs you, that's what you do, and you hope to Christ those words don't come back to haunt you:

> There's a derby game taking place on Merseyside tomorrow, [I wrote for Saturday's *Daily Mirror*]. This week has been the first time in the 44 years I've been going to these celebrated tribal battles between Everton and Liverpool when half the city hasn't given it a thought.
>
> Because to be a Liverpudlian this week was to be a student of court proceedings from London to Dallas, and company spreadsheets from Singapore to Boston, as you willed the deeds to Anfield out of the clutches of asset-stripping vultures.
>
> It was to be sad and disillusioned, ashamed and bemused, afraid and angry that your precious club had become a devalued corporate entity in a war between high-earning men in wigs and buck-turning sharks in suits.
>
> And all the time the clock ticked down towards bank repossession and possible administration.
>
> That leverage buyout merchants Tom Hicks and George Gillett were allowed to stroll unchecked into English football, and drag one of the world's most iconic clubs to the edge of the abyss, shames the men who run our game.
>
> That they have finally gone brings heart-thumping relief. That they may lose £140 million brings air-punching delirium. How beautifully ironic they now whinge about

an 'epic swindle' being perpetrated against them when that was precisely what they hoped to pull off at Anfield?

The thought of them never darkening that famous door again (save to peddle a pointless writ) means a huge weight has been lifted from everyone's shoulders, along with the huge debt the new American owners have settled.

New owners who will be cautiously welcomed simply because they cannot be any worse than the last lot, but whose actions very quickly need to speak louder than words. But sod all that.

There's a derby on Merseyside tomorrow. And I am finally looking forward to it.

The Yanks are dead. Long live the Yanks.

EPILOGUE

In February 2011 Tom Hicks and George Gillett asked the High Court to lift the ban on them pursuing claims for damages in America, against RBS, NESV and (the now) Sir Martin Broughton.

On February 17 Mr Justice Floyd effectively ruled that out by saying they could only make claims in the USA if they first went through an English court.

In his 17-page judgement he severely criticised Hicks and Gillett for taking their case to Dallas when the sale was going through in October. Describing that attempt as 'vexatious' and 'unconscionable', he said the pair had 'misled' their own lawyer in Texas, who in turn misled the Dallas court.

'I still find it difficult to imagine what possible real connection such a claim would have with any jurisdiction in the United States,' said Justice Floyd.

'I think the time has come when they need to state their case or accept that they do not have one.'

The following day Sir Martin Broughton announced he would be suing the pair for defamation over claims he had facilitated an epic swindle.

Back on the field of play, in the four months since Hicks and Gillett had left Anfield, Liverpool had risen from 19th in the Premier League to sixth.